MATTERING PRESS

Mattering Press is an academic-led Open Access publisher that operates on a not-for-profit basis as a UK registered charity. It is committed to developing new publishing models that can widen the constituency of academic knowledge and provide authors with significant levels of support and feedback. All books are available to download for free or to purchase as hard copies. More at matteringpress.org.

The Press's work has been supported by: Centre for Invention and Social Process (Goldsmiths, University of London), Centre for Mobilities Research (Lancaster University), European Association for the Study of Science and Technology, Hybrid Publishing Lab, infostreams, Institute for Social Futures (Lancaster University), Open Humanities Press, and Tetragon.

MAKING THIS BOOK

Mattering Press is keen to render more visible the unseen processes that go into the production of books. We would like to thank Joe Deville, who acted as the Press's coordinating editor for this book, Jenn Tomomitsu for the copy-editing, Tetragon for the production and typesetting, Sarah Terry for the proofreading, and Ed Akerboom at infostreams for the website design.

COVER

Mattering Press thanks Łukasz Dziedzic for Lato, our incomparable cover typeface. It remains one of the best free typefaces available and is released by his foundry tyPoland under the free, libre and open source Open Font License. Cover art by Julien McHardy.

ON CURIOSITY

The Art of Market Seduction

FRANCK COCHOY

TRANSLATED BY JACIARA T. LIRA

MATTERING PRESS

Freely available online at www.matteringpress.org/books/on-curiosity

ISBN: 978-0-9955277-0-6 (pbk)
ISBN: 978-0-9955277-1-3 (ebk)

CONTENTS

LIST OF FIGURES

ILLUSTRATIONS

BOXES

ACKNOWLEDGEMENTS

I WOULD LIKE TO EXTEND MY HEARTFELT THANKS TO ALL THOSE WHO contributed significantly to the writing of this book, through their assistance, their support, their contributions, their suggestions, their proofreading, the documents they passed on to me or suggested, and/or the opportunities they gave me to test my arguments during different symposiums and seminars:

Luis Araujo, Nicolas Auray, Vincent Berry, Alexandra Bidet, Anni Borzeix, Emmanuel Boutet, Arlette Bouzon, Florence Brachet-Champsaur, Roland Canu, Johann Chaulet, Nathalie Cochoy, François Cooren, Marlène Coulomb, Frédéric Couret, Barbara Czarniawska, Caroline Datchary, François Dubet, Sophie Dubuisson-Quellier, Paul Du Gay, Marie-Anne Dujarier, Patrick Fridenson, Danielle Galliano, Martin Giraudeau, Mathieu Gousse, Johan Hagberg, Benoît Heilbrunn, Jean-Claude Kaufmann, Emmanuel Kessous, Martin Kornberger, Aurélie Lachèze, Michèle Lalanne, Raphaël Lefeuvre, Claire Leymonerie, Celia Lury, Christian Licoppe, Alexandre Mallard, Liz McFall, Catherine Paradeise, Guillaume Queruel, Stefan Schwartzkopf, François de Singly, Jan Smolinski, Laurent Thévenot, Valérie Inès de la Ville, Lars Walter, and Steve Woolgar.

I feel immensely indebted towards Jaciara Topley Lira and Joe Deville for their amazing work on the translation. Thank you so much, Joe, for your encouragement to publish this book in English at Mattering Press, and for working so hard to have it even better than the original version!

More generally, I am very grateful to all those whose works nourished and inspired me: with a special thanks to Michel Callon and Bruno Latour.

I also owe a great deal to the colleagues and institutions which generously supported my work: all of the partners from the Œnotrace project, CERTOP, my laboratory, and the sociology department at the University of Toulouse II in

France; the Center For Retailing, the Center for Consumer Science and Handels, the School of Business, Economics and Law of the University of Göteborg in Sweden. These last three institutions welcomed me as Visiting Professor from 2009 to 2013 and provided me with the ideal conditions for writing this book. Nor can I forget the support given to me by the Education Abroad Program and the National Research Library Facility at University of California, Berkeley, to which I owe some of the essential data on which my work is based.

And finally, my gratitude goes to the natural and legal persons who allowed me to reproduce some of the illustrations included in this book (those being, and in order of appearance): the Samuel Courtauld Trust and the Courtauld Gallery in London for Lucas Cranach the Elder's *Adam and Eve*; the Kunsthistorisches Museum of Vienna for Frans Francken the Younger's *Cabinet of Curiosities*; the *Progressive Grocer* magazine for all the images I borrowed from that publication; the Saint-Michel biscuit factories for the Bahlsen advert; Claire Jonvelle and Myriam Szabo for the *Myriam* advert, produced by the CLM-BBDO agency; SFR for the Neuf Telecom advert; Volvo Cars for the leaflet on 'Offres Tentation Volvo', produced by the Unedite agency; the History of Advertising Fund for the English Advertising Association campaign; FNAC as an agitator of curiosity for the FNAC advertising spot; the journal *Mediapart* for its headline from 16 June 2010.

Of course, the statements expressed herein are mine alone.

TEASER

> In many respects, this book might *derail* some readers. All those who prefer to know what to expect, to reason on the basis of well-established analytical frameworks and not to risk wasting their time on uncertain ramblings, are thus strongly advised to go on their way.

SEDUCING AN AUDIENCE – ATTRACTING THE ATTENTION OF A READER, catching a client's attention, converting a non-believer, responding to a user's expectations, persuading a voter, etc. – often involves building technical devices which play on people's social dispositions. The excerpt above is one such device (the irony!): it is a small, rhetorical machine which attempts to play on the reader's disposition towards conservatism and/or exploration. And there are many others, especially within marketing settings, which will be my field of choice here. For example, in order to attract customers, we can use a slogan promoting their penchant for repeating a habit ('Nutella, spreading happiness every day'); suggest a loyalty card which employs calculative capacities so as to better tie them to a future routine ('5% discount on the brand's products for cardholders'); propose a brand which appeals to a propensity for altruism ('Max Havelaar: great coffee [for] a great cause'); and so on. In other words, each one of these little machines for equipping the relationship between an organisation and its audience *ascribes* an attitude to people, in both senses of the word: they *assume* that the intended targets already behave according to this or that logic, and/or *supply* them with a possible mode of action; they suggest a way of behaving which this or that person did not necessarily have *in mind* (as something inbuilt/as a possible idea) but in which they can recognise themselves or which is likely to catch their attention. With captation[1] devices, the opposition between human and non-human entities disappears, as does that between their supposed privileges and respective 'ontologies', given that artefacts play a key role in defining or activating motives for action (and vice versa).

I would like here to explore the dynamics of these devices and dispositions, by focusing on a particular disposition in greater depth – curiosity – and on the particular devices which allow it to be expressed and spread throughout society. Why curiosity? In my view, it would be better to answer this by asking the opposite and even more intriguing question on which it is grounded: why not curiosity? Why should it be curious to experience curiosity about curiosity? This book is the fruit of a twin astonishment: on the one hand, twenty years of observing commercial scenes convinced me that of the dispositions activated by marketing devices, curiosity features prominently as a force behind everyday action; and on the other, this finding only makes it more surprising that this banal disposition is almost completely absent from the current sociological lexicon, or at least it was until very recently.[2] Classical sociology, it seems, prefers conservative modes of action, first and foremost habit, which curiosity, however – with the support of a related but equally neglected disposition: boredom – calls into question. Curiosity leads us to move beyond ourselves, and thus helps us to finally experience a little boredom, or perhaps more precisely weariness, about this 'habit' we know so (too?) well; and to be curious about this curiosity (which, if not newer, is at least unusual) which calls habit into question. I am willing to wager that curiosity can help us understand how market professionals and technologies, and more generally all specialists in interpersonal relations, are able to reinvent a person's identity and their *mobility*.[3] They do this by playing on people's inner motivations, in the hope of being better able both to draw these people toward them and to make them act according to their wishes.

I propose to conduct this exploration of curiosity by starting with an analysis of *Bluebeard*, the fairy tale written by Charles Perrault, given that this story is itself a pure curiosity machine which operates at the intersection (as we shall see) of mythical history and the contemporary anthropology of this particular disposition. The fact that exploring curiosity leads me to take a detour via popular culture – as well as religion, literature, literary criticism, history, philosophy, economics, psychology, management, and others – instead of sociology, which is my primary discipline, merely illustrates the necessity that confronts the sociologist who deals with curiosity, of drawing on sources other than those from his own discipline. It also illustrates the refreshing and potentially fertile nature of an exercise which consists in using the object being considered – curiosity, that is – as the means of its own exploration.

As is often the case in stories, in *Bluebeard* it is what is said at the beginning rather than at the end that matters most. The best way of dealing with this text is to quote the opening directly:

> There was once a man who had fine houses, both in town and country, a deal of silver and gold plate, embroidered furniture, and coaches gilded all over with gold. But this man was so unlucky as to have a blue beard, which made him so frightfully ugly that all the women and girls ran away from him.
>
> One of his neighbors, a lady of quality, had two daughters who were perfect beauties. He desired of her one of them in marriage, leaving to her choice which of the two she would bestow on him. Neither of them would have him, and they sent him backwards and forwards from one to the other, not being able to bear the thoughts of marrying a man who had a blue beard. Adding to their disgust and aversion was the fact that he already had been married to several wives, and nobody knew what had become of them.
>
> Bluebeard, to engage their affection, took them, with their mother and three or four ladies of their acquaintance, with other young people of the neighborhood, to one of his country houses, where they stayed a whole week.
>
> The time was filled with parties, hunting, fishing, dancing, mirth, and feasting. Nobody went to bed, but all passed the night in rallying and joking with each other. In short, everything succeeded so well that the youngest daughter began to think that the man's beard was not so very blue after all, and that he was a mighty civil gentleman.
>
> As soon as they returned home, the marriage was concluded. About a month afterwards, Bluebeard told his wife that he was obliged to take a country journey for six weeks at least, about affairs of very great consequence. He desired her to divert herself in his absence, to send for her friends and acquaintances, to take them into the country, if she pleased, and to make good cheer wherever she was.

> 'Here,' said he, 'are the keys to the two great wardrobes, wherein I have my best furniture. These are to my silver and gold plate, which is not every-day in use. These open my strongboxes, which hold my money, both gold and silver; these my caskets of jewels. And this is the master key to all my apartments. But as for this little one here, it is the key to the closet at the end of the great hall on the ground floor. Open them all; go into each and every one of them, except that little closet, which I forbid you, and forbid it in such a manner that, if you happen to open it, you may expect my just anger and resentment.'
>
> She promised to observe, very exactly, whatever he had ordered. Then he, after having embraced her, got into his coach and proceeded on his journey.
>
> Her neighbors and good friends did not wait to be sent for by the newly married lady. They were impatient to see all the rich furniture of her house, and had not dared to come while her husband was there, because of his blue beard, which frightened them.[4]

All French readers (and certainly many people in other countries!) know what happened next:[5] along with her friends, seduced by all the things, chests, and other furniture which she had been allowed to see, Bluebeard's wife inevitably succumbed to the curiosity which drove her to explore, alone, the cabinet which she had promised not to open. There, reflected in a mirror of blood, she discovered the hanging bodies of all the other wives who had preceded her. She was so horrified by the sight that she dropped the key to the floor; this then became marked by a bloodstain, which proved impossible to remove. Returning home, Bluebeard discovered that his wife had not kept her promise, and decided that, like his previous wives, she must die. After begging Bluebeard and shouting for help by desperately calling for her sister ('Anne, sister Anne, do you see anyone coming?'), the poor woman was fortunate to see her brothers arrive in time to save her and to kill Bluebeard. The inheritance from Bluebeard allowed his surviving wife to remarry and to marry off her sisters, and to buy captains' commissions for her brothers.

In the arguments that follow, I propose to draw on this tale reflexively. In spite of Bluebeard, but also thanks to him, I intend to be (and to make those of my readers who are not already) curious about curiosity. I will try to find keys and rooms in addition to the small – all things considered! – number that appear in the story of the man with the strange shock of facial hair. As we shall see, there are two other secret rooms in Bluebeard's house that are yet to be explored. These rooms are neither those more sumptuous ones located upstairs, nor on the ground floor, like the room of horrors; we will nonetheless visit these many rooms carefully (chapter 2). Like the archaeological foundations of the house, the first forgotten room was built well before *Bluebeard* somewhere in the cellar. This room contains the complete ancient anthropological history of curiosity, and more specifically, the Bible and the cabinets of curiosity that precede, but also modify this early history (chapter 1). The second room was built later and is higher up, in the attic, and is filled with the contemporary uses of curiosity in markets, whether window displays (chapter 3) or 'teasing' devices, intended to activate curiosity further and in different ways (chapter 4). By exploring the very smallest nooks in each of the rooms in the story of *Bluebeard*, I aim to uncover a deeper level through which the tale operates (a transitional space between the two forgotten rooms), as well as to reveal both the anthropological persistence and constant renewal of curiosity which constitutes – as we come to realise by the end of the fairy tale, and occurring today as much as it ever has – one of the principle modes of action capable of changing both people and their worlds.

I

FROM EVE TO BLUEBEARD: THE DIFFICULT SECULARISATION OF CURIOSITY

IT IS WELL KNOWN THAT PERRAULT'S TALES, FAR FROM BEING ORIGINAL, are rather revised literary versions of popular tales, often drawing on oral traditions (Soriano 1977). The tale of *Bluebeard* follows this model, but in a very particular way. It follows the model insofar as its account of the dangers of curiosity, as in the themes dealt with by many other fairy tales, is far from new. However, things are nevertheless different. The story not only recounts a popular fairy tale,[1] but also possibly retells historical events. The models for *Bluebeard* perhaps include: in France, Gilles de Rais, Joan of Arc's companion, who murdered a number of children and was hanged and then burned for his crimes and acts of witchcraft (Cazelles and Wells 1999); and, in England, Henry VIII, who executed two of his six wives. We can also say, with even greater certainty, that it retells the 'tale of tales': the most obvious source of inspiration (whether direct or indirect) for *Bluebeard* seems to me to be the Bible and its story of the tree of knowledge and of Eve and the Serpent:

> Now the serpent was more crafty than any of the wild animals the Lord God had made. He said to the woman, 'Did God really say, "You must not eat from any tree in the garden"?' The woman said to the serpent, 'We may eat fruit from the trees in the garden', but God did say, 'You must not eat fruit from the tree that is in the middle of the garden, and you must not touch it, or you will die'. 'You will not certainly die', the serpent said

> to the woman. 'For God knows that when you eat from it your eyes will be opened, and you will be like God, knowing good and evil'. When the woman saw that the fruit of the tree was good for food and pleasing to the eye, and also desirable for gaining wisdom, she took some and ate it. She also gave some to her husband, who was with her, and he ate it. Then the eyes of both of them were opened, and they realised they were naked; so they sewed fig leaves together and made coverings for themselves. Then the man and his wife heard the sound of the Lord God as he was walking in the garden in the cool of the day, and they hid from the Lord God among the trees of the garden. But the Lord God called to the man, 'Where are you?' He answered, 'I heard you in the garden, and I was afraid because I was naked; so I hid'. And he said, 'Who told you that you were naked? Have you eaten from the tree that I commanded you not to eat from?' The man said, 'The woman you put here with me – she gave me some fruit from the tree, and I ate it'. Then the Lord God said to the woman, 'What is this you have done?' The woman said, 'The serpent deceived me, and I ate'.[2]

As we know, God then punishes the three protagonists: he condemns the Serpent to crawl and to eat dust, the woman to give birth in pain and to live under the domination of her husband, and Adam to cultivate the soil (and, upon his death) to finally return to it himself.

The analogy between *Bluebeard* and Genesis is as strong as it is evident: in both stories a mysterious agent (God or man) prohibits a woman from approaching one item amongst many others; that same or another item stimulates her curiosity, pushing her to contravene the initial prohibition, and either punishes her or tries to punish the person (or people) who were unable to keep their promise. In both cases, the force (incentive?) of the temptation is exactly the same: access is granted to all the trees or cabinets, with the exception of one. There are of course very considerable differences between the two stories, which might outweigh their similarities, but before exploring these differences and their meanings, I would like to emphasise the extent of the parallels we can establish between the two.

FIG. 1. Lucas Cranach the Elder[3] and Gustave Doré[4]

The story of *Bluebeard* is nothing more than a profane variation of a very old, mythical story. As such, curiosity defies the sacred: it is a disposition that is deeply linked to an old anthropological scheme, not limited to the Judaeo-Christian tradition. This scheme relies on the privileged nature of the relationship of knowledge between the gods and humankind, as in the myths of Icarus and Prometheus, and/or on their being costs for sampling and discovering what is forbidden, as in the myths of Pandora[5] and Psyche[6] (or more recently, of Lady Godiva[7] or the Lady of Shalott[8]). The mythical or religious roots of *Bluebeard* lend the question of curiosity a particular depth. It is not just any disposition; it is, on the contrary, the very first disposition which humankind gave itself; it is curiosity and curiosity alone which is at the *beginning* of our history; after God provided the main elements and the scenery, it is curiosity that sets the human adventure in motion. At least in the Judaeo-Christian imagination, curiosity therefore intervenes long before 'habit' and 'self-interest', which sociology and economics nevertheless try to impose, one set in opposition to the other, like primitive matrices for all behaviour!

The mythical and religious origin of curiosity lend it a particular quality, by reminding us of its relation to sacred questions, to the ordering of knowledge, and to respect for Scripture. Before the development of modern science, curiosity was at the heart of the tension between natural philosophy and religion, and dealing correctly with this tension was a major challenge for social order as well as for religious power. For the fathers of the Church, the problem consisted in making the teachings of Aristotle, for whom 'all men, by nature desire to know' (*Metaphysics* book Ab 980 a 21), compatible with Scripture, which forbade access to the tree of knowledge. The difficulty is best expressed in Saint Augustine's famous confession concerning curiosity. On the one hand, Saint Augustine recognises that curiosity (*curiositas*) is a passion which, like its two sisters' pleasure (*voluptas*) and pride (*superbia*), is from both a spiritual and biological point of view inherent to the human condition:

> To this is added another form of temptation more manifoldly dangerous. For besides that concupiscence of the flesh which consisteth in the delight of all senses and pleasures, wherein its slaves, who go far from Thee, waste and perish, the soul hath, through the same senses of the body, a certain vain and curious desire, veiled under the title of knowledge and learning, not of delighting in the flesh, but of making experiments through the flesh. The seat whereof being in the appetite of knowledge, and sight being the sense chiefly used for attaining knowledge, it is in Divine language called The lust of the eyes (Saint Augustine 2005: 113).

On the other hand, Saint Augustine is wary of the dangers of curiosity, which he sees as steering us towards futile and vain knowledge and distracting us from serious and pious thought:

> From this disease of curiosity are all those strange sights exhibited in the theatre. Hence men go on to search out the hidden powers of nature (which is besides our end), which to know profits not, and wherein men desire nothing but to know. Hence also, if with that same end of perverted knowledge magical arts be enquired by. Hence also in religion itself, is God tempted, when signs and wonders are demanded of Him, not desired for any good end, but merely to make trial of [...] in how many most petty and contemptible things is our curiosity daily tempted, and how often we give way, who can

> recount? How often do we begin as if we were tolerating people telling vain stories, lest we offend the weak; then by degrees we take interest therein! I go not now to the circus to see a dog coursing a hare; but in the field, if passing, that coursing peradventure will distract me even from some weighty thought, and draw me after it: not that I turn aside the body of my beast, yet still incline my mind thither. And unless Thou, having made me see my infirmity didst speedily admonish me either through the sight itself by some contemplation to rise towards Thee, or altogether to despise and pass it by, I dully stand fixed therein (Saint Augustine 2005: 114).

In his confession, Saint Augustine identifies an interesting series of types of curiosity which range in form from the most anodyne to the most dangerous. The first category includes all kinds of 'spectacle', such as the dog race mentioned in the quote, or the lizard and spider catching flies, which in the process catch our attention, or the 'frivolous' gossip which we at first listen to in order to avoid offending the speaker, but which we then find ourselves obtaining great pleasure from. All these forms of curiosity are reprehensible. It is less because of the objects of our curiosity, which are of no particular importance, and more because of their effect: they distract us from the Augustinian quest for knowledge of God and of oneself.[9] A second category (just as reprehensible) concerns the enigmatic and unhealthy curiosity we experience with regard to unpleasant sights which functions as a perverse form of distraction: 'For what pleasure hath it, to see in a mangled carcase what will make you shudder? And yet if it be lying near, they flock thither, to be made sad, and to turn pale. Even in sleep they are afraid to see it' (Saint Augustine 2005: 114). It must be said, in passing, that this second, horrific form of curiosity is precisely the kind we find operating in the last part of *Bluebeard*. It does not operate through Bluebeard's wife (who has no way of knowing what is on the other side of the door, and who turns away and leaves immediately, truly horrified by what she discovers), but through the reader: it is the 'gory' side of the tale that makes it so particularly fascinating for readers.[10] Finally, a third, more significant category of curiosity involves the search for the 'hidden powers of nature (which is besides our end)'. This is, in other words, the forbidden fruit of the tree of knowledge. Saint Augustine – like contemporaries of his such as Apuleius (Tasitano 1989) – thought that the heretical search for this type of knowledge could not be pursued other than by 'magic'. For centuries, the idea of an almost obligatory link between 'forbidden knowledge' (Harrison 2001) and 'the curious sciences' – that is to say, the heretical practices of alchemy, astrology, necromancy, Hermeticism, and witchcraft – served to disqualify and suppress (often violently and, from the thirteenth century, with the help of the Inquisition) the numerous attempts to pursue knowledge beyond the sphere of religious thought, thus impeding the development of science.[11]

This recurrent confusion concerning curiosity (considered at once natural and dangerous) was in fact supported by scholastic thought throughout the Middle Ages, including by Thomas Aquinas, who eventually attempted to reconcile the one with the other: 'Through his soul [...] man is inclined to desire knowledge; thus must he humbly restrain this desire, so as not to push his investigation of things beyond the bounds of moderation' (Thomas Aquinas, quoted in Pomian 1990). With this particular wording, Aquinas was trying to reconcile natural philosophy and religion. This attempt was based on drawing a distinction between curiosity (directed towards forbidden and therefore reprehensible knowledge) and scholarship (controlled curiosity, in other words, compatible with the teachings of the Church). The entire question was therefore a matter of appropriately directing the desire to know, of respecting the guidance of and limits defined by Scripture. Suffice it to say that these limits were very strict, and that for a long time the distinction between good and bad curiosity was completely obscured by the latter.

It was not in fact until the Renaissance and the Reformation that a breach was opened – one favourable to a freer and broader expression of curiosity. The Reformation's contribution to this greater openness was both ambiguous and limited. On the one hand, by breaking from the pontifical monopoly and advocating a more personal reading of religious texts, the Reformation introduced a more direct relationship with the world, therefore weakening the old 'scriptural consensus' that these texts had offered: the criteria of truth must be able to be discussed (Houdard 1998). On the other hand, reformers, like their predecessors, were not inclined to allow curiosity free rein. John Calvin, in particular, in his *Warning Against Judicial Astrology*, whilst supporting in what were now accepted terms the Aristotelian nature of the desire to know, denounces the 'horrible, endless labyrinth' and the 'folly and superstitions' into which men have fallen 'since they have unleashed their curiosity' (Calvin 1842: 130). In the same text, Calvin has no fear of claiming, like other demonologists whom he joins here (Jacques-Chaquin 1998b), that mathematics often serves as a refuge for astrologists in search of an image of respectability.[12]

He even goes so far as to continuously warn his contemporaries against all curiosity which is too focused on his own doctrine of Election, to the extent that behaving in this way is seen as consisting of a search for the impenetrable will of God, and thus to risk the formation of incorrect ideas about divinity (Harrison 2001).[13]

If the Reformation therefore played a role in the advent of a more curiosity-based relationship with the world, it was very limited, and in any case took place on a much smaller scale than the social changes of the Renaissance which partially preceded and accompanied it. With regards to the issues we are concerned with, these changes took the form of two major innovations: a multiplication of the number of cabinets of curiosity and the advent of modern science.

Cabinets of curiosity are astonishing private spaces, the ancestors of our modern museums (Impey and Macgregor 1985; Findlen 1994), in which, from the fifteenth century, certain individuals started storing large numbers of intriguing, bizarre, and extraordinary objects. Specifically, the strange items in these cabinets that have been subject to a magnificent autopsy in the work of Antoine Schnapper (1998) are presented in a register that occupies a space somewhere between curio and curiosity (in French 'bric-à-brac', which arrived in English with a related but distinct meaning during the Victorian era). Because of the often substantial financial resources required to assemble these collections, this was a practice dear to the hearts of Europe's finest. This was not always the case, however, given that the world of collectors included people of very diverse circumstances and wealth, including collectors of antiquities, the bourgeoisie, doctors, scientists, and so on. As for the curiosities themselves, the cabinets threw together haphazard collections of objects ranging from cultural artefacts, such as medals, paintings, Greek and Roman antiquities, to handicrafts – jewellery, for instance – to miniature heads and figurines, even to natural objects from the vegetable, animal, and mineral kingdoms. These latter objects were collected because of their spectacular qualities (for example: tulips, birds of paradise, gemstones), or their legendary connotations (the Jericho rose; a Remora fish – harmless looking but nonetheless, according to Ovid, capable of slowing down ships – basilisks, unicorn horns, and eagle-stones – a kind of geode which, according to Eastern legend, could be placed in an eagle's nest in order to encourage propagation) and/or their curative abilities: the Jericho rose, unicorn horns, and eagle-stones that I just mentioned are also known for their medicinal virtues, the first for easing childbirth, the second for healing wounds, and the third for preventing miscarriage. Finally, greatest interest was shown in intriguing objects found at the intersection of the three kingdoms, which appeared to call their separation into question: for example, fossils – animal or vegetable rocks – and coral, apparently a vegetable-mineral.

Cabinets of curiosity appeared at a very particular time, when objects were being discovered faster than knowledge itself. That is to say, they were being discovered before we had the knowledge that could categorise them, or explain their origins, or determine their exact characteristics and virtues. The collectors of these curiosities marvelled at and expressed perplexity about everything they collected. Rather than try to explain the thousands of enigmas and puzzles, they tried to record them: giants' bones, amber containing insects, minerals which attract iron, extraordinary animals, unknown objects and monsters that provoked disgust, wonder, and desire to know (Daston and Park 1998). All of these curiosities created the possibility if not of numerous explanations then at least of the likelihood of questions being left open. As Krzysztof Pomian (1990) explains – the author to whom we owe the most accomplished investigation on the subject – the logic behind these collections is that of a relationship between the part and the whole: every cabinet works as a microcosm, a synecdoche, a place which is meant to 'represent the invisible' and provide access to the entire universe. Pomian beautifully defines the items that these collectors assemble as 'semiophores': in other words, objects filled with signification intended to make us able to see what is extremely distant both in time (see: a collection of antiques) and space (see: a collection of exotic objects). To put it in Bruno

Latour's terms (1993), collectors, even if driven by the desire to know about the 'modern' in the making, are themselves very much 'non-modern': they pile up objects more than they classify them[14] and they scarcely make a distinction between the human and the non-human. The logic which motivates them is concerned with the particular, and thus neither the universal nor market value: each piece is collected according to its own merits, regardless of its exchange or use value, and without a principle of commensurability that might allow their organisation.

The desire to understand and to explain was of course very much present, but neither was it a priority – collectors were not necessarily scholars – nor could these concerns make much progress given that attention tended to be confined to singular entities, and to noting their marvellous appearance rather than their inner and often inaccessible structure. And although, from the seventeenth century, these curious collectors became interested in scientific instruments, it was as collectors' items and not as instruments of knowledge: for example, when microscopes and telescopes were collected it was as a means of multiplying fascination rather than increasing understanding about the world. That the primary attraction was the wonder of an individual object, rather than for a systematic understanding of things, can be easily explained by taking two contextual elements into account. On the one hand, the discovery of the New World and the exploration of other exotic lands opened Western eyes to numerous novelties and enigmas (some spectacular and some of great potential significance), which science, still in its infancy, was not capable of explaining. On the other hand, the continuing prestige of classical forms of knowledge and the authority of religion remained as sources of confusion. At a time when the direct observation of phenomena and experimental verification were often out of reach, it was difficult to imagine how theses propounded by the great classical authors could be called into question (see Ovid and the supernatural power of Remora). Furthermore, the weight of forms of religious authority shaped and heavily constrained collectors' cognitive processes. Contrary to what one might think, the Church was not completely alien to the art of collecting, given that the practice had largely been anticipated in its accumulation of relics, paintings, statues, and even 'giants' bones' in places of worship (Pomian 1990; Schnapper 1988). However, if 'giants' bones' or 'unicorns' horns' were being collected, it was precisely because the existence of these extraordinary creatures was mentioned in the Scriptures. Both the belief in and the weight attached to Scripture placed very narrow limits on possible explanations and discussion. Even Ambroise Paré, a sceptic amongst sceptics, could do nothing but bow in the face of dogma: he did not dare to question the existence of unicorns, confining himself instead to discussing the therapeutic virtues of their twisted appendages. If fossils were intriguing, it was because of an inability to understand how fish could be found on top of mountains. The account provided by Genesis, which was beyond question, may have featured the Flood, but the latter was hardly compatible with the rising of the sea. In order to reconcile the irreconcilable, one suggestion was that animals were generated spontaneously by rock and would only be released once they were perfect. All in all, the marvels of nature and religious dogma combined to hamper knowledge and to increase astonishment. The cabinets of curiosity were therefore like antechambers of the science to come, the paradox being that, at a time when the world was suddenly being invaded by new objects from the world over, religious objection to knowledge sharpened the very curiosity it was meant to restrain.

However, the influx of new objects of curiosity would ultimately encourage the emergence of a less superficial and more scholarly approach to knowledge, and would therefore shape the gradual emergence and increasing autonomy of modern science. It is well understood that developing independent forms of knowledge about nature was particularly risky at a time when any attempts to obtain knowledge which differed from the content of Scripture might be suspected of heresy, or even links with the Devil (Harrison 2001; Jacques-Chaquin 1998b). The emancipation and development of modern science began just before Perrault at the very start of the seventeenth century; it became a key topic in academic circles in the following decades (Kenny 2004), and triumphed with the Enlightenment. Two major factors contributed to completely turning the image of scientific curiosity around (and thus to converting a desire for knowledge that was blasphemous and condemned by the Bible) into a force that would benefit society.

The first contribution was that provided by the English scholar and philosopher, Francis Bacon, who between 1603 and 1605 managed, for the first time, to develop a method of reasoning compatible with religious Scripture but nevertheless able to overturn the subordination of knowledge to religious authority. The first part of the argument consisted in arguing that since God had endowed man with cognitive skills, the knowledge of the world was neither forbidden nor above our capabilities: 'God hath framed the mind of man as a mirror or glass, capable of the image of the universal world' (Francis Bacon, quoted in Harrison 2001: 279). This formulation is very subtle. On the one hand, to claim that the knowledge of the world is accessible to man does nothing more than repeat the classical Aristotelian position which the guardians of Scripture had long since conceded. However, on the other hand, to say that God conceived the human spirit as a mirror, capable of directly reflecting the state of the world, was to open the way for a new approach. Largely favoured within Protestantism (to which Bacon personally adhered), this consisted in proposing to complement the reading of the great book of Scripture, and the Bible, with that of the new 'book of nature' (Mukerji 1983; Findlen 1994).

The second part of Bacon's argument was just as astute and innovative. The idea involved conceding the existence of forbidden knowledge (that which produced pride) in order to better emphasise another kind of knowledge, that which, on the contrary, would promote charity – the greatest of theological virtues, in other words. Once again, the concern to separate 'proud knowledge' and knowledge guided by charity falls within a longer philosophical tradition, given that it reminds us of the distinction drawn by Thomas Aquinas between curiosity and scholarship. However, at the same time as connecting with previous ideas, Francis Bacon managed once again to innovate, by suggesting that it was possible to define the proud or charitable nature of knowledge in light of its usefulness. With this new criterion, it then became possible to distinguish between knowledge acquired through vanity or pride, guided only by the 'pleasure of curiosity', and virtuous knowledge, directed not towards the personal satisfaction of the senses or of the mind, but towards a search for knowledge that is useful in life. This would repair the damage caused by the Fall. By providing a new reading of Genesis, this twin argument manages to overcome the dogma which had stood in the way of scientific progress. The promoters of the new sciences had finally found a way of developing their work without overly offending the religious authorities and risking the wrath of the demonologists. Robert Boyle referred to Bacon in order to defend his experimental philosophy and a practice of science consistent with reading the book of nature; the members of the Royal Society, who first resisted Bacon, Boyle, and Newton's pioneering curiosity (Ball 2013), finally recognised their debt to Bacon, who had given them legitimacy and had opened the way for their activities to take off (Harrison 2001).

The second contribution to the emancipation of science and the acceptance of curiosity came from authors such as Descartes and Montesquieu. Descartes' original contribution, shortly after Bacon and long before Montesquieu, also consisted in addressing curiosity not from a religious point of view, but through a methodological approach. Based on the idea that the intellectual capabilities of man were limited, Descartes argued that these capabilities could not encompass everything, or else there would be a risk of errors of judgement. He therefore condemns unbounded curiosity, and in particular the curiosity which is aimed, according to him, at the pointless inventory of all natural entities. He does this in order to argue in favour of a desire for knowledge that is deliberately limited to objects that we can tackle with the tools provided by reason and method (Pomian 1990; Harrison 2001). Later, and after *Bluebeard* had been written (1697), Montesquieu agreed by saying that

> [w]hat makes the discoveries of this century [eighteenth] so admirable are not the simple truths that we have found, but the methods for finding them [...] It is not a single brick in the edifice, but the instruments and machines for constructing the whole building (quoted in Jacques-Chaquin 1998a: 19).

Without a doubt, and as has been demonstrated by Christian Licoppe (1996), the previous 'curiosity for curious things' played an important role in the development of modern science throughout the second half of the eighteenth century – the period between Descartes and Montesquieu. This occurred through the organisation of spectacular experiments where a curious public (generally deliberately chosen either at the time of the experiment, or when it was later recounted) was called upon to give its approval to the events observed and the conjectures inferred. However, this was ultimately a period of transition: a 'curiosity-based' knowledge regime was, little by little, sidelined in favour of methods of argumentation revolving around the usefulness and exactitude of scientific proposals. A science playing on the curiosity of public experiments was replaced by a 'cooler' form of knowledge, determined less by the excitement of visual and collective perceptions than by the possible usefulness of the knowledge produced. This was whether this knowledge was employed by political authorities (in France); by economic and financial institutions (in England); in the internal organisation of museums and the establishment of their catalogues (which contributed (especially in Italy) to 'codifying the culture of curiosity that defined the experience of the collection' (Findlen 1994: 44);[15] in the drafting of laws meant to explain the reproducibility of the phenomena studied; or in the increasingly hushed, closed world of scholars' studies and the academies – for instance, in the Académie des Sciences in France or the Royal Academy in England (Licoppe 1996).

Thereafter, the Enlightenment completed the liberation movement of *libido sciendi* (the craving for knowledge) from religious tutelage: the limitations of science and human curiosity were, from then on, not cultural, but technical and cognitive (Jacques-Chaquin 1998a). Paradoxically, accompanying the triumph of knowledge over religion was a disenchantment not only with prior beliefs, but also with curiosity. This was also a process which clearly demonstrated the decline of analogical thinking (which, for example, claimed nuts could heal the brain) in favour of taxonomic thinking (which tried to reduce the world to a finite series of universal criteria) (Foucault 1973). Consider the case of ornithology, for instance. We see a move from Rondelet's impressionist sixteenth-century classifications (birds with strong beaks, singing birds, birds living beside water, and so on), towards the morphological classifications of Francis Willughby a century later (based on anatomical criteria (Schnapper 1988: 61)). The singular is finally reconciled with the universal: with the development of robust methods of classification, able to draw together a series of singular events within the same structure – what Descartes had feared so much (uselessly overloading the memory through the vain science of the inventory) finally made sense. With the upsurge of taxonomy, collections were ordered and divided, with curiosity taking a step back in favour of examination. Employing the general laws of physics and chemistry, and supported by the use of methods of dissection and an analytical approach, single objects were split into ever more simple elements. The irreducible strangeness of creatures thus became the simple expression of universal combinations. Paradoxically, science had triumphed over both the Church's prohibitions on curiosity as well as over the forms of guilty curiosity which its practices were meant to arouse:

> In the last decades of the eighteenth century, naturalists increasingly turned towards observation, experimentation, and reconstitution. As Cuvier said in 1808, 'natural history [...] which the general public and even some scholars still have rather vague ideas about, started to be recognised for what it really was: a science whose aim is to use the general laws of mechanics, physics, and chemistry to explain particular phenomena demonstrated by different natural entities'. This leads us to apply classificatory criteria to natural phenomena which no longer owe anything to visual inspection. Thus, minerals are now classified according to their chemical composition, which is only revealed thanks to the destruction of the samples being studied and the use of measuring instruments. And animals are classified on the basis of their anatomy as studied under the microscope; this means that specimens have to be removed from their jars, in which they had been preserved and exhibited, so they can be dissected to the point where very little is left. As for fossils, they are now classified in relation to their original organisms, which involves comparative anatomy, whilst being integrated into a time-based, reconstituted series, thanks to the presence of fossils in strata whose position allows their order of succession to be inferred. The golden age was coming to an end. We were now entering the age of laboratories and fieldwork (Pomian 2004: 35–36).

At the same time, curiosity began to become 'economised', which completed the general sense of disenchantment: over time, the commercial potential of curiosities was seized upon by traders: these grew in number, invaded the world of collectors, contributed to and organised collections, authored catalogues, and converted the previously private accumulations of the collectors into a market for collected objects. The market became the place where both collectors and scientists obtained the curiosities which fascinated and interested them (Findlen 1994: 170 sq.), as well as the place where these same objects were put into circulation. If we could give only one example to illustrate the consequences of this movement of commercialisation, it would have to be the fate of the poor unicorn: traders supplied such a large number of narwhal tusks (those twisted horns so dear to collectors) that they ended up ruining the unicorn legend by both demonetising and discrediting it (Schnapper 1988). In other words, science and forces of economic transformation joined together to restrain curiosity, collections, and the number of collectors. The very last source of hesitation was that of the *Encyclopédie*,[16] torn between its own ambition for knowledge and the risk of vain curiosity (Jacques-Chaquin 1998a), under the influence of La Bruyère's brutal satire against tulip collectors (Schnapper 1988). However, this hesitation was no longer produced in the name of religion, but was rather grounded in knowledge guided by reason: these were the dying embers of a long debate, which had already moved towards an era of tempered or even forgotten curiosity.

We have now reached the time when the major divisions that structured modernity since the Reformation ended as they became brought together: after Protestants had launched their own modern project by attempting to separate the divine and the Church, scientists in many ways prolonged their efforts by seeking to separate the world of things from those of the state and religious authority (Shapin and Schaffer 1985). Eventually, in the eighteenth century, the new separation of the economy from religious and civil control resulted in the disentanglement of all of the political, religious, and economic elements which the old world had mixed together. Just as Protestants had built their doctrine on the definition of a direct link between the subject and the word of God (the Bible), scientists had founded their knowledge on the establishment of a direct link between the work of a researcher and the things he studies. Now, with Adam Smith at the forefront, the new economists also intended to break away from their old political affiliations (associated with the heritage of mercantilism) by proclaiming the transcendence of market forces. This would protect economics from all human and spiritual domination for the benefit of the dictatorship of 'interest', created *ex novo*, as a new, natural disposition (Hirschman 1980). The economic, the political, and the religious were each separated while the manner in which they could be recombined was reinvented: 'The laws of commerce are the laws of nature and consequently the laws of God' (Polanyi 1957: 117); laissez-faire had to be respected in order to respect the divine/natural order to things.

The proliferation of goods was accompanied by a general movement towards materialism, science, and economics. Contrary to what is understood following Weber, Protestantism did not play a privileged role in this development: the love of gold, finery, possessions, and the search for profits for profit's sake, which Weber postulated as the consequences of capitalist behaviour, in fact preceded the advent of the economics of accumulation (Sombard 1966: 32). Similarly, at the root of the modern economic world we find Veblen's pre-capitalist 'leisure class', which was born out of the disappearance of both the feudal system and the predatory nature of the aristocracy. If the lower classes were still limited to a subsistence-level existence (Veblen 2013), then the new leisure class was giving pride of place to salons, speech, and manners, as well as to luxury and comfort, presents, feasts, and ostentatious behaviour. Of course, the leisure class (inclined to spend) was quickly replaced by the middle class (inclined to save). Long before Weber's Protestants, rich Italians (such as, starting in the fifteenth century, the architect Alberti) pushed problems of household management to the fore by discovering that it was possible to become rich not only by earning a lot of money, but also by spending less (Sombart 1966: 106). However, the middle class's inclination to save was – in fact similar to Weber's Protestants, who followed – purely relative. Whatever the middle class men did not personally consume was done so by those that surrounded them: for example, by domestic servants (Veblen 2013: 49) and wives who were responsible by proxy for the master of the house's consumption. The former did so out of duty and the latter to guarantee the household's reputation:

> It is by no means an uncommon spectacle to find a man applying himself to work with the utmost assiduity, in order that his wife may in due form render for him that degree of vicarious leisure which the common sense of the time demands [...] the wife [...] has become the ceremonial consumer of goods which he produces (Veblen 2013: 57).

This duplicitous behaviour is not the late flowering of curiosity. On the contrary; curiosity has been coextensive with the history of modern capitalism. In fact, the double articulation of production and consumption was based less on a hypothetical division of duties between Protestants (inclined towards saving and production) and Catholics (inclined towards spending and consumption), and more on the intimate entanglement of saving and consumption behaviour amongst all of the actors involved:

> Many of the seventeenth- and eighteenth- century English businessmen of Protestant faith who built up their enterprises by careful reinvestment eventually used large portions of their wealth to become the new gentry, building great country houses on their newly acquired estates and filling them with lovely artifacts (portraits, chairs, murals, and chinaware) that testified to their high social station. These entrepreneurs are easy to type as Protestant businessmen in the Weberian sense if one simply ignores the way they lived at home. But such ignorance is costly. It masks the fact that *pure ascetics or pure hedonists were rare in early modern Europe; most people, whether Protestant or Catholic, combined the two tendencies* (Mukerji 1983: 3–4, my italics).

The worlds of collecting and consumption became progressively blurred, at the mercy of a movement of 'publicisation' and democratisation. The English historians McKendrick, Brewer, and Plumb (1982) and the sociologist Chandra Mukerji (1983) have clearly demonstrated how, throughout the eighteenth century (after *Bluebeard*, then) there was a craze for the exotic and for novelties amongst the working classes. The private collections of old, which had required considerable wealth, took on different and more accessible forms. This involved new, less costly activities: growing seeds and bulbs in the garden for show, buying ribbons and printed textiles which brightened up wardrobes, and visiting zoos and botanical gardens, which gave people a cheap way of discovering the extraordinary animals and plants that had been brought from the New World and the colonies. However, the progress of science and the progressive generalisation of the unusual ultimately resulted in disenchantment. The commercialisation and the assignment of monetary value to everything eventually imposed interest as a substitute for all other passions (Hirschman 1980). From then on, economics became concerned with self-interest, and sociology with habit, with both forgetting all other motives of action, including curiosity, which, as we shall see, was abandoned to the market.

2

BLUEBEARD: TOWARDS THE MARKETISATION OF CURIOSITY

WE CAN SEE THAT VENTURING INTO BLUEBEARD'S CELLAR AND DELVING deep into the foundations of the 'wonderful house of horrors' helps us to better understand who this enigmatic man is and what is at stake in his tricks, beyond his particular case. *Bluebeard* appears at a pivotal moment, just before modern science established itself, and just before the generalisation of consumer society. Perrault wrote his tale at a time when collecting practices were reaching their peak, while also coming into competition with quests for gold, success in business, and material pleasure. With an eye on these historic changes, we can now, therefore, study the differences between Genesis and the character of Bluebeard on the one hand, and, on the other, the relationship between Bluebeard's collecting practices and this new economic configuration.

The main difference between Genesis and *Bluebeard* concerns, of course, the main protagonist. Bluebeard combines, in a single figure, the Serpent (traitor), Adam (spouse), and God (punisher), whilst at the same time being quite different from each. The blurring/differentiation of these figures is the fruit of a certain identity crisis: Bluebeard imagines himself neither as the weak Adam[1] of the inaugural garden of Eden, nor as the more contemporary husband who accedes willingly to his partner's wishes, also the subject of the tale's 'moral' (see below), but rather as the domineering (if dated) figure invented by God to punish Eve. In its own way, the tale begins the movement towards secularisation, of which it is also a product: there is no imperious God in the story, nor a tempting serpent, but rather simply a man, however frightening he may be. This point is worth emphasising: with the exception of his enigmatic hirsuteness, which is only there to focus the reader's attention, Bluebeard is far from the fantastical creatures which normally fill fairy tales; he is neither ogre, nor giant, nor sorcerer.[2] Bluebeard is of course monstrous, but no more or less so than the 'serial killers' of the past (before Perrault: Gilles de Montmorency-Laval and Henry VIII, and after: Landru[3]) and the present. The character could even be considered more pathetic than frightening: he is a 'man of possessions', a misogynist and misanthropist who dreams of himself as both God and master, unable to become either, and who is rejected because of his blue beard, perhaps because he is not, or is no longer, blue-blooded. Bluebeard is frustrated because it is not he that is attractive to others, but rather his riches. So he kills his successive wives because they let him down; this is undoubtedly because they break their promises but equally because they systematically fall for an illusory materialism, one which, paradoxically, he also suffers from. Nor does the tale explore a universal mythical question, but rather delivers an anachronistic testimony about an era which is coming to an end: the central character, his businesses, and possessions, already have one foot in the future modern middle class, while his behaviour demonstrates that he still has one foot in the old world. Bluebeard is nostalgic about a mythical time, characterised by attitudes and values which tend to be, if not disappearing, then at least becoming less relevant (respecting promises, authority, obedience, the primacy of spirituality over material goods, as just a few examples). He is, however, marked by the inaugural zeugma which defines his identity according not to who he is, but to what he has ('There was once a man who *had* fine houses, both in town and country, a deal of silver and gold plate, embroidered furniture, and coaches gilded all over with gold'; my italics) including his fateful beard ('But this man was so unlucky as to *have* a blue beard'; my italics). In light of these shortcomings and contradictions (as with so many victims used as scapegoats), he condemns his wives as if he is vainly trying to forget that he is just like them, and was so long before they were, having become unworthy of the values he defends.

Bluebeard is therefore a character who is both trivial and mysterious, but for reasons which we did not expect: he is intriguing less because of

BOX 1. *BLUEBEARD* AND PSYCHOANALYSIS, OR THE MISFORTUNES OF MISPLACED CURIOSITY

Since Bettelheim (1976), it has become conventional to reduce tales to psychoanalytic fables. Bettelheim himself used *Bluebeard* as a way of applying his universal analytic framework, and in order to explain that the blood on the key signified that the heroine had had extramarital relations whilst her husband was away; thus the tale would be seen as confronting us with a sexual curiosity which it of course condemns.[4] If I were to adopt the same approach (on which Freud's successors were so keen) of tracking down the juicy motive, I could attempt another explanation, based on an inversion. In this case, I could place the woman in an active role with the husband adopting a passive one: on the one hand, the woman deflowers the forbidden room using a phallic key, risking a bloodstain which cannot be removed; on the other hand, her husband limits his speech and remains in the background. From this inversion, it would therefore be possible to deduce that Bluebeard is impotent. Everything would then become clear: the character would compensate for his sexual shortcomings not only with his absence, but also by putting his power to the test, as well as by transferring activity onto his wife/wives, and then finally by killing the person who represents him as the substitute for an impossible relationship (Eros and Thanatos: the theory is well known!). Psychoanalysis could even support this audacious interpretation, by referring to one of its historical variants – one that appears much later but which is equally troubling: the case of Louis XVI, a king who, when experiencing difficulties consummating his marriage and forced into political inaction, found himself (almost) like Bluebeard, distracted by his hobby of locksmithery, before this double inaction condemned both him and his wife to the fate we well know! In fact – and abandoning the historical variant I mention 'just for fun' – the theory about Bluebeard's impotence seems more reasonable than Bettelheim's interpretation. It has the advantage of proceeding carefully based only on the elements provided by Perrault, without having to involve lovers who are difficult to locate in the story (although admittedly, there are plenty of cupboards in which to hide them!). We can see that a psychoanalytic approach is never short of imagination (or fantasy?!). However, I believe this exposes it not only to the risks of over-interpretation, but also to the dangers of a certain obliviousness to other, more likely interpretations. By focusing too much attention on motivations which may not exist, we in fact end up not seeing all the rest – as in (upstream) the clear and pregnant precedent of Genesis, and (downstream) all the economic lessons which stories convey quite explicitly; no hermeneutics, other than reading carefully, is needed to explain these. Undoubtedly it is Gustave Doré who best grasped (by accident?) this point: his engravings show heavily dressed figures facing objects which are as bare as they are intrusive, perhaps to signify the extent to which the body is so much less important to this story than objects. The same could be said, of course, for the – very intense – ways in which the figures regard these objects.

the enigmatic colour of his beard or the sexual content of the tale (see Box 1), and rather because of how he is positioned economically. The character is trivial in the sense that he is attached from the outset to a completely materialistic economy, where people are defined by neither their birth (like princes), nor their origins (like in the Middle Ages), nor their job (like modern subjects) but their possessions. Bluebeard is a fairy-tale character in a tale of facts,[5] immersed in a purely materialistic universe. He nonetheless remains mysterious because he is a man about whom we know nothing, other than the fact that he has a lot of possessions, 'both in town and country'; in other words, everywhere and nowhere. We do not know by virtue of what economic logic his possessions were acquired (inheritance, through private income, production, trade?); they were accumulated, but it appears they cannot be alienated. Bluebeard can therefore be considered as an ambiguous figure who encompasses all of these elements: assets, savings, production, and consumption/ostentation.

It is here that we touch upon the connection between curiosity and economy which would become established in the years to come. Curiously(!), the analogy we were most expecting is the one which is least effective:[6] Bluebeard no longer corresponds to the figure of a collector of curiosities, despite the presence of numerous cabinets at the time: the collector from Castres (Pierre Borel, who was a contemporary of Perrault, himself knew of sixty-seven in France alone; furthermore, during this period there were 'hundreds, if not thousands' of cabinets of curiosity in Europe (Pomian 1990). As an initial approximation, one could certainly say that Bluebeard was a collector; twice over, perhaps, given that he collected both objects and women. In this respect, he corresponds to a traditional collector of curiosities, accumulating objects and animal carcases as well as human bodies in the form of mummies, shrunken heads, and other more or less well-preserved monsters (Pomian 1990; Schnapper 1988). However, whilst diversity in collections was the rule, and homogeneity the exception, the women that Bluebeard collects are identical. And if he is collecting them, it is only because he is unable to find the perfect wife who follows his wishes, and not, apparently, because he initially intended to multiply his crimes and trophies. But as for the rest, all the goods he possesses, in other words, Bluebeard has an entire collection of objects, the wealth of which actually masks great poverty: it all boils down to either containers that are rather hollow ('two great wardrobes', '[crockery]', 'strong-boxes', 'caskets', 'apartments', and a 'little closet'), or to contents like precious stones and metals and therefore to the value they represent. We are confronted with a one-dimensional and pecuniary approach which is demonstrated by the rather vain repetition of the words 'gold' and 'silver', which little by little dissolve the real value of the associated objects ('silver and gold plate' (twice!), 'coaches gilded all over with gold', 'gold and silver', 'jewels'). The emergence and invasion of a monetary standard actually extinguishes the very principle of collecting, given that, by using the same yardstick to make the collected objects commensurable and fungible, they lose their irreducible singularity.[7] There is therefore a second major difference with Genesis: in *Bluebeard*, it is no longer a matter of forbidden knowledge but rather vain material seduction – as if the symbolic fruit had become literal; as if sacred knowledge had turned into profane tastes. In the tale, the protagonists' appetite is, in fact, not for fundamental knowledge, but rather for quite vain objects of pleasure, until they reach that abyssal, ultimate emptiness: the forbidden room – the only true cabinet of curiosity in the story, which is filled only with the women who thought it was full.

FIG. 2. Frans Francken II[8]; Gustave Doré[9]

The materialistic and vanity-driven universe which Bluebeard honed to test his victims is indeed the antechamber of the movement to come: that of the economy's emancipation from old forms of control and social relations, and towards a new order which is based on consumption and the 'natural' circulation of goods in the commercial sphere. We have reached the tipping point between the economy of the *Ancien Régime* (literally: Old Regime) and the emerging commercial economy of the middle class. This is demonstrated by the tale's ambiguity, which, from the first to the last lines, defines a universe that is both economic and domestic.

Right from the beginning, the tale shifts dizzyingly between economic calculations and filial relationships. Filial relations take precedence over every calculation, since children are faced with the traditional obligation to accept the suitors proposed by their parents. However, in this case the situation becomes more complicated given that the two daughters are available for just one marriage. This introduces the question of choice into the heart of traditional family relations of authority. The lack of interest and embarrassment which this problem (respectively) presents initially leads Bluebeard to delegate the management of this choice to his potential mother-in-law ('He desired of her one of them in marriage, leaving to her choice which of the two she would bestow on him'). It is then up to her to offer her daughters the choice, in a manner of speaking, of a non-choice (this second delegation is implicit in the following wording: 'Neither of them would have him, and they sent him backwards and forwards from one to the other, not being able to bear the thoughts of marrying a man who had a blue beard'.) The opening scene thus confronts us with a particularly original situation of impossible calculability, the opposite of that faced by Buridan's donkey (Cochoy 2002): instead of a single economic agent, Bluebeard – or his possible mother-in-law – faces an inescapable trap, consisting of the rational choice between two potential, almost identical wives (two sisters between whom one cannot a priori differentiate: they are both said to be 'perfect beauties', and it is only afterwards that we find out who is the younger and more naive of the two). Ultimately, it is the two potential wives who are driven towards the choice of which one will have to be chosen! This choice is yet more complicated because the agents, far from having a preference, demonstrate an identical aversion to the object to be chosen; they thus find themselves in a situation akin to that of Buridan's donkey, as evoked by Christian Schmidt, who had to choose not between two equally desirable quantities of food, but between two poisons (here there is only one). Now, Schmidt tells us that in such a situation, one possible and rational option is abstention, and that this must be taken into account as a real choice (Schmidt 1986: 77). However, in the tale, a choice other than abstention is at play, through the presence of both obligation (the sisters know that one of them will have to yield) and calculation. It is calculation that leads one of the girls to consent, for, after experiencing the festivities offered by Bluebeard, she believes that in the final analysis her suitor's possessions will have sufficient appeal to overcome the repulsion which his blue beard inspires in her ('the youngest daughter began to think that the man's beard was not so very blue after all, and that he was a mighty civil gentleman'). The difficulty of choice is resolved by a process of calculation which includes, on the one hand, the revelation of additional information about Bluebeard (the attraction of his wealth), and, on the other hand, the revelation of physical and cognitive differences between the two sisters (one is younger and therefore more naive). Whereas the first element turns a negative preference into a positive preference, the second means they can resolve their indecision (if one of the sisters was not more naive than the other, we might assume that their calculation would have been identical – to either marry or reject Bluebeard. This would have meant the problem remained unresolved. It would thus have had to be referred to the mother for arbitration, or a convention, such as the birthright of the eldest,[10] would have had to be applied. Thus, we can clearly see to what extent the tale both brings into play and calls into question the old way of managing alliances. It opens up the sphere of personal dependencies to expressions of individual preference and rationality, whilst implicitly announcing the aporias that accompany this development (possible errors in calculation, logical deadlocks, a reworking of personal dependencies, among others).

The blurring of the economic and the domestic continues in the rest of the tale, this time in relation to place. What Bluebeard offers his wife is an economic space in the sense that it is a question of choosing, exploring, consuming, and evaluating the objects that are 'supplied'. It is important to underline the extreme degree of licence which he grants his wife: not only is she authorised to visit (almost) every place in his home, but she is also allowed to show these to her acquaintances ('to send for her friends'), and also is given an almost total freedom of movement; she is thus far from being imprisoned in the home behind locked doors, as an overly hasty reading of the tale might lead one to believe ('to take them into the country, if she pleased'). If it were not an anachronistic expression, one could say that Bluebeard presents his house almost as if it were a self-service emporium, where one can come and go as one pleases, and of course, where one can approach the objects without fear of being hindered by human mediation. Despite this initial impression, however, the economy that is portrayed remains strictly domestic: the universe of exploration in fact constitutes a closed circuit; it is closed by the unbreakable link that then existed between marriage and the allocation of a household's assets. The supplied objects have no price and are inalienable. We are clearly in the presence of consumption that is preferential and non-rival: the economic relationship in this case is confined to visual exploration and does not involve the acquisition of goods. If the tale does provide forms of material seduction, then this is done in the manner of 'window-shopping'. Indeed, this is a forewarning of future market configurations (see chapter 3), which here remains highly private and illusory, narrowly enclosed within the domain of personal property and, for the moment, far removed from the open markets which are to come.

Finally, the combination of economy and family extends to the denouement. On the one hand, after the death of Bluebeard, the distribution of his inheritance commences with activities of calculation and allocation being set into motion: the heroine, who inherits all her late husband's assets, wisely uses a portion to marry off her sister, another to purchase captains' commissions for her brothers, and herself uses the remainder to remarry. However, the way these different sums are employed elegantly demonstrates that we remain completely immersed in an economy of accumulation and unearned income: at Bluebeard's, there is no production; goods do not circulate but rather stay within the circle of kinship; women have no other economic existence other than through marriage, while for men, it is through the acquisition of commissions under the Ancien Régime. The intertwining of both spheres – economic calculation and the domestic economy – reminds us once again of the extent to which the economic is not unaffected by strong ties, and vice versa (Callon and Latour 1997). What is at play in the tale is not a world of personal attachments and non-calculation which then tips over into a world of calculations and individual freedom, but rather a change in proportions between these different entities. The move is towards more flexible family relationships and an extension of the rational assessment of situations.

In this movement, the motives of self-interest and curiosity play roles which are as significant as they are subtle. In the tale, self-interest does make an appearance, but simply as something that is in the service of curiosity. The distinction between these two types of motivation, and the way in which they are brought together, appear to be clearly visible in the two sequences which follow Bluebeard's temporary departure.

There are three characteristics proper to the first of the two. First of all, in this sequence, that which we explore is neither surprising nor curious, for Bluebeard has already (and quite meticulously) explained, revealed, and made accessible the content of each room. For visitors, it is above all a matter of experiencing the simple excitement that arises out of being able to come and see for themselves all the things that they have heard about and aspire to see and/or possess. This is an aspiration that is no doubt more general than linked to the tale's particular plot: unlike Bluebeard's wife, her invited friends were not provided with any specific preparation for the visit (at least, not that we know of). They therefore discover things that they had not necessarily coveted beforehand. Then, the sequence is collective. The sense of excitement appears to be shared by all of the invited friends ('They ceased not to extol and envy the happiness of their friend') and with the emphasis almost exclusively being placed on the degree of wealth; it is this that encourages their expression of a common passion. This is the third characteristic: everything involved in this sequence concerns the seductive nature of material goods: rooms 'all so fine and rich that they seemed to surpass one another', mirrors 'in which you might see yourself from head to foot', but paradoxically, where the reflections are admired less than the frames – 'the finest and most magnificent that they had ever seen'. Here, the commercial value of things takes precedence over their function. All in all, what occurs in this sequence results less from curiosity – which, as we have seen, involves bringing a certain mystery into play, a personal point of view, or adopting a certain attraction to the singularity of the objects in hand – than from a novel orientation grounded in a world that is more transparent, in points of view that are more widely shared, and in an attraction towards the exchange value of these coveted items. In fact, the first sequence plays not with curiosity but with self-interest, with desire, with material pleasure, with an early form of a 'Ladies' Paradise'. It plays with the seduction of the false market represented by Bluebeard's inaccessible, private offerings, which takes the form of a proto-consumer economy in which goods can be desired and looked at, but not taken away.

The contrast between this first sequence and the one that follows it is as violent as it is systematic: they oppose each other on every point. The transparency and accessibility of the rooms in the first is matched by the opacity and absolute injunction which characterise those in the second. The collective exploration of the permitted areas of the house is followed by Bluebeard's wife's solitary secret visit to the last room. The shift from a multiple and shared visit to an exploration that is individual and secretive, is accompanied by a change in motivation. It is possible to detect this change in the first sequence when the admiration expressed by the group of friends is contrasted with the attitude of Bluebeard's wife, who 'in no way diverted herself in looking upon all these rich things, because of the impatience she had to go and open the closet on the ground floor'. Thus, a naive expression of self-interest is opposed by the almost irresistible force of curiosity, a term which Perrault very significantly saved for this last sequence: 'She was so much pressed by her 'curiosity' that, without considering that it was very uncivil for her to leave her company, she went down a little back staircase' (let me be clear that the word curiosity has not appeared in the story apart from on this one occasion; it appears again later as a central motif in the story's first 'moral'). Between one location and the other, the purpose that guides the gaze is effectively no longer the same. This is revealed in the extraordinary game of mirrors between the two sequences, with mirrors themselves playing a crucial role in the tale, dominated as it is by the issue of the gaze and by the Augustinian theme of curiosity as the 'concupiscence of the eyes'. In the first sequence, we may be thrilled to stand in front of the mirrors and to gaze at our reflection 'from head to foot; however, it is in fact their frames that we subject to particular scrutiny (see above). In the second, we are frozen with fear when confronted with the 'floor [...] covered over with clotted blood', this bloody pool, whose boundaries we cannot see but within which, on the other hand, we can clearly see reflected: 'the bodies of several dead women, ranged against the walls'. In each mirror, the women can always see themselves from head to toe but they are neither the same mirrors nor the same women: whereas the first type of mirror is blinding, drawing attention away from the very image which it should help to anticipate, the second illuminates, by revealing too late the cost of not looking properly or looking too much. Whereas the first stimulates self-interest, at the risk of being blinded, the second ensnares the heroine in the trap of curiosity, at the risk of fatal self-knowledge.[11]

In the tale, Bluebeard therefore plays with not one, but two motives for action. He arouses self-interest in order to subordinate it to curiosity. By acting in this manner, he teaches us that there is nothing spontaneous about curiosity: although natural to humankind, in order to spur us to action, this is a disposition that must still be activated. To do so, the character proceeds sequentially. First of all, he uses the greed[12] of his targets, including, of course, that of his wife: if, during the collective visit to Bluebeard's house, she seems hardly aware of the economic seduction that enthrals her friends, it is not because she does not share their taste for riches but because, on the one hand, she has already experienced this opulence during the initial festivities, and on the other, because she knows what the others do not: the existence of an enigmatic room which – she believes – will be able to reawaken her interest, already blunted by the inaugural festivities and the first weeks of marriage.[13] It is at this point that the second aspect of Bluebeard's ploy intervenes: by providing a lot of information (except about one aspect) and by referring to the last key and the last room as mysterious and forbidden (and not without previously indulgently describing and opening all those rooms preceding this reference), the character creates an appetite. He arouses a hint of homology, and invites his wife (but also the readers, along with her) to co-produce the tale, through anticipation. Using the example of *Little Red Riding Hood*, I have previously demonstrated how all 'captation' operations aimed at catching our attention consist of mobilising the logic of ballistics, according to which the actors who engage in operations of captation first try to construct a model which follows their target's path, so as then to build a device suitable for meeting this trajectory and intercepting it (Cochoy 2007a). What is interesting about *Bluebeard* is that the 'catcher' delegates this ballistic operation of calculation to its target. Unlike the wolf who asks Little Red Riding Hood questions in order to be able to guess her trajectory and to intercept her, Bluebeard does not settle for building an unequivocal model in order to anticipate the logic behind his wife's actions and to trap her. Furthermore, his intention and the model's determination still remain subject to caution: we will never know whether our man wanted to manipulate his wife to be certain of satisfying an urge as perverse as it is morbid, or whether he simply wanted to put her to the test, secretly hoping to finally find a woman who lives up to his wishes. In fact, let us not forget the number of fairy tales which feature the same kind of seemingly unlikely trial, consisting of successively subjecting a large number of people to the same test which they all fail, but which, however, allows the appropriate person to be identified *in extremis*: this is the case in Andersen's *The Princess and the Pea*; it is also the case with Perrault himself, whether with Cinderella and her glass slipper, or with Donkeyskin and his fine-fingered ring.[14] There is here the heritage of the values of both chivalry and courtly love, from which Bluebeard cannot be completely excluded, given that, as we saw, he manifestly still has one foot in this world (he is a fairy-tale character amongst fairy-tale characters) and the other in the modern world to come (he is a man of property, driven by 'business', rationality, and material possessions). Therefore, the model's construction and the fatal 'captation' (i.e. seduction) are delegated to the wife. Bluebeard suggests that she build her own history (in every sense of the word: both tale and trajectory) but based on the scenario and resources which he has deliberately arranged for her (even if it is only up to her to open the door or not and to thus seal her fate; she can only do so using the doors and keys with which she is provided).[15] Bluebeard gives his wife all the keys (real and figurative) she needs to be able to build and express 'the algorithm that suits'. In the process, he invites her to pursue her exploration according to a dual sequence that proceeds from the awakening of self-interest towards the awakening of curiosity. Thus, the model to be built borrows from the highly 'scripted'[16] register of riddles or mathematical sequences: Bluebeard's wife is implicitly led towards anticipating what the last room might contain, on the basis of and according to what she saw in the preceding rooms, without however, being formally made to do so. Therefore, the initial arousal of her self-interest serves as a first step in awakening her positively directed curiosity towards the forbidden room, which is later tested. His wife thus progresses at the mercy of an expertly crafted combination of rational expectations and passionate dreams. The fact that these expectations and dreams are finally disappointed in no way invalidates the strength of the cognitive device which has been deployed in order to awaken curiosity. On the contrary: its failure functions entirely as a sign of its remarkable effectiveness (which saddens Bluebeard just as much!).

I would like to conclude the analysis of the tale by highlighting its superb ambiguity (or perversity?). This tale is built up pragmatically by Bluebeard (but not necessarily by Perrault; see below) to condemn curiosity, but also to stimulate it, to pay tribute to it, and even to excuse it. With *Bluebeard,* we are in the presence of an eminently introspective tale: the horrible husband awakens not only his wife's curiosity, but through her, ours as well. Even before the story has begun (see the enigmatic title), the reader's cognitive enrolment in its central motif is fascinating in itself. In fact, *Bluebeard* should be seen as a marvellous illustration of the literary power of curiosity. It is perhaps the most beautiful of tales, because more than any other it intrigues its readers, gives them goosebumps, freezes them with terror whilst also warming their appetite for knowledge. It pushes them irresistibly forward until the last door, until the last page, preventing them from stopping or interrupting their reading. The reader is torn between the pangs of pleasure that come from wanting to know the rest of the story, and the fear of discovering what exploring the secret chamber and breaking the promise made to the unsettling blue-chinned character will bring. Certainly, this introspective twisting between the substance and the form of the story increases a problem of which its predecessors were aware but protected themselves against: Saint Augustine was wary of the romantic nature of his writing, while Apuleius warned his readers against the seductions of his rhetorical methods (Tasitano 1989). The same introspective twisting also constituted an insurmountable dilemma for the demonologists: by subjecting the curious sciences which they sought to combat to such a forensic examination, they did nothing more than heighten the charms of the curiosity they wished to condemn – charms which they in turn fell victim to (Jacques-Chaquin 1998b). Nevertheless, Perrault's position regarding this same difficulty is different, and even radically innovative. Far from being concerned about the contradiction between the form and the substance of his story, the author instead pushes the contradiction to culmination. His tale works not only as a parable but also as a virtuoso rhetorical invocation of curiosity.

This rhetoric consists namely in a dizzying interarticulation of two styles – suspense and ellipsis – which are to curiosity as prosody is to poetry, narration to the novel, grammar to language, and the like. Ellipsis deprives us of information about Bluebeard's previous background, including the origins of his highly unusual beard, his wife's identity and history (even though we at least know her sister's first name), what happened between the wedding and his departure, and so on and so forth. The use of this style creates gaping holes in the story which themselves operate as mysteries and arouse the reader's desire for them to be filled. This desire becomes ever more strong and prolonged because it can never be satisfied. Suspense, in turn, is connected to two complementary methods. The first consists in punctuating the story with information, pregnant with meaning but truncated, whose full significance only becomes clear once the gaps are filled – perhaps later ('he already had been married to several wives, and nobody knew what had become of them'; 'except that little closet, which I forbid you, and forbid it in such a manner that, if you happen to open it, you may expect my just anger and resentment')... or perhaps never ('Bluebeard told his wife that he was obliged to take a country journey for six weeks at least, about affairs of very great consequence'[17]). Distilling the information in this way creates a sense of great expectation, pushing readers forward but also working on their imagination, with every movement reinforcing another.

The second method consists in stretching out the tale at those moments when time is supposed to be passing more quickly, slowing things down almost unbearably (Perrault's systematic and collective tour of the whole house is described in ninety-three words and a single paragraph, whereas the heroine's exploration of the small chamber alone stretches to 173 words across three paragraphs, with the division into paragraphs adding to the effect of suspense). The method of slowing down time repeats again and again at the end of the story. It first appears when everything indicates that we will finally and immediately discover the contents of the forbidden room ('she went down a little back staircase, and with such excessive haste that she nearly fell and broke her neck'). Perrault then interrupts the progress (or rather the race which he has just promised us!) towards the denouement by adding a paragraph of suspense ('Having come to the closet door [Are we there? Well, no, not yet!], she made a stop for some time, thinking about her husband's orders, and considering what unhappiness might attend her if she was disobedient; but the temptation was so strong that she could not overcome it. She then took the little key, and opened it, trembling'). The method is used a second time, of course, as soon as the door is opened. This time, Perrault achieves the miracle of revealing a sight that we might a priori suppose appears at the speed of light over a seemingly interminable period of time: 'At first she saw nothing, because the windows were shut. After some moments she began to perceive that the floor was covered with congealed blood, in which the bodies of several dead women were reflected, ranged against the walls'. The effect expected by the opening of the door is cancelled out by the closed windows; the instantaneousness of the vision is interrupted by the time her eyes need to become adjusted to the darkness. Finally, when the heroine's pupils have sufficiently dilated, the horrific spectacle is only revealed extremely gradually and follows an indirect trajectory: it starts from the door, moves to the puddle of blood, then to its reflection, and finally from the reflection to the bodies. What is remarkable here is that Perrault is not content with writing. The author is handling material that is more visual than literary; he is scripting a cinematographic scene before its time and generating fear through the clever movement from a bird's-eye view to a low-angle shot, prefiguring the art of a certain Alfred Hitchcock. The horror in the chamber, far from marking the end of the story and the suspense, shifts immediately to yet further revelations. It would no doubt be tedious of me to meticulously describe, in the way I have done up until now, the variants of the time-stretching methods employed at the end of the story (that, nevertheless, are just as remarkable) as Bluebeard's threat becomes ever more pressing. In order to keep things brief, let me just mention, however, the interminable dialogue between Bluebeard and his wife, the quarter of an hour she is given to pray before he will cut her throat, and from that moment, the agonising wait (which takes the style of a countdown) for the brothers, who by chance have promised to come by that day (but nothing in this tale is for sure, given that promises have the questionable effects that we have seen). The sense of expectation is heightened by the time it takes for a laborious exchange of information and glances between the two sisters (one at the top of the tower, the other at the bottom), with the obsessive repetition of the same dialogue, emphasised by the reiteration of 'time' and the stammering of the rhyme (the poor afflicted girl would shout to her from time to time 'Anne, sister Anne, do you see anyone coming?' And Anne the sister would reply: 'I see nothing but a cloud of dust in the sun, and the grass greening').[18] The expectation is in vain; the hope raised by a moving dust cloud is dashed when it turns out to be nothing but 'a flock of sheep', with the wait then further prolonged by a final lengthy exchange with Bluebeard (an exchange which hovers between efforts to plead and an attempted execution), before the two brothers finally arrive and triumph over Bluebeard (but not before a last chase). From narrative ellipses to suspense, and from textual effects to visual methods, it is thus clear that the curiosity which the tale seemed to have the ambition to condemn, paradoxically constitutes the procedure which binds it together. This ambiguity is the last of the tale's curiosities, which sustains the startling contradiction embedded in the two morals at the end of the story:

> Moral: curiosity, in spite of its appeal, often leads to deep regret. A thousand examples appear each day. To the displeasure of many a maiden, its enjoyment is short lived. Once satisfied, it ceases to exist, and always costs dearly.
>
> Another moral: apply logic to this grim story, and you will ascertain that it took place many years ago. No husband of our age would be so terrible as to demand the impossible of his wife, nor would he be such a

> jealous malcontent; he is meek and mild with his wife. For, whatever the color of her husband's beard, the wife of today will let him know who the master is.

The moral, which always appears as the final key to a tale, takes the form here of a Berlin key; in other words, a key with two blades that are not identical but symmetrical (Latour 1991): whereas one gives us access to the cellar which we have now explored in depth, while presenting curiosity as a passion as dangerous as it is illusory, the other allows us to lock up and leave, so that we can climb the very long staircase that takes us towards the chamber of novelties, towards a world where we cannot but accept our part in an irrepressible curiosity (feminine, according to the tale) and towards a certain egalitarianism, or even the potential inversion of gender relationships. As Barbara Benedict (2001) argued, curiosity expressed the transgressive desire to go beyond assigned roles and categories, especially between men and women. We must now borrow this staircase, from which a gentler atmosphere flows, in order to climb from the cellar of 'historical' curiosity to the attic of its renewal in markets. Thanks to the detour via the cellar and the return via the tale, we have seen that one part of Bluebeard's character draws on his genealogy in an older world and its value in the new, and, fortified by this dual identity, another employs the nascent figure of self-interest to test the old demons of curiosity. Thanks to the tale and the exploration of the attic of commerce (which was later added to the wonderful house of horrors), we shall see that, despite Bluebeard's death, it is also possible to implement the opposite strategy of appealing to the extremes of traditional curiosity in order to satisfy the interests of contemporary commerce (and with one often merging into the other).[19] Lorraine Daston and Katherine Park explain it well: curiosity became 'a highly refined form of consumerism, mimicking the luxury trade in its objects and its dynamic of insatiability' (Daston and Park 1998: 310).

Bluebeard foreshadowed the shift from the economy of the Ancien Régime to the economy of the market, in that the tale was grounded in the appeal of material possessions, of monetary values, of window displays, and the like. However, the journey was far from complete: the tale exhibited 'things to be seen' rather than 'things to be acquired': it promoted an economy confined to the domestic sphere – Aristotele's *œconomia* rather than Adam Smith's – an economy without production or consumption; in other words, an economy lacking prices and the circulation of material goods. By contrast, the contemporary economy is its opposite: things are now displayed to be bought; goods are less to be collected than to be produced and consumed; things do sometimes remain immobile, but never for long: they circulate in the market as they do in our lives; the logic of flow and exchange tends to prevail over the old logic of stock and property (Vatin 1987). Sitting behind all these changes, curiosity, far from having disappeared, plays a preeminent role. However, both curiosity and the role it plays are not the same as they used to be. Now, curiosity works as a way of stimulating self-interest rather than the other way around; curiosity has today lost its previous air of sin; it has become both more discrete and more obvious: within contemporary markets, curiosity is self-consciously appreciated and cultivated by traders but also more or less consciously cultivated by their clients.

In order to demonstrate how these changes have occurred, the mechanisms behind them, their effects, and what is at stake, I propose that in the following chapters we analyse three examples of how curiosity is being used in contemporary markets. The first is the use of curiosity in the arrangement of the display windows of an American grocer in the 1940s; in this example, curiosity takes on many innovative forms, each centred around competition (chapter 3). The next two examples (both in chapter 4) relate to 'teasing'. One concerns the design of new packaging for Kellogg's cereals in 1955. Here, curiosity appears both as an internal component of the packaging and as an external means to promote it. The third and final example is that of the 'Myriam' advertising campaign in 1981. Myriam is one of the most famous campaigns in the history of French advertising. This campaign introduced the 'teasing' device (in other words, a series of mysterious posters aimed at preparing the audience for the final revelation of a commercial offer), and thus turned curiosity into the driving force, designed to elicit a response from the consumer. Although the choice of each of these examples is somewhat arbitrary, I hope that together they will form a heuristic whole. On the one hand, this set of examples shows that each particular device – displays, packaging, advertising – is capable of renewing and enriching the social use of curiosity in markets. On the other hand, a particular actor corresponds to each device: a small shopkeeper arranging his display window, a large company managing its packaging, and an advertising professional who offers himself as a mediator to all the others. Therefore, it clearly emerges that all the market actors – shopkeepers, manufacturers, and intermediaries – and beyond them, all the actors in society whom they address, are, for better or worse, engaged together in the game of socially activating curiosity.

3

'PEEP SHOP'? AN ANTHROPOLOGY OF WINDOW DISPLAYS

LET US START WITH AN ARTICLE ON SHOP WINDOW LAYOUT PUBLISHED IN the magazine *Progressive Grocer*. Launched in the United States in 1922, this is a professional magazine aimed at supporting the modernisation of small independent and traditional grocers, faced with competition from new forms of distribution (such as chains of shops in the 1920s and supermarkets at the end of the 1930s). Apart from articles written by specialised journalists, *Progressive Grocer* publishes testimonies provided by the grocers it targets, who, from time to time, share tips about the job with their peers (Cochoy 2010a). This kind of contribution is immensely interesting as it gives us access to explanations regarding real professional know-how on curiosity. It is as if Bluebeard and Perrault had agreed to give away and exchange their methods, techniques, tricks, and little secrets with their peers, and as if we could simultaneously explore this exchange in secret and clandestinely observe the school of wizards – like Lucius from Apuleius' Golden Ass, or the demonologists of yesteryear. Proceeding in such a manner spares us the kind of enquiry, subject to possible errors and/or oversights, which I have had to resort to thus far.

Access to this type of knowledge and its relationship to curiosity is provided for us quite explicitly in an article from February 1940 entitled 'We put curiosity to work in our shop window' with the subtitle: 'Shop window displays which arouse the curiosity of passers-by always lead to sales, says a trader in Kansas'. In other words, this article purported to be the testimony of a grocer from Kansas, much renowned for giving advice and concrete examples. The expression 'arouses curiosity' is deliciously ambiguous given that it encompasses both the manipulation of curiosity (as an external device meant to attract customers) and the activation of clients' prior propensity to be curious. The relevance of these two interpretations is explicitly confirmed and completed in the article's opening proposal, based on using the display as a device to arouse curiosity:

> There isn't any part of the store which will draw more trade, pay bigger dividends, or stir up more interest than the display window. My slogan has always been, 'Displays built right will sell on sight'. In putting this slogan to work the whole secret lies in your definition of the word 'right'. To me it means a display that is different – unusual for some reason or other so it will arouse people's curiosity (*Progressive Grocer* February 1940: 58).

Just like Emmanuel Didier's (2007) statistical objects, curiosity is both constructed ('built right') and at the same time seized upon, activated, 'expressed' ('arouse' people's curiosity), in line with the classic paradox so well identified by Latour – and of course, before him, by the actors themselves as soon as they became concerned with achieving results and not idealising their practices or putting them on a pedestal – according to which '*les faits* [facts] *sont faits* [facts/made]': no fact can exist independently from its construction. Conversely, what is constructed is always based to a certain extent on facts (Latour 1999).[1] In fact, setting curiosity to work (in Bluebeard's house or in the display) means awakening the curiosity of the subject (whether wife or consumer). The one does not go without the other: that was the lesson from Bluebeard; this is also what our window dresser from Kansas teaches us. However, we still need to know what alchemy lies behind this strange construction-activation of curiosity; this activity of 'making someone do something' or this 'performance' (Callon 2007) of the 'curious captation'. It is here that our shopkeeper from Kansas brings us something new by presenting three techniques for activating curiosity that are very similar to the figures of 'advertising magic' that Roland Canu (2011b) describes so clearly.

In our witness's account, the presentation of the three techniques is preceded by a very broad and innovative definition of the curiosity which underpins them, a curiosity that provides guidance towards something 'different' and 'unusual'. Curiosity is therefore closely linked to the theme within marketing of differentiation, whilst being applied to it in a very particular manner. On the one hand, there is classical differentiation with which we are well acquainted, and which, after Chamberlin (1962) and its implementation in marketing (Smith 1956), consisted in modifying the definition of the product in the hope that specific characteristics associated with this modification will encounter preferences not satisfied by the market. On the other, we have what we could call 'curious differentiation', proposed by our modest grocer: contrary to the other more well-known forms, this type of differentiation is not aimed at any prior preference, other than the prior preference for the absence of prior preference; our grocer intends to play on people's propensity to be surprised, to be attracted by the unknown, to choose novelty, and/or to like surprises. This, as we will see, is what makes it so significant.

The techniques used to arouse and construct this type of disposition are each based on managing the window display as a curiosity device. Before examining them in turn, note that the choice of the object which brings them together – the display – is not in the least anodyne. For those who have just read *Bluebeard*, it is a choice that might admittedly be somewhat surprising.[2] The image that we remember from the tale is from its final episode, that is to say it is the memory of a closed, opaque door and an association between curiosity and secrecy: the less I see, the more I want to know what I might be able to see. With the closed door and the secret room, we find ourselves at the antipode of the window displays and the shop that is on view and open to all. However, let us not forget too quickly that the tale is sequential and that the final episode is preceded by a tour of other rooms; a tour which, conversely, plays on maximum transparency and visual accessibility. What is interesting about the display is that a single device unites and links precisely those properties of the devices proper to each of the tale's two sequences, according to an economy of means designed to maximise its effectiveness. Just like the final door in *Bluebeard*, the display takes the form of an obstacle and a screen – a separation capable of hindering the movement of the body and the senses and therefore of stirring desire. Furthermore, the visual access provided by the display is often deceptive, given that it is not the shop itself, and in addition, the duo, consisting of the window and the display space behind (often enclosed by a background), operates as a particularly thick and opaque door, so much so that when we first approach it, we cannot see just how thick and opaque it is. However, as with our previous tour (of Bluebeard's rooms), the display attempts precisely to present itself as a transparent opening, as a faithful representation of the wider universe to which it is supposed to give access. The display is closed, but this closure, whilst filtering the other senses (touch, smell, sound, and even taste, despite the deceptive French expression '*lèche-vitrine*'! (Literally: window-licker – in English, window-shopper)), gives the eye almost unlimited access. Like the door, it marks both the separation between a private space (here, commercial) and a public space. However, like the door, it is also intended, in its own way, to allow passage between the two (Leymonerie 2006):[3] the display is an open-closed door – open to the eye, closed to the body. The display is open to view, thus encouraging the 'concupiscence of the eyes', the very foundation of curiosity (see above, 'Teaser'). However, this transparency is arranged: the view is neither direct (the objects are 'represented', and those that I see are not necessarily and/or exactly those that I will find, buy or consume in the shop) nor free: the objects are organised in a certain way and I cannot 'move around' them other than according to the very limited set of angles that the window dresser has chosen for me. But this is exactly the point; the visual opening is intensified by the closing off of the body. What conditions curiosity here is at once the illusion in which the customer experiences seeing (knowing) everything and the practical difficulties involved in using this knowledge, this total possession and perspective – the display manages to achieve, in a gradual and intricate way, that which the different rooms and the secret cabinet in the tale did but in a manner that was too brutal and divided; by luring the viewer with the impression of immediate access and at the same time obstructing it, the display produces the time lag that is fundamental to the operation of any curiosity device. The display's invisible door is even more attractive because it opens up a world which it prevents us from reaching – the display 'holds' us: it prevents us from advancing and captivates us at the same time.

Once again, the display connects two devices that are clearly different in the tale. We have just seen that this device associates the visual accessibility of the rooms with the opaque closure of the cabinet. The ploys thought up by our grocer combine, as we will see, two sub-elements from the same scenarios: the effects of mirrors, on the one hand, and of locks, on the other.

THE EFFECTS OF LOCKS

Let us start with the game of locks. First, the analogy between the lock in the tale and the shop's window display is not obvious, as the two devices possess opposing characteristics: whereas the lock, with the exception of the keyhole, constitutes a space that is perfectly opaque, the window display offers a view that is perfectly transparent but hermetically sealed. The analogy therefore operates on another level. Not in the radically different physical configurations of the two devices, but rather in their proximity to each other as 'observation devices', and in the effect of this proximity on their users. In order to understand this effect, we should begin by referring to Jean-Paul Sartre and his famous text on the subject of the keyhole:

> Let us imagine that moved by jealousy, curiosity, or vice I have just glued my ear to the door and looked through a keyhole. I am alone and on the level of non-thetic self-consciousness. This means first of all that there is no *self* to inhabit my consciousness. [...] This means that behind the door, a spectacle is presented as 'to be seen', a conversation as 'to be heard'. The door, the keyhole are at once both instruments and obstacles; they are presented as 'to be handled with care'; the keyhole is given as 'to be looked through close by and a little to one side', etc. Hence from this moment 'I do what I have to do'. No transcending view comes to confer upon my acts the character of a *given* on which a judgement can be brought to bear. My consciousness sticks to my acts, it *is* my acts; and my acts are commanded only by the ends to be attained and by the instruments to be employed. My attitude, for example, has no 'outside'; it is a pure process of relating the instrument (the keyhole) to the end to be attained (the spectacle to be seen), a pure mode of losing myself in the world, of causing myself to be drunk in my things as ink is by a blotter in order that an instrumental-complex oriented toward an end

> may be synthetically detached on the ground of the world [...] Moreover I cannot truly define myself as *being* in a situation: first because I am not a positional consciousness of myself; second because I am my own nothingness. In this sense – and since I am what I am not and since I am not what I am – I cannot even define myself as truly *being* in the process of listening at doors. I escape this provisional definition of myself by means of all my transcendence [...].
>
> But all of a sudden I hear footsteps in the hall. Someone is looking at me! What does this mean? It means that I am suddenly affected in my being and that essential modifications appear in my structure – modifications which I can apprehend and fix conceptually by means of the reflexive *cogito*.
>
> First of all I now exist as *myself* for my unreflective consciousness [...] This means that all of a sudden I am conscious of myself escaping as myself, not in that I am the foundation of my own nothingness but in that I have my foundation outside myself. I am for myself only as I am a pure reference to the Other [...] It is shame or pride which reveals to me the Other's look and myself at the end of that look. It is the shame or pride which makes me *live*, not *know* the situation of being looked at.
>
> Now shame [...] is shame of *self*, it is the *recognition* of the fact that I *am* indeed that object which the Other is looking at and judging. I can be ashamed only as my freedom escapes me in order to become a *given* object. Thus originally the bond between my unreflective consciousness and my Ego, which is being looked at, is a bond not of knowing but of being. Beyond any knowledge which I can have, I am this self which another knows. And this self which I am – this I am in a world which the Other has made alien to me, for the Other's look embraces my being and correlatively the wall, the doors, the keyhole. All these instrumental-things in the midst of which I am, now turn toward the Other a face which on principle escapes me. Thus I am my Ego for the Other in the midst of a world which flows toward the Other (Sartre 1984: 259–261).[4]

The lock in the tale on the one hand, and the window display on the other, are both extremely close to and distant from a Sartrian lock.[5] First let us compare

Perrault's and Sartre's locks. There are many differences between them that at first sight render the parallel inoperative: firstly, whereas in Sartre, the inquisitive person knows that he is being observed, Bluebeard's curious wife would no doubt have abstained from being inquisitive had she known what she was about to see and the exact punishment that would result.[6] In addition, in Perrault this visibility requires the door to be opened, whereas in Sartre it is rather the opposite: seeing means avoiding the risk of being seen by those being watched on the other side of the lock. We might be surprised by the fact that Perrault chose the opposite solution to Sartre for his tale, given that the keyhole – ever since doors equipped in this way have existed! – is the archetypal curiosity device.[7] But if we think about it, there is only a difference of degree and style between direct observation through the lock (which means the key may not be placed inside) and indirect observation, subsequent to the key being used (preventing one from looking through the keyhole).

In the tale, the decision to open the door rather than voyeuristically peep through the keyhole has perhaps less to do with some deep reason, to which Perrault holds the secret, than with the story's overall structure, which imposes the one outcome rather than the other on him. As such, opening the door rather than looking through the keyhole is, as we have seen, a good way to draw out the action and suspense, in a way that is likely to engage the reader in the very experience of curiosity (using the third person means the point of view cannot be shared; it is difficult for two people to look through a keyhole, and even more difficult to have a lasting view when the viewing angle is limited and the objects to be seen are immobile!). Secondly, this choice is justified because the set of keys already exists and because one of the keys will play a subsequent role as proof the action was committed. Lastly, and in this specific case, as only Bluebeard and Perrault know, it is not necessary to resort to a device that would prevent those who are being watched (on the other side of the door) realising that they are being watched, and for good reason! Aside from these contextual factors, in both Perrault and Sartre the keyhole, however it is used (with the eye or the key), remains a curiosity device able to arouse the self-consciousness of the person or people who use it,[8] even if the ways in which this is done are somewhat different: whereas in Sartre, self-awareness comes from the intervention of people behind the voyeur's back, in Perrault it comes from both the same kind of intervention (Bluebeard's shadow hovers behind his wife's conscience, although admittedly, alas for her, intermittently) and from the very object being observed on the other side of the door. This is because the butchered women stand for both a reflection of a broken promise and the fate promised to the wife who is looking at them (and unfortunately, unlike his wife, Bluebeard intends to keep his promise).

However, does this make the keyhole necessary for the phenomenology of self-consciousness described by Sartre? Or does the window display operate just as well (or worse) than Sartre's door? Unless neither the keyhole nor the window display plays a direct role? Does the activation of self-awareness not depend more on the irreducible attributes of the subject who is observing, and of those who are looking at him and of the surrounding society? Another well-known text, Jean Starobinski's analysis of the young Rousseau confronting some confectionery, helps us examine this question:

> Jean-Jacques, miserable apprentice, coveted only in secret. Roasts, fruit or sweetmeats (not to mention girls, of whom he knew nothing) – all of these he ogled with sidelong glances, followed immediately by blushes. Even if he had cash in his pocket, he was ashamed to enter the pastry shop, for then he would be obliged to point out the object of his desire, thus betraying to the others the appetite that held him in its grip. This caused him insurmountable embarrassment. 'I catch sight of the women behind the counter and can already imagine them laughing amongst themselves and making fun of the greedy youngster... But two or three young people over there are looking at me'. He feels dangerously exposed. If he exhibits his desire, the gazes focused on him will immediately turn hostile. When he restrains his greediness and goes hungry, he convinces himself that the others are 'devouring him with their eyes'. The would-be eater suddenly discovers the risk of being eaten. A reinvigorated commandment weighs upon his conscience. 'Thou shalt not covet' – not even what you can buy honestly. Rousseau will not permit himself to be caught redhanded in the act of desiring, for this this would exhibit a culpable weakness, a shameful need. Before he can be slandered

> by a single gesture or word, his imagination leaps ahead: in the gaze of the onlooker it glimpses adumbrations of irony, anger, and mockery. Paralyzed, he is a timid Tantalus, repressing his desire while feeling it swell within him: 'I am frightened by everything and discover obstacles everywhere. As my discomfort grows my shame increases. But in the end I go home like an idiot, consumed by longing and with money enough in my pocket to satisfy it, but not having dared to buy anything'. Desire, thus disappointed and heightened, must invent new gratifications. It will seek itself in ways more oblique or more direct. Who is spying on his actions? Rousseau has no idea. His 'eyes lowered', he cannot recognize faces in the distance, which only increases his alarm. He is the victim of anonymous scrutiny by an unidentified spectator. Thus he is subjected to a ubiquitous peril. The hostile witness, who is nobody in particular, in effect becomes everybody. Things quickly get out of hand. Under the scrutiny of the witness (that is, under the presumed scrutiny of a faceless witness) Jean-Jacques' relation to the object he covets is completely distorted. The distance and the lighting change, and a new obstacle crops up. Desire, knowing that it covets a forbidden object, can no longer reveal itself openly. It is obliged to dissumulate. From now on, it will be the hidden desire of a forbidden object (Starobinski 1989: 14–15).

Rousseau's confession[9] and the analysis provided by Jean Starobinski refer to a case very similar to the process described by Sartre: whenever other people observe a look of desire, a feeling of shame and of doing something forbidden is created in the person who is surprised or observed. For all that, the way the two situations are organised, and the methods of explanation, are quite different. With Starobinski/Rousseau, the imprecise description of the context of interaction is inversely proportional to the meticulous introspection of the subject (and also, as we shall see, to the more subtle but no less significant pressure of society). With respect to the objects, I have neither door, nor keyhole, nor window display capable of arousing shame or framing the gaze (retrospectively). Rousseau's shame is present before entering the shop (indicated by the very discreet metonymy of the counter) and this shame, as with Sartre, awakens self-consciousness. It may be delayed, but it is just as sharp, taking the form of the superlative introspection so particular to the *Confessions*. In neither scene is there a focus on the door, the lock, or the window display which separate them. In other words, at no point is this feeling of shame connected to *things* other than the subjects themselves – the person being observed and those who are observing him. Or rather, there is an object which lends support to this shame but it is only the object of desire itself, and not the mediations that might inhibit or arouse the desire and shame. In the absence of any technical intervention whatsoever, Starobinski therefore has no other choice than to seek, quite logically, the reasons for shame in both the subject and the society that surrounds him.

With respect to the subject, we are not dealing here with a generic, universal, and unknown spectator. On the contrary, the character – the young Rousseau – is as distinctive as he is famous. Starobinski strongly emphasises the irreducibility of the subject by later creating a contrast between Rousseau and the 'normal man'. Whereas the former 'convinces himself that others "are devouring him with their eyes"', the latter 'accepts not knowing how others see him' (1989: 15). For the author – who, without any other forms of transition, establishes an equivalence between 'a normal man' and 'us'; in other words, everyone but Rousseau – the difference lies in the fact that, contrary to Rousseau, 'we' possess a well-reasoned social attitude that does not draw us into making assumptions about the benevolent or malevolent nature of other people's looks, given the wholly undefined and a priori unknowable, and therefore equally probable, nature of the attitudes with which we are confronted:

> So as not to cut off the possibility of dialogue, we generally leave open a range of possibilities. Among the attitudes we ascribe to others, favourable thoughts more or less compensate for hostile intentions. Thanks to our polite precautions of politeness and the conventions of language, all eventualities combine, in the absence of more ample information, to create neutral uncertainty, a wavering ambiguity. This affective ambiguity, which is not without its dangers, results from mutual respect for an elusive liberty. In everyday intercourse, we readily accept the uncertainty that prevents us from making assumptions about the true feelings of others, thereby

> protecting our independence. We do not think of complaining about the perpetual oscillation between a phantom of benevolence and a phantom of wickedness, knowing full well that for our interlocutors our feelings are no less hypothetical than those we believe we can read in their eyes. Jean-Jacques, however, cannot bear uncertainty. With a rapidity characteristic of all his emotions, he rules out every possibility but one: hostility (Ibid: 15).

The originality and skill of Starobinski's analysis lies in his continual combination of psychology and sociology in inverse, counter-intuitive and perfectly symmetrical proportions. In an opposition in which the irreducibly singular 'Rousseau' figure is on one side, and the extremely general nature of the normal man on the other, we might have expected him to propose two opposing forms of explanation: the clinical in the case of Rousseau and the sociological in that of the normal man. However, in neither is this the case.

In the passage just quoted, we see that the analysis of 'the normal man' involves a highly psychological sociology which chooses to reconstruct likely social behaviour not according to a range of external forces, affecting different categories of people, but according to a form of reasoning oriented around an 'average' social figure. This is identified by the author according to an introspective anthropology, quite similar to that kind undertaken, in a Weberian tradition, by sociologists like Raymond Boudon and Jon Elster. Conversely, as we will see later, when explaining Rousseau's behaviour, Jean Starobinski decides to distance himself from the clinical psychology that the case nevertheless seemed to call for, focusing instead on quite a wide range of accidents and external social factors.

Indeed, his use of the category 'normal' implicitly appears to point to its opposite, the pathological, and even more specifically, the psychiatric. Is it not in fact paranoia which appears to emerge from Rousseau's attitude, not only in the passage analysed by Starobinski, but also in the other circumstances of his life? Many authors have not hesitated to provide this diagnosis, both prior (see below, and Wilkins 1959) and subsequent to Starobinski (Farrell 2005; Glass 1988; Lilti 2008), by examining the delusion of persecution from which the philosopher suffered from at the end of his life, in other words exactly when he was writing the *Confessions,* at the risk of transferring this late-onset paranoid affliction to the writing of his childhood memories. However, even if Starobinski himself admits that the scene of Rousseau's shameful greed is a 'precursor to the paranoia of Rousseau's final years', he prefers to distance himself from this kind of analysis[10] by refusing to choose between psychology and sociology. On the one hand, the literary critic takes Rousseau's personal psychology into account, by interpreting his shame about the disapproval of others as a 'projection' of a 'condemnation he feels inwardly' given that passing the act of punishment onto others is perhaps a way of making it more bearable ('There is an economy of suffering: better to be the object of others' hostility than to suffer inner conflict and torment'). Yet, on the other, Starobinski wants to relate this psychology to the social conditions that gave rise to it.[11] He mentions the position of the typical 'citizen of Geneva' and the pressure it puts on Rousseau to himself invent his own position:

> Although no one really cares about mediocre existence, Rousseau imagines a reproachful gaze precisely because the *idea* of an omniscient and just God was an inextricable part of the Genevan heaven [...] To breathe the air of Geneva was to breathe the conviction of man's original lapse and to bear all the weight of God's potential wrath. The vigilance of the Consistory meant that the atmosphere of the city was always kept heavy with suspicion of scandal. The Company of Pastors kept an eye on everyone and everything. It was quick to denounce and stigmatize libertines for the least offense to law and order. It observed, reprimanded, and condemned [...] Believing himself to be under scrutiny, Rousseau restrains his lusts and forbids himself to give in to desire [...] By the time the *introjection* is complete, the suspect has been found guilty, convicted on the testimony of an accuser he carries within himself. Then and only then are all the necessary conditions satisfied, allowing an inverse *projection* to recreate the persecuting witness where none exists [...] We are now in a better position to distinguish between society's role and Jean-Jacques' initiatives and reactions. The environment supplied the all-seeing religious police and austere morality, quick to suspect vice and condemn it, as well as the social inequality that left Rousseau's family in a position of resentful humiliation. Though a 'citizen', he was only a

> 'representative', being in fact stripped in fact of privileges accorded him in law. Confronted with these circumstances, Rousseau invented his response. Guilt feelings, protestations of innocence, and flight are not behaviours strictly determined by the environment. An element of personal interpretation is required, an extra option (Ibid: 18–20).

Starobinski is an astounding author because he understands the shame and paralysis Rousseau feels when faced with these sweet treats; he shows us that Jean-Jacques, far from being a victim of his own psychology or an external sociology, instead invents his position at the meeting point of singular suffering and setbacks which do not reduce his behaviour to a personal flaw, or to external factors, but nonetheless give a meaning to the feelings driving him and to the inhibition affecting him.

Nonetheless, and for that which concerns us – let us not forget that the only justification for this long detour via the literary history of curiosity is that we are better equipped to continue our anthropology of the window display, using the highly exotic and hardly literary case of our grocer from Kansas! – what is at stake exists neither at the level of Rousseau, or intellectuals (even those as brilliant and shrewd as Starobinski) but at the rather more ordinary level of customers and products, and above all among those whose job it is to bring the two parties closer together in the service of financial gain. The important point of view is that of the vendors, who, whenever considering a customer entering or potentially entering their shop, cannot know whether they are facing a new incarnation of Rousseau or Starobinski's 'normal man'. They thus have no choice other than to ignore psychology and sociology, and instead to try to overcome the irreducibility of character and the inevitability of social determinisms.[12]

How can this be done? Sartre set us on the right path by emphasising the importance of the 'keyhole' device, that, by intervening between the subject and society, manages to exceed, or rather *displace* each. The market puts all of its efforts into understanding each and every case that presents itself (as it is) and into organising the setting that will orientate it accordingly. It is as if the pastry chef had noticed Jean-Jacques' discomfort yet would not admit defeat. As if, instead of assuming the reason behind the missed sale was the combined intervention of an irreducible psychology and sociology, he had asked himself the question 'what to do' to overcome such inhibition – to either 'ward off the Rousseau effect', or to encourage 'normal', more well 'disposed' customers, and so avoiding the singularity or universality of psychology (either Rousseau's or that of the normal man), and the inevitability of sociology (which operates over and above the configuration of action).

The problem, Rousseau noticed, was due to physical pressures stemming from a configuration too restricted for the triad involved:

> It is as if his world were too narrow to permit the simultaneous presence of desiring consciousness, coveted object, and censorious witness. The confrontation of these three elements resulted in an intolerable malaise. One of them had either to disguise itself, change its nature, or disappear (Starobinski 1989: 21).

But as Starobinski is only following Rousseau, he has no choice other than to list the solutions examined by his character, excluding all the external forces influencing the organisation of the situation. With Rousseau, it is precisely 'desiring consciousness' which yields, whereas the 'coveted object' and 'censorious witness' remain unaltered. In order to escape embarrassment, Rousseau is therefore able to '[avoid] the witness' gaze', or, when this is impossible, find in 'imagination' a 'substitute' object, or even invert the relationship, 'stand still and leave it up to the object of desire to make the advances' (this is in other parts of the story); or better (!) still, make a paradoxical turn to 'theft' to calm shameful desire. Theft is his saving grace indeed, because it gives him the means to escape the looks he so dreads.[13] Of course everything changes when the adjustments to the potential difficulty of the situation are the result of the two other poles (object and witness) being rearranged. The market professional is counting not on the importance of psychology or sociology, but on technologies capable of radically altering expectations, and of putting regular customers at ease, in a way that works for him and whatever customers' motivations and identities.[14]

The grocer is not confronted with one particular case, but with a range of different ones. Therefore, his problem is not that he must in some instances adjust to the Rousseauian counterpart (a rare event), and in others to that of the normal man (most often the case), but that he must contend with a *continuum* of attitudes, ranging from being afraid of being looked at by another person, to free and 'liberated' expressions of personal desire. Or rather, his job involves building on the two situations that engage the subjective relationship to the window display. On the one hand, a social tie is brought into play (to the real or imagined risk of disapproval, and therefore the shame dealt with by Sartre and Starobinski). On the other, there is the promise of a corporeal tie to the things (to the hope of discovery, and to the pleasure that also motivates the subjects being observed by the two authors[15]). In other words, the seller's analytical position requires a logic according to which Starobinski's Rousseau and his 'normal man', far from being radically different from one another, coexist in each of us, as corresponds with the theory of the plural actor so well described by Bernard Lahire (2011).

As well as 'each of us', the grocer can or must also deal with 'all of us', particularly when it is a matter of doing so through a window display, whose inevitably rigid physical arrangement is intended for an audience whose members it cannot differentiate between.[16] Here it becomes possible to extend and improve Sartre and Starobinski: Sartre because, as we will see, the presence of a crowd rather than the sudden appearance of 'somebody' can noticeably change the factors involved in curiously exploring the world; Starobinski because the configuration of the people present can affect the feeling of the person who is observing and who knows he is being observed. A fundamental property of the market is that it is both a collection of things and a collection of people. Real markets, far from opposing warm-hearted human society to the cold adjustments of accountancy mechanisms, and far from revealing the contrast between social interrelations and the anonymity of the market, instead bring together and place centre stage the 'crowd' (a 'society' in other words) that has no fear of oxymoron and paradox, given that although it is 'social', it is simultaneously 'anonymous' and 'marketable', and given that it concerns a gathering of people whose lack of mutual relation in no way means a lack of interaction.

The crowd should be added to a more extensive list of collective figures, well known within sociology, including the community (grounded in the integration of people who identify with a cohesive group constructed in opposition to what is alien to it), the network (grounded in exchange relationships and individual acquaintanceship), the public, and social classes, or categories (grounded in a shared interest or objective properties and/or on recognition of this sharing). Of course the crowd has a close relationship with these different categories, to the extent that it sometimes merges with them. Both classic (Le Bon 1960; Tarde 1892; 2006 [1901]) and more recent works (Arnoldi and Borch 2007) ground the crowd in the feeling of acting in a very large group that shares a common direction, and which does not necessarily require the physical presence of the people concerned. Nowadays, such crowds articulate themselves in ways that connect together community belonging, networked relationships, and/or the putting into play of a set of precise characteristics – such as taking part in a well-defined profession or activity. This kind of crowd, like the 'public' – in other words, at once scattered but nonetheless extremely vibrant – can be observed within financial markets (Arnoldi and Borch 2007; Hertz 1998), but more readily on the internet. The digital crowd meets through collaborative work (Beaudoin et al. 2001), the world of free software (Coris 2006), online video games (Boutet 2008), sharing knowledge through 'wiki' systems (Roth et al. 2008) and discussion forums (Conein and Latapy 2008). These apparent crowds, far from continually emerging and existing spontaneously, establish subtle forms of connection to companies, as in the case of communities of Wi-Fi enthusiasts (Calvignac 2010), and are now even the subject of a tripartite form of strategic exploitation. The first consists in the establishment and management of 'customer communities' and multiple 'user accounts', 'pseudonyms', 'blogs', and 'forums' (Amine and Sitz 2007; Sitz 2008); the second is grounded in the use of 'viral marketing', closely linked to networks of targeted publics (Mellet 2009); the third is 'crowdsourcing', which does its best to set the public 'to work' by encouraging internet users to carry out a range of activities that they love: taking photos, making videos, writing articles for the press, and so on (Dujarier 2008).

In view of the subject being considered here, I will, however, stick with the most common and narrow definition of crowds: the community that brings the window display into play is in fact this anthropological entity, this concrete multiple body, and this temporary and situated human agglomeration (swarming and sometimes grumbling) that can sometimes transport us, in both the physical and moral sense of the expression. Our immersion in the crowd, thus defined, confronts us with an unusual social imperative – that of learning to exist with but also of acting beside, and even with, these people whom we do not know and whom we encounter for the duration of a shared moment, without this necessarily involving verbal exchanges. This situation of 'living in or with the crowd' is part of the history of collective social practices, whether this occurs in the sacred form of religious effervescence (Durkheim 1985), or during more profane events, including collective crimes (Tarde 1892), political protests (Vergnon 2005), musical performances (Hennion 1993; Ferrand 2009), or sporting events (Bomberger 1995), and, of course, the daily experience of markets (de la Pradelle 1996) or the city (Goffman 1974).[17]

Within the narrow meaning of crowds, I will refer to an even more limited variant. Certainly, market crowds can be very dense, noisy, and insistent, as in the world of fairs or auctions (Arnoldi and Borch 2007), but, especially in the retail trade, they can appear as more modest, discrete, and hushed, as simply a gathering of people. If concerned with this latter kind of crowd, one must take into account not only the dynamics of interaction and reciprocal expectation (Eroglu and Harell 1986; Eroglu and Machleit 1990; Eroglu et al. 2005; Dion Le Mée 1999; Cochoy 2008a), but also the 'influence of quantity' – in other words, the impact of imperceptible physical exchanges like brushing against one other (Underhill 1999), or even the almost invisible cognitive or sensory processes that are trying to be understood by sociologists of the senses and 'atmospheres' (Sauvageot 2003), specialists in 'atmospheric marketing' (Grandclément 2004), 'sensory marketing' (Hultén et al. 2009) or more recently promoters of 'neuromarketing' (Fugate 2007 ; Lee et al. 2007, Senior and Lee 2008).

Nonetheless, it is important to emphasise at this stage that the social contact which unfolds around window displays does not stop at interaction but extends and continues with objects. Certainly, the window display establishes a very clear separation between the world of people (who are walking in the street), and the world of things (exhibited but also protected from the other side of the glass).[18] However, this separation is paradoxically only there to arouse transgression, to divert people away from social exchange and towards the trading of objects. The window display is therefore to be seen as a device for shifting people from the singular social dimension, so dear to sociology, into the multidimensional sphere of commerce. The latter combines social resources and readily accessible materials, and enriches the social exchanges between people which take the form of hybrid interactions between people and things. The window display thus involves a reconfiguration of social dynamics, in which interpersonal ties are balanced against 'inter-objective' ties (Latour 1996) – in other words, the ties that each of us have to objects. The effect on different forms of social relationship of ties bound to objects is a classical issue, given that it involves processes that have been thoroughly explored by the sociology of consumption, ranging from ostentation (whereby we acquire this or that good in order to impress others (Veblen 2013)), to distinction (which turns consumption into the prop for social classifications (Bourdieu 1984)). However, the same question might also enrich this sociology if we cease to consider the objects solely according to their social function, and instead become interested in both their objective properties (their taste, texture, sensory, or conventional characteristics) and the way in which the interaction with these properties redefine the subject (Gomart and Hennion 1999).

Let us consider the properties of the window display. In a slightly reconfigured version of Starobinski's schema, in which the pastry chef gives way to the glazier, the window display connects three elements: a window, subjects, and objects. The first is only relevant by virtue of the 'suspended access' it institutes between the two others. The tension established between visual accessibility and the hindrance of physical access is intended to draw attention and to turn the window display into a 'device of desire'. The latter places subjects and objects in a peculiarly interactive relationship, given that the window display addresses the first (subjects) about the second (objects), but without itself being able to see any of them. It is also an object that places us in front of a *crowd* of things, not just in the conventional descriptive sense of the word, but also in the highly social sense outlined above. In fact, there is nothing that should prevent us from thinking about the relationships between the objects in the same terms as we do those between the subjects, even if, of course, by virtue of the differences in the shaping of the elements in question, the social configurations observed in each case will likely be very different.

Three 'societies of things' are involved in the window display. The first is the 'crowd' of articles on display. These articles have stable, deliberately hierarchical relationships that are nonetheless united by the principle of 'collection'. The collection is predicated on the fact that the display's attractiveness relies specifically on its ability to make the collection of objects that are gathered together greater than their sum: just as in the story of *Hänsel and Gretel*, the image of the house assumes precedence over the gingerbread (although it takes us there) in a grocer's shop, and the coherence of collections plays a highly significant role in directing consumers towards the elements they are comprised of (Cochoy 2008b). This schema is yet more relevant to the window display, where the 'layout' of things is even more important because it cannot be 'broken up', or rather, not yet: the paradox of commercial collections is in fact that the coherence of their constituent elements is used to encourage their separation. However, two other crowds of objects are, paradoxically, even more important and are upstream and downstream of the first. Upstream, the ordinary customer has to deal with the things which she or he has (or does not have) at home. Their presence, or lack thereof, but also, and especially, the relationship between these things weighs heavily on purchasing decisions, to the extent that a consumer's preferences often express more accurately those of their cupboards: we are missing certain things, but an absence is also noticeable between them, so much do their respective values often depend on their combination. If an ingredient or element is missing, then sometimes all of the other objects, despite their presence, suddenly become useless and rejected, cast into a kind of functional void. Vinegar is nothing without the oil that makes it possible to prepare a vinaigrette; a suit can hardly be worn without matching shoes; toothpaste is of no use without the toothbrush that holds it; and on and on. Conversely, the overabundance of certain things can hinder their purchase – for example by prompting in their owner a feeling of guilt, of extravagance, futility, and waste. I want these glasses, but I already have a pair; I am interested in this new phone, but mine still works perfectly; etc. Downstream, the collection of products offered for sale plays its part – products that have a metonymic relationship with both the collections of the window display and the ordinary customer. There is no way this collection can be fit into the window display; rather, it extends it by offering new displays (admittedly often less artistic and sophisticated) but that are all the more attractive because now we have unrestricted access to the goods we desire – and our desire is yet greater because we were initially impeded. When facing goods, a customer's personal collections (or those more public ones contained in the window display) influence every choice in the end, much like the witness does in Sartre and self-awareness does in Starobinski. The customer must juggle the desires created by the window display, the injunctions posed by 'the preferences of the cupboard', and the delicate interplay of the successive choices between them. The time given to this or that choice limits or increases the time available for those that follow (Cochoy 1999); the volume or value of the objects already gathered is a constraint on possible new purchases in terms of satiation, physical limitations, budgetary limits, or a bad budgetary conscience.

Let us go back for a minute. Previously, Starobinski explained Rousseau's shame by focusing his analysis on the character's psychology and sociology, while excluding all other considerations. Here we have a typical case of Bruno Latour's argument on the forms of 'social theory' that perhaps have 'no object' (1996): if I deprive myself of the objects that support social relationships, or am deprived of them, I need to look for explanations elsewhere, either in the subject's inner self, at the micro, subjective level, or in society, at the macro, objective level. Starobinski is sufficiently rigorous to use both.[19] Sartre's case is a little different: the existentialist philosopher related the awakening of self-consciousness to a scenario reduced to three elements: the voyeur, the witness, and the lock, or rather its 'hole' – in other words, 'nothing' other than the access it provides to grasping pure subjectivity in action. But, however tenuously, the keyhole's precise technical arrangement plays an essential role in connecting the visual access the hole provides to the door's opacity, both by permitting observation, and by distributing and multiplying the positions of the observer and the observed, whether it is the person or people being observed through the keyhole being seen, unwittingly, or the voyeur who sees without being seen, on this side of the keyhole, or when the same subject is finally caught and 'seen as a voyeur'. It is obviously the absence of a door and a keyhole 'behind him' which is the cause of the voyeur's shame and (as a result) his self-awareness, rather than the keyhole and the door in front of him. Even if this is not his main concern, Sartre thus puts us on the right path: if the device is reintroduced, the explanation moves from the subjects or society to the setting that connects one to the other. On this basis, we can extend the comparative anthropology of the devices I already outlined. Taking them fully into account means managing not to limit oneself to the idiosyncrasies of this or that consumer, constrained by his own forms of moral or social conformity (for Starobinski), or his own existential experience (for Sartre), and instead going back to the *agencement* (arrangement) of the situations that rework psychology, sociology, and, ultimately, the subjects' modes of existence.

From this perspective, the window display proposes a highly original compromise between the restricted technical interface of Sartre's keyhole and the maximally open and unequipped nature of the gaze for Rousseau. As just described, the window display puts both dimensions into play: that of the crowd and that of the materiality of things. As we saw earlier, in this respect the devices are very dissimilar. With the window display, instead of having one large, awkward subject in front of a tiny keyhole (as in Sartre), or a subject whose gaze is free and limited only by that of others (as in Rousseau), we have, as it were, a kind of gigantic keyhole in front of which smaller subjects crowd. However, the difference is not only one of size and shape. Added to this lateral difference – how many subjects it is possible to have in front of the keyhole – is a difference in the depth of field: whereas Sartre only focuses on the voyeur's point of view (while Starobinski notes that Rousseau believes he can feel the gaze of others), the window display also directs us to consider the point of view of those who are behind the voyeur. These two differences with the window display now combine their properties to wholly invert Sartre's keyhole problem and Rousseau's guilt complex. With the window display as an expanded keyhole, those who see the voyeur from behind his back are no longer prevented from seeing what is being seen, nor are they driven to vague fantasised guesses. They are, rather, provided with a new opportunity to experience the same view that he does, and to do so with him. In these kinds of situation in which everything happens as if several viewers were able to look through an immense keyhole together, the voyeur's potential attitudes and those of the witnesses potentially become reversed. On the one hand (in the background), some might want to join the voyeur and share his experience – rather than, without knowing the particularities of what is being observed, condemning it as a 'generic' situation of 'misplaced' curiosity (which is clearly illustrated by the sheeplike behaviour of groups of onlookers) – and in so doing discover or convince themselves that alongside the curiosity that they assume to be guilty or forbidden (see the tradition ranging from Genesis to *Bluebeard*), there is an innocent, licit, and even 'communicative' curiosity. On the other hand (in the foreground), the voyeur, who is also aware of this possibility because things are occurring behind his back but also alongside him, far from experiencing shame, might instead feel encouraged and then become carried away as his own excitement becomes shared. Ultimately, the Sartrian effect is spectacularly inverted: whereas the sociotechnical configuration around a small keyhole provides the opportunity for the arousal of self-consciousness, an analogous configuration around the window display conversely operates as an opportunity for this same self-consciousness to dissolve into the truly collective experience of the commercial crowd – being dissolves into nothingness. The window display brings into play, or rather 'plays on', the double articulation of the gaze, which hinders *and thus* stimulates desire, according to Corneille's maxim: 'And desire increases when the effect recedes'. This is indeed about playing a game: the idea is to create a fictitious, festive situation, or one that is out of the ordinary; the device delimits an acceptable space for voyeurism. This space rests on both the (material) setting of the window display and the (conventional) rules of the game, both of which render it acceptable. Thanks to the game, there is an expectation that a person's curiosity is aroused, but also that this is achieved by surrounding them with other people whose curiosity is equally aroused, so as to tip the whole crowd over to the side of the voyeur, thereby creating a crowd that pushes rather than condemns – establishing a 'mass curiosity', as it were.[20]

Of course, there is nothing new about this type of situation in which the interaction with things eventually prevails over exchanges between subjects. We have already come across this in Bluebeard's spacious apartments, albeit with one radical exception: the difference between interest and curiosity: whereas the group of friends gives in to the collective agitation of their interest, his wife's well-hidden curiosity enables her to avoid succumbing to the general trend and to preserve her identity. Eventually she breaks away from the group to go and satisfy – elsewhere, discreetly, and alone, and in an almost Sartrian manner – her own curiosity. More precisely: just as Bluebeard's apartments showed, a singular display can itself be enough to arouse curiosity. This is the Kansas grocer's whole point: to combat this inadequacy, to prepare devices that can make a window display just as enticing as the secret room (replacing, of course, the vision of horror with things that are appetising), then to closely bring together the two motives of curiosity and interest that the tale tended to split asunder. As we shall see, the window display appeals to an interest-driven curiosity (its orientation is economic and rational) and a curiosity-driven interest (in which economic concerns are subordinate to cognitive exploration). Taking this particular effort into account leads us to put the somewhat generic virtues of the 'window display' device to one side, in order to take a closer look at the layout of 'those specific window displays': the window displays from the interwar period imagined by our grocer from Kansas. The grocer makes good use of these generic properties, but in order to advance these further, we should now closely align the window display's hyperbolic keyhole effect to the mirror effects that we already mentioned and will now present. This will demonstrate how to go about completely transforming the window display into a device able to provoke interest-driven curiosity and/or curiosity-driven interest.

THE EFFECTS OF MIRRORS

The grocer's story presents two variants of how this troubling mirrored keyhole device is used. The first relates to the reflexive use of both the window display and customers themselves on Valentine's Day, through the organisation of a photography contest that would select the best photo of the specially made-up window display:

> There are many ways of arousing curiosity. Among the best are contest windows – they always more than pay their way in this respect. Take, for

example, the snapshot contest we ran in conjunction with a Valentine window: We trimmed our entire window, which is 15 feet long by 8 feet deep, in red and white crepe paper, and throughout it hung large red hearts cut out of cardboard. By displaying fancy heart-shaped box candies and all kinds of fancy Valentine candies in bulk glass jars along with suitable foods for Valentine parties, we made a window that shouted 'Valentine!' even if you were across the street. Then we used a contest as a curiosity-arouser. At the back of the window we placed a large cut-out red heart made of cardboard, with this message on it: '$3.00 to the person bringing in the best snapshot of this window'. Numbers of people took pictures and entered them, and the contest excited comment and interest among customers who didn't take snapshots. Windows of this type, and in fact all contest windows, because they are unusual, are always good for a write-up in the local papers. And these write-ups alone are worth more to us as advertising than the few dollars we put up for prizes (*Progressive Grocer* February 1940: 58–60).

FIG. 3. *The Progressive Grocer*, February 1940, p. 127

The second consists of a metaphorical crow showing the passing foxes a large cheese in the hope that these foxes will be seduced into removing a piece, risking their money in a game based on guessing its weight:

> A 'Cheese Window' once attracted a lot of trade for us during a time that was ordinarily slack. We displayed all kinds of cheese, filling the window chock-full of cheese in packages, jars, glasses, in tinfoil, and in bulk. In the center, at the back of the window where it could be easily reached by our customers, we featured an enormous cheese weighing 523 lbs. which was made in Wisconsin especially for our store. In conjunction with this window we again used the contest idea, this time giving prizes of cheese to persons guessing nearest the weight of the big cheese. But the main attraction of this sale and the thing that really sold cheese for us was this sign in the window: 'Free – cut yourself a piece of cheese. If you guess the correct weight of the piece of cheese you cut, it is yours free. If you don't guess its correct weight you must purchase the piece you cut off at our special price this week of [XX]¢ per lb.[21] Their curiosity aroused and their guessing skill challenged, our trade went for this promotion in a big way. Not only did we sell nearly all the giant cheese while it was on display but we sold many, many packages of the other cheeses shown in the window – kinds people would never think of if they weren't reminded by a display (*Progressive Grocer* February 1940: 127, 130).

Both window displays draw on two distinct approaches: on the one hand, they both play on the draw of a contest; on the other, each of these contests is a variant of the same game of mirrors that, for the person competing, consists in assessing the effect of an image which he himself projects (by choosing the point of view and the frame for the photo; by guessing the weight of the large cheese or by cutting a piece) in order to ascertain his future state (winner or loser). What we are dealing with here is a version of the very old and traditional branch of curiosity, long condemned by religious authorities and demonologists, and grounded in divination, in predicting the future. In *Bluebeard*, this version features indirectly: the mirror of blood reminds us of Snow White's mirror; in

FIG. 4. *The Progressive Grocer*, February 1940, p. 59

the same way that the queen sees the future in her mirror, the pool of blood and its ominous reflection inform the heroine – a little late, admittedly – about the fate that Bluebeard has in store for her. However, with the window displays, the playful thankfully replaces the tragic: the contests at the heart of the game of mirrors on display present us with dynamics of personal and/or reciprocal expectations that are no longer reminiscent of Sartre's famous keyhole. We are instead reminded of the equally well known beauty contest alluded to by Keynes when he outlines the behavioural dynamics within financial markets:

> Professional investment may be likened to those newspaper competitions in which the competitors have to pick out the six prettiest faces, from a hundred photographs, the prize being awarded to the competitor whose choice most nearly corresponds to the average preferences of the competitors as a whole; so that each competitor has to pick, not those faces which he himself finds prettiest, but those which he thinks likeliest to catch the fancy of the other competitors, all of whom are looking at the problem from the same

> point of view. It is not a case of choosing those which, to the best of one's judgement, are really the prettiest, nor even those which average opinion genuinely thinks is the prettiest. We have reached the third degree where we devote our intelligences to anticipating what average opinion expects the average opinion to be. And there are some, I believe, who practice the fourth, fifth and higher degrees (Keynes 1936).

As we know, the image of the beauty contest allows Keynes to explain the phenomena of speculation and the resulting risks. Keynes' argument makes a distinction between two types of agents who might come together in market-places: some are interested in the real value of things, estimating the price they are willing to pay for a company's shares, based on the hopes of profit inherent to the economic activity concerned; others are interested in market value; in this case, the company's value does not depend on its fundamentals but rather on the value that others are likely to assign to it, according in turn to the value that others are likely to assign to it, and so on and so forth.[22] The tragedy of this situation is that the existence of the second type of actor very quickly squeezes out the first: the mechanism of reciprocal expectations soon leads all the actors to play the game, unless they are willing to go bankrupt and/or leave the market, given that no one person can be more right than the market as a whole. Speculation can thus be defined as a game of mirrors in which the same projected image endlessly reproduces itself until it becomes completely detached from reality, forms a bubble, and only crashes once, albeit too late – a restorative force renders it possible to identify the gap that has opened up between the economy's fundamentals and the market's own introspection. The lesson learnt from the beauty contest is clear: if the profit expected from such a contest depends on aggregating the choices made by all the participants, it is more rational and profitable in the short term to try to anticipate the workings of this aggregation – from the second to the nth degree – than to depend on criteria that define external beauty, as supposedly required by a first degree assessment.

Keynes' proposal – expressed only four years before the publication of our article on the window displays of Kansas – is useful in two ways: because of what it teaches us about the market, but also about beauty contests, given the fact that in our case, the beauty contest and the market are not in a metaphorical relationship but are instead completely entwined (one of them is simultaneously the referent and metaphor of the other). Broadly speaking, Keynes' image first teaches us that market and contest both operate through the same curiosity and the same excitement, stemming from the frisson associated with the appeal of the unknown, the pleasure of uncertainty, and the risk inherent to gambling (an excitement, thrill, and pleasurable uncertainty which everyday gamblers and market players share[23]). What is unknown in contests is less the product on which they are based, and more the subject – including their relationships to themselves and others: Will I discover the price of the cheese? Will I win the prize? And if it is not me, who then? In the Valentine's Day window display contest, and Keynes' beauty contest, the pleasure and curiosity of the market is that of reciprocal anticipation, competition, and/or expectation; of a 'thrill' which economic science and financial theory have since tried to organise and reduce with their models and instruments (Martin 2005; MacKenzie and Millo 2003; MacKenzie et al. 2007), but which the actors on the ground continually test and tame through their own commitments (Arnoldi and Borch 2007). However, neither are reciprocal anticipation, competition, and expectation necessarily substitutable, nor do they necessarily operate in all situations. Furthermore, the stakes are different in each activity. Once again, it is by referring to Keynes that we are able to see things more clearly, insofar as he gives us ways of identifying the processes at play in each of our devices.

The case of the competition about the weight of the cheese (with its two variants: guessing the weight of the whole cheese or guessing the weight of the piece you have cut yourself) is on the face of it the simplest. The competition's characteristics bring into play, in a simplified form, the logic of the first kind of agent described by Keynes. In fact here, in whichever version, winning does not mean taking part in a game of mirrors in which the expectations of a group of participants are matched with one another (as in the Keynesian stock market and beauty contest case): it is rather a quite simple game of mirrors between each participant and their own expectations. Both of the cheese game's variants simply appeal to a reflexive curiosity – each person asks themselves the same internal question: 'Will I provide the right estimate?' When it comes to guessing the weight of the entire cheese, this is because there is only one real weight, regardless of the players' estimates. The deployment of a personal reflexivity specific to the game is even more manifest when it is a matter of estimating the weight of the single piece which has been cut: on each occasion, the estimate being made is different from and cannot be reduced to the other estimates: instead of having to compete against a group of other agents in order to assess the weight of the same piece of cheese (from the same series of playmates in Keynes' example, or from the same cheese in the first variant, or from the same window display in the photograph contest), each successive person is involved in a competition in which they are the only participant, and in which they aim to assess the weight of their own sample. In both cases (assessing the weight of the entire cheese or one of its pieces), everyone competes against him/herself – we are thus dealing with two types of 'single-player game' and not with 'multiplayer' games, as they are now called by the video-game industry. This configuration has two consequences: in both variants, each individual estimate is wholly unaffected by the others. In these two cases, the competition as a whole, combining each individual game, is a non-zero-sum game in which theoretically all the participants can win, no matter what the other players win or lose. In both, it is fascinating to note that the winning strategy is the one used by those who would always be losers[24] in Keynes' game: in order for us to win a prize, after having correctly guessed either the cheese's entire weight or that of the piece we have cut, we do not need to be concerned with the estimates of others,[25] but rather with the single cheese (or the single piece), with its fundamental value (its mass), as evidenced by the very material test that takes place before or after (respectively) it is weighed.

Let us go further by now investigating the case of single-player games according to the terms of game theory. The first game consists in offering a prize in case the cheese's exact weight is guessed. As it costs nothing to participate and the gain is positive, all potential players are advised to play. The second proposed game involves offering the product itself in case its exact weight is guessed and making the contestant pay for the price of the cheese if not. When it succeeds, the game's rate of return (the quotient between the gain and the bet) is infinite because the bet costs zero.[26] When it fails, the game's rate of return is neutral, given that the loser leaves with the equivalent value in cheese that was bet on (i.e. the price of the cheese[27]). Here also the result of the game is obvious: in games like this, one's interest in playing – even in playing as much as possible, or even indefinitely – is because one's chance of winning will always be more than zero, even if very small, and with at worst a neutral outcome (it will cost me no more than it will yield). In fact, the average gain is more than zero across *n* bets, given that out of *n* bets, as *n* approaches infinity, the probability of winning at least once increases until it approaches 1. Therefore, even if I were to win one in a thousand times, my average gain is positive and greater than zero.[28] Whether I am rational or a gambler, I am once again literally caught in a gambling trap, given that the more I play, the more I increase my chances of achieving a positive outcome. As we have seen, therefore, the two games both operate (in theory) as formidable curiosity 'captation devices'. They are like two unavoidable whirlwinds, with the power to drag customers into the shop, into the game, and then into making a purchase.

Taking part in the second game (guessing the weight of the piece that we have ourselves cut off) would not be so simple in reality, however. Understanding this problem means subjecting the (very small, very basic, and very modest) model of game theory that I have just outlined to the test of experimental economics (as our grocer from Kansas did ahead of his time!). Yet, when confronting the results of such a game, experimental economics would still not be out of the woods, whether the behaviours observed corresponded to its model's predictions (all potential participants decide to take part in the game), or conversely, a difference appeared between the model's prediction and the actually observed behaviours (some decide not to play). In the first case, it would be impossible to decide whether the model was effective and whether the players were rational – for three reasons. Firstly, it may well be that taking part in the game is not (just[29]) the expression of a calculation (one that actively encourages participation), but rather simply expresses an almost unconditional preference for gambling and the accompanying experience of curiosity.[30] In this case, winning the cheese would no longer be the objective, but rather the potential consequence, and a completely secondary one – of an activity that on its own is enough to satisfy their involvement. This is especially because, in this specific instance, the potential loss is almost nothing. Secondly, taking part in the game can also result in the intervention of a collective dimension, one that literally 'pushes' the customer into the game, to a degree in spite of himself. This dimension is clearly captured by the illustrator who depicts an audience 'surrounding' the person playing. Once again we find here the sharing effect that is part of 'the expanded keyhole' described earlier, and the corresponding loss of individual judgement that results from submitting to collective emotion. When we play a game, we often do so in situations where we make a spectacle of ourselves, and in a situation of shared involvement and curiosity.[31] As soon as a 'single-player game' involves spectators, it is, formally, no longer entirely what it claims to be: the preference for the game no longer only involves a calculation but also the game that results, which consists of playing in order to make an impression on those who can see us playing. In other words, even if the presence of an audience does not directly affect the player's calculations, it might nonetheless weigh on his decision to be involved in the game.[32] The audience inhibiting the young Rousseau or Sartre's voyeur could, if formatted in a certain way, play a diametrically opposite role and actually encourage players to take licence with the rules. Finally, and from a completely different perspective, involvement in the game might result from an error in calculation, from ignoring a certain amount of 'implicit data' that were present in the situation but not made explicit when the game was introduced. In fact, the game becomes radically more complicated if we take into account either (in the case where the player loses) the charging of a hidden investment – the shop's mark-up – or the cheese's relative price, in relation to other similar cheeses being sold ('outside the game') by other grocers elsewhere in town. In both cases, it is eminently possible that the whole calculation is unfavourable. This means our preference comes to be for a cheese with a known price, rather than trying to obtain it for nothing in a situation where, if we lose, we do not obtain the precise value for the cheese in which we invested (given that the margin has already been deducted) and/or where we might well be paying more than we would do in other grocers.[33] A final point concerns the preference for cheese or money. Even in cases where there is in fact no gain – where that which is handed over in cheese is worth exactly the price being paid – a player might prefer money, either because he does not like cheese (except when it enables gambling), or because the cheese is infinitely less fungible than money (accepting cheese means rejecting the fungibility of the corresponding amount of money).

Interpreting the results of an actor's lesser involvement in the game is precisely symmetrical: it might reveal a lack of calculative skill – if we use as a reference the 'explicit' presentation of the game without mentioning the gain or the local competition – or not realising that, in this specific case, it is in our interest to play. However, conversely, it might also reveal a 'better calculation', sensitive to the slightest fungibility of the cheese, given the existence of a profit margin and the competition. If a player abstains it could be the result of an aversion to the game (or the cheese) and/or an ability to avoid being influenced (or influenced by players opposed to the game).

No doubt (and paradoxically), theoretical economics would argue that this material is nothing to kick up a fuss about. It believes these kinds of painstaking analyses are unnecessary; that they are parasitic 'overflows' that a model either cannot or need not consider. In fact, the job of economists is to 'stylise' reality so as to distil some of the pure elements and mechanisms that operate in a given situation; from this perspective, unless one understands nothing about the intelligence of their profession, it is completely absurd to reproach economists for not including in their analyses all these 'details' so adored by sociologists. Contrary to what some people believe, economists are perfectly aware of them but choose specifically to get rid of them in order to come as close as possible to the trends underlying the 'noise' that inevitably surrounds the operations of the market (as the cast-iron law of economic knowledge goes, there is no model without simplistic hypotheses and simplifications). Experimental economics is more flexible than theoretical economics because it is willing to take some of these overflows into consideration, but it does so in order to adjust them according to objectives it has itself set. Experimental economics is not afraid of concretely 'reworking' these configurations, whether by bringing both the world and the model closer to one another or by adapting them (Giraudeau et al. 2007). Certainly, this way of making 'reality twist', while paradoxically, 'twisting reality', sometimes means finding a way to avoid twisting at all:[34] the contortions that experimental economics imposes onto the elements that it manipulates merely brings it closer to the underlying operations of the economy in which facts are continuously 'twisted', reworked, and shaped to fit models that might lend them meaning (and vice versa), as has been clearly demonstrated across the recent work on the 'performativity' of the economic sciences (Callon 2007).

According to experimental economics, the overflows we have described can of course be put down to an inadequate preparation/presentation of the game. In the case of our competition, in order to overcome these problems the game's designer would repeat the experiment, specifying, for example, that the cheese 'on offer' in the event of a win is offered at cost; he would allow winning the cheese to be convertible into money; he would rearrange the situation so that an audience would not be able to disturb a player (for example by reducing the size of the opening that provides access to the cheese); he would choose players without prior experience of (or a known taste for) gambling; he would specify that the situation was a monopoly, and make it not possible for a player to leave the game to go and play on another table; and so on. Or rather, the experimenter would choose which of these different 'adjustments' were necessary, in line with the objectives he had assigned to the experiment. For example, if the experiment's objective were to test the impact of a preference for gambling on the calculations of agents (thereby also loosening the model's hypothesis of perfect rationality), we would avoid filtering participants according to this criterion, while making sure we were as strict as possible with each of the others.

However, what is fascinating about the situation being described is that without the help of a specialist in experimental economics and using only its own, it operates reasonably well in this process of restrictive and selective readjustment of the players' calculation – that is, at least according to one of its dimensions: concealing the competition and the implicit bet represented by the payment of a commercial markup. On the one hand, the game's temporality, which lends the bet its credibility whilst concealing within it the cheese's unit price, rejects any economic calculation 'beyond' the game. This is concealed by giving prominence to the playfulness of the activity and the fact that it is free (see in the display the bold lettering in 'Free – cut yourself a piece of cheese'). On the other, the shop's location pulls players away from other offers: it is important to note that in order to play, one must 'take the tour' – so leaving the street to move into the store interior, and migrating from the window display outside to enter the shop. This migration further reduces the possibility of (mentally or physically) turning back towards the competition, so that in the end the window display paradoxically transforms the market into a pure externality. Conversely, this same migration by players on the other side of the window display, outside the shop, becomes part of the game's spectacle and an incentive for those who remain outside to play: the players are part of the window display. It is not just the cheese game that is on offer, but also the playful experience it stands for: watching the players on the other side of the window, the customer can already see himself playing, as if he were looking at himself in a magic mirror.[35] Of course, this 'living mirror' is only activated intermittently when people burst into the window as they arrive to take part in the game (and, despite themselves, to promote it). The rest of the time, however, the aforementioned placard takes over quite well: just reading a lottery advert inevitably means seeing oneself a little like a winner. The placard and/or the players' *tableau vivant* thus combine their respective 'reflections' to intensify curiosity and the appeal of the game. Here, curiosity is 'distributed' and 'arranged': it is located in the window display and/or in the actors, with the idea that what is in the window can be activated by the actors (and vice versa). This effect is reinforced by the extreme subtlety of the games' connection to one another. The first game, consisting of guessing the price of the giant cheese, is genuinely free. However, it leads the player into sliding towards the second, which is only 'almost' free, inasmuch as it results in taking the risk of paying the (admittedly 'special') price for the piece from the very same cheese, whose weight we will have failed to guess correctly. Because of a simple isomorphism, this second game is now very likely to be perceived like the first, despite entailing a market action.

Like a laboratory of experimental economics, the window display therefore adjusts the game, simplifies the number of hypotheses, defines an interior and exterior, and provides the terms of a calculation that, despite the lack of absolutes, is nonetheless defined and framed as if there were. Of course, the organisation of the game is aimed less at testing a model than maximising results: beyond experimental and theoretical economics, the approach is a pragmatic economics, one likely to increase sales, as the conclusion eloquently recalls:

> Their curiosity aroused and their guessing skill challenged, our trade went for this promotion in a big way. Not only did we sell nearly all the giant cheese while it was on display but we sold many, many packages of the other cheeses shown in the window – kinds people would never think of if they weren't reminded by a display (*Progressive Grocer* February 1940: 127).

The second window display, for its part (dedicated to the Valentine's Day photo competition), operates according to a very different register. Whereas the cheese game did not involve anyone else as part of the incentive to play the game, or as part of the calculation to be made, the Valentine's Day window display defines a far more subtle game, one that is fascinatingly close to the beauty contest described by Keynes. Certainly, and contrary to the very clear rules that govern beauty competitions, the criteria that will inform the selection of the winning photo of the display are not stated. However, far from altering the mechanism of reciprocal expectations, the vague nature of these criteria only exacerbates it. Whereas in Keynes, the winning choice involves guessing the average preferences of the players, who in turn are trying to guess the same average, the Saint Valentine's game increases the uncertainty surrounding both the content of the expectation and the agents that lie behind it. It increases the uncertainty about content because the question common to both games – 'What must one do to win?' – in this instance involves not just (as in Keynes' games) the concrete anticipation of other people's choices – 'what will the others do to win [as a rule]?' – but also guessing the rule towards which the common question is directed. Uncertainty is therefore extended to the agents of expectation, given that it is not just a matter of guessing what other players will do (who endlessly act in the same way) but also of anticipating what the grocer's criteria will be. And that is not the end of the dizzingly intersecting suppositions: will others anticipate the criteria? And what should I do once I have imagined what others will do to anticipate these criteria?

Speculating about the course of such speculations might run the risk of undertaking an intellectual exercise as futile as it is fragile,[36] if another of the game's dimensions – Valentine's Day – did not reinforce the way it engages players. Coupling the game to Valentine's Day means making a 'contest' and the 'game of love' synonymous; it means finding a way of hybridising the cold world of the competition and calculation, and the much warmer world of personal feeling and emotion. Of course, the game of love being proposed here can both surprise and disappoint: taking a photo of a window display is far less sexy than taking a photo of a beauty contestant... or your beloved! But this choice is the one best adapted to the situation: when we are in love, the most beautiful person is inevitably the one whom we love; there is 'no competition'. However, for this very reason, it is much more convenient to shift the object of the beauty competition to something other than the choice of the most beautiful face! By offering itself as a step on the road to Valentine's Day, the window display therefore proposes a connection between market trade and romantic exchange. This is a matter of adopting the opposite view to the young Rousseau who, as Starobinski tells us, does not yet know what a girl is! And the implied genders are of course perfectly reversible: what counts for the male sweetheart also counts for his female lover. Our Valentine's Day contest teaches us that this property also extends to consumers' characteristics: we encounter once more mimetic desire, so dear to René Girard (1965); we become interested in the objects that interest others. As we saw, in this window display as enlarged keyhole, this process concerns our neighbours: I become ever more interested in the window display as others become interested in me.

However, the Valentine's Day competition teaches us that not only does this process apply to the anonymous and local relationships between people collectively observing a window display, but also, and perhaps especially, to the relationships between ordinary customers and their loved ones that are, by contrast, highly personal, even when the latter are absent, and perhaps even because of this absence. As the anthropologist Daniel Miller (1998) demonstrated so perfectly, the consumption of goods is one way of celebrating social bonds. Shopping is very often done out of love, not for oneself, but for the people we love. We could even say that buying for them in their absence is a way of rendering them present. Now, just as the homology between the two cheese contests led to the transition from one game to the other, the homology of the questions involved in the double Valentine's Day game is a wager on their mutual reinforcement: Will they like my photo (taken from outside the window display)? Will she or he like the present that I will give them (potentially obtained by crossing the display's threshold)? In the juxtaposition of these two questions, there is a dimension of being *driven* towards seduction, in which seduction becomes a force that is both equipped and that can carry someone away. Moreover, by creating a shared time and space, in which everyone is simultaneously able to experience the same questions, the Valentine's Day display manages to unite and reinforce the two forms of being 'transported' that I have identified: on Valentine's Day, what leads us to give gifts is both a singular passion for a beloved (between two lovers) and the collective sharing of this same passion (between the crowd of customers as a group of lovers, which is what they are supposed to be during this period).

The highly particular force behind the commercial version of Valentine's Day is once again perfectly captured by the illustrator, whose drawing, had it been a photo, would logically have had to win the prize! In fact, the illustrator understands that the best view of the window display is the one that manages to bring together, create, and then unite a double collective of people and of things. The photo competition plays a decisive role here. At a time when amateur photography was not only a mass activity (Jenkins 1975) but also fetishising personal ties (as both Bourdieu (Bourdieu 1996) and Barthes (1981) identify so clearly), the Valentine's Day window display uses the photo competition not only as a means of playing on a homology of seductive gestures – in which the photo of the window display both replaces and echoes lovers' photos – but also as a lever to potentially intensify the onlookers' crowd mentality. But what can they see that is so worthy of being photographed? The presence of cameras, which objectifies and renders public unique sets of views, spectacularly increase the voyeurism that is inherent to the operation of the window displays. Their use implements a recursive display, one that takes the form of a new game of mirrors: as I watch people watching (and taking photographs), I am drawn to look at (and photograph) what they are looking at (and taking a photo of), rather as if I were forced to take into account the reflection in the shop window, in which the onlookers gaze at both themselves and the reflection's 'bonding' effects.

Far from simply highlighting the ability of the window display contest to bring about the lateral grouping of the onlookers, the illustration also depicts, in a particularly suggestive way, the window's dynamic ability to make these same onlookers move towards the shop interior. The large heart in the centre not only – as we have already seen – combines love (the heart) and calculation (three dollars), it also draws people in with a zooming movement that has to be followed if we want to get more information. The most global assessment (I see the heart; I see the money) initiates a sentence that can only be completed by moving a little closer to read the small print: first we see '$3 for the person who', but one has to take a few more steps forward to be able to read who this person is and what they have to do to acquire the promised money. We are even more inclined to move forward as the association between the large heart and money is not on its own intriguing, even though each element is inherently tempting. We thus find ourselves implicated – that is to say we are caught in a sequence that we are free to leave at any moment, but from which we tend to find it hard to break away. *As we proceed*, we find ourselves being led to do one thing in order to obtain something else, corresponding to the way that revelations are co-produced – between tempting and being tempted – which is an integral part of curiosity devices: eating an apple to acquire knowledge, turning a key to uncover a mystery and, when confronting a competition, taking part in a game to discover if we win – or rather, buying a product in order to discover a game's result. This very last hesitation, between two formulations that are similar but with very different outcomes, reveals how in many cases a customer risks being mistaken about what is really at stake. He finds himself trapped in a new game of mirrors – what we might call a game of smoke and mirrors. This latter type of optical illusion enacts a subtle shift: taking part in the game means entering the shop, and this movement simultaneously leads to the discovery of different things, things we would not initially have been able to see. The entire art of engaging consumers here consists in making a target advance not through forward steps, but rather like a crab, both forwards and sideways, which rather neatly corresponds to the form of 'commercial rebound' so well analysed by Christian Licoppe (2006) – in effect, a rebound consists in making an offer at the best possible moment, over the course of a conversation on a quite different subject.

None of this analysis would be complete if I failed to mention the third and final device used by our grocer from Kansas. Unlike the two others, this one is not grounded in the logic of the contest, but rather on the principle of collection, already indicated above. Its principal interest for us is that it reveals how the targets of experts in curiosity are more diverse than we might have imagined:

> Last Easter we trimmed our window with crepe paper in seven bright colors, using paper tubing alternating the colors. For variety we made up large pom-poms with crepe paper. These showed up fine. At the center and back of the window we placed Donald Duck and a flock of Easter egg dyes. Flanking that at one end we had a six-foot paper bunny. Throughout the window we placed plush bunnies in many sizes and colors. [...] We sacked all our colored Easter eggs in cellophane and put them in the window, together with all kinds of Easter candies. Then we filled toy carts, baby buggies, baskets, autos and engines with small Easter eggs and covered each unit with cellophane. Fancy boxed Easter candies, vases filled with Easter eggs, sand buckets filled with colored eggs for children and real colored eggs in nests were placed around the window. On various colored cutout signs 16 inches long, made of heavy cardboard, and cut in the shape of eggs, we had selling messages: 'This merchandise is all for sale', and 'Leave your order now', and 'Thanks for stopping to look at our display'. By the time Easter had arrived we had sold all the plush bunnies, Donald Duck, the vases, and all the toys and buckets (*Progressive Grocer* February 1940: 60).

As we have seen, from Genesis to *Bluebeard,* the captation by curiosity was above all, directed towards women. We have now discovered how, with the secularisation and commoditisation of the world, neither gender is any longer able to avoid it. With the third and final window display, we ultimately discover that to the universality of gender is now added age: as a device to provoke curiosity, the purpose of the window display is to re-enact the original setting for the temptation of innocence, by attracting children in order to attract their parents. Working on the dispositions of these targets – arousing their curiosity – involves working symmetrically on the arrangement of the objects that are the object of their desire. The idea is clearly to connect a psychology that is intensive and exclusive (focused on people's inner being) to an extensive and

FIG. 5. *The Progressive Grocer*, February 1940, p. 58

inclusive sociology (extending to things that are nevertheless to be attached to people). It is not a question of mobilising a society that already exists, but of constructing a society that is yet to come; of composing a 'common world', or a 'collective' to be 'assembled', to employ terms so dear to Bruno Latour (2005). It is a composition that rests on three elements.

First of all, as I have just indicated, it involves including children in the sphere of decision-making which the social sciences have tended to assume is exclusively reserved for adults. With the window display, the identity of the subjects legitimately able to participate in exchange no longer depends on set rules but is rather defined at the centre of the exchange itself. It is as if, through the technical configuration of voting equipment, a level of taxation that conferred the right to vote in an election was set at the same time as when the voting took place. Catherine Grandclément and I together have shown elsewhere (Cochoy and Grandclément 2005) the degree to which this comparison extends far beyond a simple analogy, by risking a comparative anthropology of the 'isolating device' that is the polling booth, and the 'gathering device' – also known as the supermarket trolley! – both of which appeared shortly before our Kansas window display (the polling booth in 1913;[37] the trolley in 1936 (Grandclément 2006)). Thanks to its narrowness, opacity, the height of the shelf, and the small size of the voting envelope, the polling booth reminds us that choice in a democracy is individual, secret, reserved for adults, and unique (respectively). However, in this specific case, it is only a reminder: the technology is only there to embody, summarise, and reinforce the pre-existing voting rules, as framed in law. In a strictly symmetrical but inverted way, because of its push-bar and seat, and its transparency and generous storage space, the shopping trolley is intended (respectively) to accommodate more than one person – by providing a separate place for children – and to enable choices to be made that are public, and of which there are many. In this case, far from being established in advance, the rule is the fruit of a chaotic evolution, characterised by appropriations and re-appropriations of the device by both consumers and manufacturers (Cochoy 2009). The window display operates in the same way: the breadth of its aperture marks an initial phase in a long history of welcoming children into places that offer provisions, at a time when the interior of a shop was still very hostile to them, with its high counters and goods that tended to be hidden behind the grocer, often concealed in opaque containers (Cochoy 2008b).

The composition of a common world, which is the window display's responsibility, therefore involves establishing extremely close ties between the objects themselves, as if trying to clearly demonstrate – according to a schema to which I have already referred to and that I would now like to explain – that besides the society of people, there exists a 'society of things'. The window display mixes toys, characters, and sweets (Donald Duck, Easter eggs, soft toy rabbits, sweets, toy carts…) as if it were a matter of making food fun through juxtaposition and contamination,[38] but also with the help of extras ('crepe paper in seven bright colors', 'large pom-poms with crepe paper') and an entire series of syntactical operators that clearly highlight the effort made to arrange and choreograph these different elements ('we trimmed', 'we made up', 'we placed', 'we arranged', 'we sacked', 'we filled'…). In the staging of the window display, we are in the presence of a new instance of the curiosity cabinet: in fact this time the collector is no longer an individual who haphazardly gathers curious things about which the collector will gain familiarity (as with the cabinets of yesteryear), but rather a shopkeeper who skilfully arranges already familiar objects that have associations that might arouse curiosity (as with contemporary window displays). As I said, the strategy is similar to that used by the witch in *Hansel and Gretel* (see above, chapter 2), except that here, in addition to the house of sweets, we have objects that bring it to life: thanks to the presence of the various characters, the objects form a society; they come to life and form a circle that customers are invited to join. This is in fact the third element in the window display's attempt at composition, where the trick consists in connecting the first two: after having assembled the children and their parents *on one side*, and the sweets and toys *on the other*, the whole idea is of course to unite one with the other.

On one side... and on the other: this rather heavy expression, which we tolerate in academic literature because elegance of language must sometimes be sacrificed for clarity of expression, is for once exceptionally appropriate, provided we want to give it its literal meaning. By separating the public and the commercial offer *on either side* of a totally hermetic partition, the window display establishes a strict division between humans and non-humans, a division of which not even the Moderns would dare to dream, even though they establish this kind of apartheid as the basis for their representation of the world (Latour 1993). And yet the paradox lies in the fact that here this physical division between the two types of entities that inhabit the world is entirely dedicated to its own dissolution. The 'merging' magic of the window display operates both downstream and upstream of the gaze.

Downstream, the window display's particular arrangement is designed to overcome the resistance of Rousseau by removing people as much as possible – the opaque curtain enclosing the background is there for this very purpose. It is as if the pastry chef had understood, from initial careful tests at the edge of his shop with a new self-service approach, that by slipping away and hiding he was better able to extend his influence. Upstream, the window display's particular location contributes to inhibiting the emergence of a Sartrean self-consciousness. It encourages the subject to abandon himself to the objects: the window display opens onto the street – in other words, into a public domain, in which neighbours are anonymous and almost objectified individuals, and where, except for exceptional odd gestures, nothing happens that might be considered scandalous. Between the upstream opaqueness of the curtain and the downstream anonymity of the street, everything is thus played out between the customer and the objects displayed for him to view. The configuration of this setting thereby reinforces both the detachment of the subject from the public, and his attachment to the objects in question (except of course for the more limited public composed of those who crowd together and watch the scene, in that they share the same sense of fascination and excitement). Paradoxically, the more inert these objects are (frozen as a group in a meaningful relationship with one another), the more active they are; the more inanimate they are, the more they possess a soul. The tranquillity and stability of their relationships with one another is reassuring – both these properties and relationships mean that we fear neither their disapproval nor their gaze, as there is no risk of being observed. The inanimate objects re-establish vision as one-way by neutralising any possibility of being looked back at.[39]

It is the socialisation of objects that finally results in the absorption of the subject, thus reversing any Sartrian introspection: if I objectify what I observe, as in Sartre, then I expose myself to becoming aware of the eyes of the subjects observing and objectifying me. However, if, as in the window display, the things being observed are socialised and pull me into their own social world, just as the rabbit leads Alice into Wonderland (or into the window display – it depends!), what is happening in the present, and any people passing by in the background, becomes unimportant (Lewis Carroll tells us that Alice is a 'curious child'[40]). As the result of an astonishing reversal of perspective the customer is indeed carried away by the crowd (but by a crowd of objects) with almost no-one on the side of the subject – in the illustrator's picture, the customers are rare, *stationary* – objectified, in other words – sharing nothing other than the same sense of contemplation that comes from confronting the intense and dense social life of the objects that is offered up to their gaze on the other side of the glass. Society truly has migrated into this other world, and it is thus best to go towards it in order to recover moral and social life by building new relationships with the objects that compose it. Here, we really are facing a last game of mirrors which brings about its abolition and its transgression: the appeal of the window display leads the customer to suspend *reflection* so as to move towards action (abolition); it is an invitation to go *through the looking glass*, to venture around the window display in order to enter the shop (transgression).

Returning from wonderland and leaving a dream – a delusion? – waking up, and returning to consciousness in some way always leaves a feeling of ambivalence: on the one hand, we still have the magnificent memory of the world that we briefly glimpsed; on the other, we feel creeping doubt about how real this world is, and how relevant. What, then, is the point of our trip to the land of window displays, and if we look more closely, to the land of a single window display as presented by a grocer from Kansas – a character about whom we know no more than we do about Bluebeard, other than that he is no doubt less frightening but also rather more boastful – and illustrated with drawings (which we can say are to photography what fiction is to reality)? Where is the window display *really*? Outside or inside the story? Unless the story itself is the true window display, as the title on top of its printed pages seems to suggest, does *Progressive Grocer* not function as the 'window display of all window displays', with the magazine showing a thousand displays in its own pages, each more seductive than the next, in the hope of persuading its advertisers and readers to place their adverts and lend it their attention for its greater ultimate profit? (Cochoy 2010a).

One doubt leads to another, causing me to examine the risks involved in my own impulse. Have I not just conducted an 'experimental exercise of experimental economics' that was undoubtedly too long, confused, and finicky (at best) or even misplaced, inappropriate, and off topic (at worst)? As classical economic sociology is constantly warning us, economics is rarely enough to fully understand the economy. After all, does it make sense to undertake all of this calculation when the episode I just described should have warned me from the very start? What is the point of calculation when addressing children who can barely count? I would like to offer three answers to these questions. Firstly, exploring the anthropology of window displays in the way that I have allows us to use a method of expression rather similar to that in Nathalie Serraute's *Planetarium* – of reliving in slow motion and gathering together a thousand tiny cognitive instances that were hinted at, experienced, and for the most part, most certainly abandoned, but which most certainly begin again each time we contemplate these commercial displays from the street. Secondly, calculation is not necessarily numerical. When a figure is missing, either because it is not on the goods (Cochoy 2002), or the subjects are still too young to read and to handle figures (Cochoy and Grandclément 2005), economic rationality (in other words, a concern to make the best choice between what is on offer and our preferences) nevertheless finds a way of expressing itself in the form of what I have called elsewhere a 'qualculation' (Cochoy 2008) – in other words, an appraisal of things based on a perception of their other qualities. Lastly, as François Cooren (2007) has clearly demonstrated, calculations are much 'warmer' than we think: 'Is there not [asks Cooren] a little warmth, even if diffuse, in the ties that unite us to these beings whose relative weight we estimate?' Now, the 'warm' dimension of calculation can make it brief and impetuous: in front of the window display the rational assessment of what is on offer can easily take the form of a sudden emotion; does not the hope of gain, the silky seduction of a prize, the promise of a discount, a gift or reward arouse in us a certain childlike happiness, one capable of implicating us in feverish consumption? So far, we have seen to what extent this kind of emotional calculation is supported by the clever combination of a mute commercial offer and a silent scenography, whose paradox consists in how it comes to life and brings us to life despite (or by virtue of?) its immobility. Now we must investigate how these sorts of combination, far from ending on the surface of a window display, proliferate, and are transformed both inside and outside the shop.

4

'TEASING'

WINDOW DISPLAYS ARE CLEARLY NEITHER THE PRINCIPAL NOR THE ONLY way to arouse commercial curiosity. Contemplating a window display is always about being located at a precise moment in the trajectory of marketing objects and subjects, between past offers and future novelties; it is also always about having someone (or something) behind you as well as in front of you. Behind you, on the side of the street, and in public space, the window display is caught amongst the infinitely wider discourses of rumour, the press, and advertising; in front of you, on the side of the shop, and its private space, the objects shown in the window display are themselves enveloped in the more local coverings of packaging – covers that we must pass through should we want to consume them. I would now like to turn to these two spaces, which both prepare (in the case of advertising) and prolong (in the case of packaging) the curiosity operative in the window display.

I intend to demonstrate that packaging is a paradoxical driving force of curiosity. Packaging activates the tension inherent in every 're-presentation' (Latour 1995). On the one hand, the text it features tells us what things are contained within. On the other, this text and what it says, cannot convey everything about these things and therefore cannot represent exactly what they are. It follows that packaging inevitably activates this tension, even if unintentionally: it creates a gap, a horizon of expectations, the desire to have things clear in one's mind and to use one's own senses to assess the balance between the cover's promises and the properties of its content. Thanks to the invention of 'teaser campaigns', advertising takes advantage of this gap itself by re-enacting the spatial difference between the packaging's outer message and inner content, in the form of a temporal gap between the promise being hinted at, and the promise being realised. It is these two methods of arousing curiosity that I would thus like to analyse, first by studying in greater detail the way they work, based on two suitable cases, then by considering one of their recent metamorphoses, which invites us to journey through a new 'wonderland'.

PACKAGING (TEASING, SCENE 1)

With only a few exceptions, packaging is as opaque as the window display is transparent. The box – by hiding its content, while at the same time providing a few indications about its nature and postponing the discovery of what is inside until later – uses Bluebeard's three old tricks: an appeal to curiosity, the progressive revelation of content, and the preparation of a surprise. Packaging moves us towards making a purchase so that we can rip off the cover, just as the heroine in the story is always made to turn a key in order to be able to see what is on the other side of the door – with the associated pleasure and risk of surprise, which are to a person what the event is to a story.

Nevertheless, it is precisely concerning the surprise and its meaning that the tale and the packaging differ, or rather begin to differ. The tale makes a very clear choice to destroy the heroine's dream with the occurrence of the 'nasty surprise', which we saw is also paradoxically an exquisite surprise for the reader: it is indeed the shiver produced by the unexpected discovery of the corpses that lends the tale its appeal, as if the taste for morbid spectacles at one time condemned by Saint Augustine had suddenly became acceptable, to the extent that it is offered to children. The tale therefore sets up a nasty-but-nice surprise, oscillating between the negative and positive according to whether we adopt the heroine's or the reader's point of view (this is a judgement that in turn can vary according to whether the reader himself identifies to a greater or lesser extent with the heroine[1]). Packaging sets up a far more complex set of operations, both regarding expectations and their satisfaction, given that fearing the worst and hoping for the best can, depending on the case, turn into a nice or a nasty surprise, or simply into a lack of surprise, when upon opening the box the buyer encounters a near-perfect match between the container and its content. Whereas the tale's heightening of ambiguity only involves varying points of view, and while the nature of the final secret is utterly unambiguous – highlighted, in particular, by the repetition of references to 'hooks' – the uncertainties surrounding packaging involve the evaluator as much as that which is being evaluated: a judgement as to whether a surprise is 'nice' or 'nasty' involves both the multiplication of points of view, as well as the multiplicity of the objects being subject to inspection.

However, and contrary to the version of the tale set in stone by Perrault (which constantly repeats the same scene and is intended to be read identically), packaging confronts us with a far more fluctuating set of situations. The countless experiences of opening packaging have tended to bring about an evolution in the results of the task. Over time, a spectacular inversion between the proportion of nasty and nice surprises has been produced, in favour of the latter. How can we explain such an inversion? Historically, packaging was first perceived as an opportunity for potential fraud. By pushing the assessment of content beyond a commercial setting, the public was right to suspect that it was only being used to conceal a lack of correspondence between the proclaimed and actual content, to the benefit of the shopkeeper (Strasser 1989). Nonetheless, as irony would have it, through an extraordinary reversal that is integral to the functioning of the device itself – this is the first surprise of the surprise device – ever since appearing, packaging has actually presented itself as a tool employed for eradicating the fraud it was believed to supposedly encourage. Here, the word 'reversal' must be understood not only in the figurative sense of a turn of events, but also as meaning an actual inversion of the inside and outside, as if turning a coat inside out; as though the package's content had migrated onto the surrounding surface, to the point that reading the text on the box becomes even more reliable than taking a detour into its content. In fact, packaging has the incredible virtue of being able to teach us more about the content it conceals than the content can do by itself: it enables us to be given information about a product that no sensory experience of the same unadorned product could ever provide us with, such as details about its composition or its origin. At the beginning of the twentieth century, in the context of major national legislation concerning product quality and safety – the French Law of 1905 on the prevention of fraud (Canu and Cochoy 2005; Stanziari 2005), the 1906 Pure Food and Drug Act in the United States (Presbey 1929; Frohlich 2007), and others – the law turned these sorts of specificities into statutory obligations, and thus into contractual commitments. Instead of operating as an opportunity for fraud, packaging has become one of the best means of preventing it, given that once the information on the boxes had been signed with the manufacturer's name, it offered the means of finding and punishing potential fraudsters, to the extent that now (and as was recently underscored by Alexandre Mallard (2009)), the scandals that we still occasionally encounter within markets (Besançon et al. 2004) are an exception to the ordinary situation, namely the most common, which rather demonstrates that extreme trust is the law of the market, and that breaking it is the exception.

From this point of view, social sciences lag behind the path pursued by the history of the market. Economic sociology (and more particularly the sociology of quality) has paid considerable attention to the question of information asymmetries, by focusing either on the economics of quality (Karpik 1989; Stanziari 2005), or the dynamics of product description (Callon et al. 2002; Cochoy 2002). In economics, information asymmetry is represented as a tool available to the seller that inevitably works against the buyer, as a perversion of the market: since we assume the actors are opportunists, the one who conceals something from his partner inevitably takes the opportunity to trick him for his own benefit, in order to achieve a larger profit. There is the canonical example of the used car market: in this market, the seller knows more than the buyer and, if the product is faulty, he will not hesitate to conceal this information and sell it at the normal price, thus making what is a dubious profit, to say the least (Akerlof 1970). In other words, in the economics of quality, the 'surprise' is implicitly assumed to be unavoidably 'nasty'; in a market filled with rational actors, the partial concealment of an aspect of a real situation inevitably lends itself to the deliberate exercise of fraud.

However, with respect to these issues, economics, and even more so sociology, have intervened at the wrong time. When writing his famous article, even

Akerlof conceded that actors on the ground did not wait for the formulation of his model before establishing their own diagnosis and developing sets of solutions that he is very honest to list: he mentions guarantees, brands, chains, certification systems – 'even the Nobel prize, to a certain extent', explains a mischievous note written by the prize's future recipient, evidently reluctant to recognise the merits of certain laureates whose own arrogance is mocked in the article! How very unlucky: the one time an economist appeared to be receiving the unanimous praise of sociologists, to the point of becoming excited about the heuristic power of a pure, tough model, perfectly fashioned and indexed according to a series of extremely simplistic hypotheses, of the kind loved in economics and hated in sociology, no one – except the brilliant Akerlof himself! – noticed that this model had been obsolete ever since its creation. One does not need to be a specialist historian of the markets to know that the guarantees, brands, chains, and labels that Akerlof mentions in support of his argument are not his own inventions, but rather antidotes that have long existed as a counter to the emergence of opportunism in situations of informational asymmetry.[2] In other words, the economics and sociology of quality are of very little use: their arguments and results are perfectly correct and even enlightening, but they are also completely redundant in relation to what actors (perhaps except for some of Akerlof's colleagues) already knew, and were doing, long before their formulation.[3]

On the other hand, it is surprising to observe the extent to which these works have ignored the role played by the resource of surprise (this time in the positive sense of the word), even though the organisation of nice surprises is the only form of information asymmetry with which the professionals are still free to play, ever since the nasty surprise of fraud was seriously hindered by the mechanisms of contractual obligation that govern the management of packaging. The 'nice surprise' does however lend another sense to information asymmetry as *desirable* asymmetry, and in particular as information asymmetry desired on both sides: both on the supply side – proven by the recurrent use of contests, gifts, 'bonuses', praising 'new releases', and teaser advertising (see above) – and on the demand side, as revealed in the emblematic example of the receipt of gifts.

BOX 2. THE GIFT PACKAGE: THE ECONOMICS OF SURPRISE

Within economic sociology, ever since Mauss, we have gone on endlessly about gift-giving. However, generally we have done so from a rather disembodied perspective, restricting ourselves to questions that are both accounting-related, involving the opposition between what is given freely and what is calculated, or social, oriented around gift-giving as the basis for a collectivity. More innovative works have demonstrated the extent to which gift-giving and market exchange, far from being mutually exclusive, are mutually reinforcing (Callon and Latour 1997). The gifts that circulate in the context of the market economy are an excellent illustration of this intricate relationship between gift and market; on the one hand because in this kind of economy offering gifts develops the underlying market, and on the other because thanks to the gift and counter-gift, presents themselves are a powerful vector of commoditisation and socialisation (Winnepenninckx-Kieser 2008).[4] However, no matter what their merits, perhaps none of these approaches take into sufficient account the material nature of gifts.

However, taking their material nature into account allows us to be able to consider the relationships between gift and market differently. As these gifts very often appear in the form of packages, presents take us into an economy of surprise where, even before the delay separating gift and counter-gift occurs, the delicious suspense of discovering the former is in operation. Gift packages employ a form of hyperbolic informational asymmetry, given that they produce even more pleasure by being completely hermetic, opaque, and mysterious. More specifically, they appear simultaneously as a form of 'anti-packaging' and sublimated packaging. The gift is anti-packaging because it conceals everything and says nothing, whereas conversely, ordinary packaging shows almost everything and says a lot. However, it is sublimated packaging in that it takes the two fundamental incentives for packages to their limit, consisting in splitting the act of consumption in space by establishing a hermetic boundary between the container and its content, and in time, by separating the moment of purchase from that of consumption. This double characteristic of the gift package shifts the problems of the market and the gift somewhat: whereas the wrapping paper detaches the object from its market origins (Brembeck 2007), the curious excitement of unwrapping cancels out, at least for a while, the horizon of the counter-gift so as to focus the subject's attention on the pleasurable struggle both with the wrapping and of discovering the object.[5]

Packaging (or arranging the surprise that goes with it) clearly brings the deliberate (or obligatory) exploitation of information asymmetry into play. However, it shows us that rather than inevitably leading actors towards valuing the lowest price, economic calculation can on the contrary inspire them to be honest and/or generous, to the extent that, in this case, rationally taking advantage of the information asymmetry leads, in a spectacular turn, not to the depreciation but rather to the preservation, or, in the best case, to the enhancement of the quality in question.

The preservation of quality is the most common. This is where the surprise (from the economist's point of view, who is completely surprised to see calculation not being taken to its limit, despite such a wonderful opportunity to do so!) is the absence of surprise: this is the situation where the opening of a package confirms the accuracy of all the information intended to describe its content – as if the actors had not given into opportunistic temptation. In the second case, the package does not contain exactly what the packaging had promised, but this discrepancy operates in favour of the buyer, in the manner of a 'nice surprise'. This surprise could take the form of a quantitative surplus – the package contains more product units than indicated on the label – but also a qualitative gain that is rarer and/or harder to assess, when the product is decorated with, or accompanied by, more qualities, objects, or services than the label was able, or wished, to announce. In each of these scenarios, it is as if the logic of the 'efficiency wage', dear to labour economists, had migrated towards the market for goods and services, in the form of an 'efficiency bonus'. In the same way that in the labour market the payment of a salary above the market rate allows an employer to expect greater commitment from his employees (Shapiro and Stiglitz 1984), going beyond the promises of the packaging is to play on the strengthening of customer loyalty. Who has never experienced the satisfaction of discovering that an ordinary product bought at a cheap price was much better than its packaging and/or price might have led us to expect? It must be noted, however, that very often actors find it difficult to resist the temptation to reveal the logic of this bet after its implementation (like a secret we cannot keep), either directly, with comments such as 'x% extra product free', or indirectly, and in a way that is perhaps more rhetorical than literal, as exemplified by the hilarious tics of 'Monsieur Plus', the hero of the famous adverts for the Bahlsen cookie company.

Monsieur Plus invente la noisette au biscuit.
Bahlsen
Bahlsen
Kipferl

FIG. 6. Monsieur Plus, Bahlsen[6]

What the information asymmetries in packaging employ most often, however, are neither errors of judgement, involving mistaking a poor quality product (in Akerlof's case) or a more abundant or better quality product (in the case I just mentioned) for the standard product, nor the hope of consumer loyalty or a repeat purchase if they are satisfied, but rather the excitement provoked by the promise of the packaging and the obstacle that this nevertheless presents. This gap establishes a differential; a tension, in the physical sense of the word, whose emergence often calls on desire to resolve it. In this case, the surplus value attached to the use of informational asymmetry is quite different from the pattern described by Akerlof, both in terms of supply and demand. On the supply side, this surplus does not lie with the negative or positive variation of the content's quality but rather in the 'game' played by the packaging itself: it offers both the potential for a mismatch and/or fun. On the demand side, this surplus activates an asymmetry which differs from classic forms of information asymmetry. Whereas the latter is not perceived by the customer, the new asymmetry is, on the contrary, sensed as an expectation of 'something different and desirable' that nevertheless remains, if not a mystery, then at least an object worthy of discovery. The added-value here does not stem from a particular input but rather from the input of novelty or the hope of novelty. The device is very close to the excitement of a striptease, which draws the spectator into being involved in an enjoyable sequence of expectation and discovery, as we shall see from following a 1955 campaign carried out by Kellogg's (the cornflakes manufacturer) in order to promote a new form of packaging design.

The choice of cornflakes is all the more significant as this product played an emblematic role in the history of packaging. The Quaker Oats company, to make a profit out of investments in expensive machinery designed to guarantee continuous production, had the idea of packaging its product to distinguish it from other cornflakes, which tended to be lower quality and sold loose. This enabled them to combat fraud by establishing competition oriented around quality, to invent a market for breakfast cereals, to promote their brand name, and to conquer the whole American market via its national advertising campaigns (Chandler 1977). Along the way, the development of breakfast cereal played a decisive role in extending the activities not only of cereal farmers, but also of the railways that assured its national distribution, as well as in both the growth of the paper industry involved in manufacturing the cereal boxes, and the considerable expansion of magazines responsible for advertising (Presbrey 1929: 438).

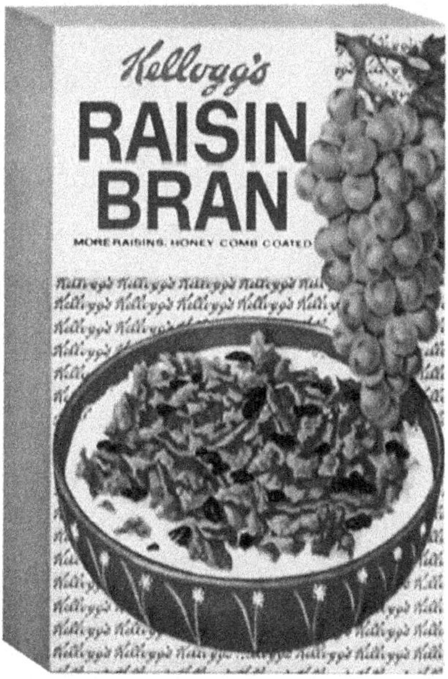

FIG. 7. *The Progressive Grocer*, December 1957, p. 38 (detail)

Packaging transforms a logistical constraint into a playful device. As in a striptease scenario, it manages to convert the fleeting encounter between a consumer's gaze and a richly coloured scripted surface into a scenario seen as likely to extend over time. This is what is clearly demonstrated by the rhetoric of the Kellogg's packaging which consists of a representation not only of the product, but also its origins (a fresh bunch of grapes), and its destination (an appetising bowl of cereal with raisins).

By proceeding in this way, this packaging breaks from the product's lateral position amongst its competitors and enrols the consumer in a longitudinal and longer-term experience of consumption. From this perspective, the device genuinely employs a technique of manipulation. For the psychologists Beauvois and Joule (1987), manipulation refers to any strategy designed to lead people into doing something that they would not have done spontaneously, but without either forcing or duping them. The trick is sequential: manipulating someone consists of involving them in a step-by-step decision-making process. Over the course of the process, people will obtain all the information they need in order to make a rational choice, but they will only receive it progressively. The most appealing information is provided at the beginning, whereas negative information is only revealed at the end, before the final decision. Experiments show that once people have been attracted to and are involved in the decision-making process, they find it difficult to go back and abandon choices that were previously considered, even once they eventually possess those elements in the assessment that, from the perspective of a purely rational choice, should lead them to abandon their initial plan.

The 'raisin bran' packaging clearly places the consumer within this type of sequential decision-making process. However, in this case, the manipulation is reinforced from two sides. The first reinforcement involves a subtle temporal trick. What should logically be considered as the first stage in a sequence of manipulation – that is to say, the initial offer made to the consumer – intervenes here as the second stage, in a longer story that links consumer and product *even before* they have encountered one another in the shop. In fact, in the imagery of the lovely bunch of fresh grapes, the consumer is meant to understand that she or he is already implicated in the product's lifecycle. Thus, from the moment of the first visual contact with the packet, the subject is already being drawn in. In other words, the consumer is discreetly led into following the logic of a striptease, in a literal sense, in which excitement comes from reading, ordering, and working out the promises associated with the progressive discovery of vignettes within a very real 'storyboard'. He is at the very centre of a linear story that moves from production (the grapes) to consumption (the cereal, raisins, and milk in a bowl), while being invited to complete this story, and to commit himself to the next stage of buying the packet so that the narrative – running from production to consumption, via the purchase – becomes well-ordered. This is how real life corresponds with the life that is depicted. This is how desires and promises are fulfilled. Everything happens like in a game of strip poker, in which players have to 'pay to see' the cards (open the box) so as to discover what the story is all about.

The second reinforcement stems from the customer's cognitive enrolment. Paradoxically, the packaging's material striptease is both much 'hotter' and more universal than the sexual striptease of specialist clubs. It is much hotter because, with the packaging, the (usually male) spectator is not restricted to passively watching a striptease. On the contrary, he is invited to take part, to get to grips, physically, with the performing entity, as if the spectator were able to touch and undress the striptease artist and even leave the club with her in order to continue the operation at home. It is far more universal as it is neither limited to an adult audience nor in any way towards a single motivation. On the contrary, it is addressed to men and women, adults and children: anyone who finds themselves attracted to a very long list of motivations and pleasures.

Far from being a fragile metaphor arbitrarily chosen to deal with the appeal of packaging, the logic of the striptease is clearly the pragmatic logic which professionals themselves use, as we can see from the entire advertising insert from which my example is taken, shown here:

FIG. 8. *The Progressive Grocer*, December 1957, pp. 35–40

This Kellogg's advert is presented as a six-panel 'storyboard' published in the magazine *The Progressive Grocer*. The wording of the advert consists of a spectacularly reflexive and 'back-to-front' use of the striptease: each of the new elements and advantages of the new packaging are presented in sequential fashion, in a folded leaflet that ranges from employing 'nudity' to the 'appropriate clothing'.

The sequence begins with an intriguing cover that at first conceals everything else, as long as the leaflet remains folded: that of an enigmatic 'naked box' with only the Kellogg's logo visible. This logo is repeated obsessively on the box's surface, like the texture of a skin, or as if it had been drawn by Andy Warhol, the artist of the moment (particularly in the advertising sector!). An unknown hand deepens the mystery of the packaging by placing a first 'garment' onto the box: 'Fresh from Kellogg's of Battle Creek: Packaging with a Purpose'. But what purpose? It is only by unfolding the leaflet that in the next three panels we discover (in the real sense of the word) a set of similar boxes, this time modestly covered with product names and graphic illustrations, which gradually reveal themselves bit by bit. The world of clothing is not only suggested by the supportive navy-blue velvet in the background, but also by presenting the products according to the logic of a real fashion show, with all the elements that make up the complete collection of cereal boxes being exhibited from left to right. Finally, the last two panels, covered with text, reveal the deeper meaning of the Kellogg Company's 'purpose': the fifth page announces that 'The purpose of these new packages is simply to sell; to sell the fastest selling cereal even faster. Faster selling for you, for us – faster buying for your customers. Everyone benefits. These new 'bank note' packages on your shelves are as good as money in the bank'. The last panel provides impressive evidence of the scope of its campaign: 'Biggest ad campaign ever: Selling to 160 million people', and so on. This advert is aimed at professionals in retail distribution and in making profit; here it is Kellogg's that is trying to tease the grocers so that they, in turn, can tease the consumers, so that 'everyone benefits'. By proceeding in this way, the campaign partly reveals a final game of bodies and clothes, in which each market actor and mediator hides behind the other: the grocer behind the consumer; the manufacturer behind the grocer; the trade press behind the consumer; the grocer and the manufacturer; and on and on (Cochoy 2008b).

In the final analysis, product assessment involving the progressive revelation of packaged information does not have to be abstract, cold, and descriptive, distant from the 'flesh and bones' of products. On the contrary, thanks to the curiosity that is aroused by this way of getting to know economic objects, the packaging itself becomes as warm and tangible as its content. Through curiosity, packaging tries to build 'attachments' (Gomart and Hennion 1999); it tries to warm up the relationships of consumption; it attempts to help us find the sensory glow of the goods that, throughout its history, it has tended to conceal (Cochoy 2004). Packaging does this by showing the products directly through narratives, through appealing arguments, and representations, or, indirectly, by playing with ideas, values, identities, and symbols.

The Kellogg's advert, however, acts as a hinge between two devices: on the one hand, it features packaging and the ways in which it can be designed so as to magnify the power of seduction; on the other, this scenario is itself presented as an advert, whose discursive trick consists in intensifying the narrative sequence that is inherent to this specific form of packaging, while using the same type of procedure, albeit this time applied to advertising. We thus understand that the methods for arousing curiosity are layered, involving not only a game at the level of each constituent element – window display, shelves, and grocer's bank account; the brand, product description, and box's contents; the discourse, the 'storyboard', and how the advert unfolds – but also the ordered way in which these themselves are 'packaged'; the forms of advertising that cover the commercial spaces that enclose the forms of packaging that, in turn, house the product.

ADVERTISING (TEASER, SCENE 2)

The advert thus occupies a position that looks over others,[7] giving it a particularly unique role in terms of instigating commercial curiosity. The carnal game of unpacking the multiple layers inherent to packaging is in fact often largely prepared further upstream by the advert that appears like a first virtual envelope, a first appeal, and a first piece of bait in the game of arousing curiosity. With the first veil of the advert lifted, people should be led into removing, one by one, the other layers that separate them from the product they desire, or are made to desire. However, this game reaches maximum intensity when the advert itself, even before it has indicated the other coverings that are its very job to point towards, mimics the next game, becoming no longer just a metaphorical striptease, as with the Kellogg's packaging, but sometimes a literal striptease, as in the case that follows. It is this spectacular manner of arousing curiosity that I would now like to focus on, by examining an extremely famous advert that – at least in France – is considered to be an archetypal masterpiece of 'teaser' advertising (Lendrevie and Baynast 2008).[8]

This advert, known as *Myriam* and remembered by all those who lived through the beginning of the 1980s, consisted of a series of mysterious posters that appeared at the end of August 1981, on 900 4 x 3 billboards across Paris and six other French cities (Le Monde 1988; Devillers 2001; Mantoux 2010). The first poster shows a pretty woman in a green bikini with a beach in the background, between a blue sea and sky. This anonymous person announces, in an inset that acts as a speech bubble: 'On 2 September, I'll take the top off'. No other information is given on the poster: just as we do not know the names of the blue-bearded man and his wife, we do not know the name of the model in the green bikini, or of course the advertiser's identity and intentions. On 2 September, we find the young woman in the same place and the same position, except that she has indeed removed the top half of her bikini and has thus unveiled her bosom. This new shot announces: 'On 4 September, I'll take the bottom off'. The fascination of this slow-motion 'soap opera' and the incredulous anticipation of full nudity, as presaged by the initial promise, inevitably leads to major questions in both private and public, echoed in the media, as people excitedly await the day after tomorrow. On 4 September, Myriam does indeed take off the bottom of her bikini. However, this time the photograph is taken from behind, with the comment: '*Avenir*, the billboard company that keeps its promises'.[9]

FIG. 9. Avenir, the Billboard Company that Keeps its Promises

The singular notoriety of this campaign is no doubt connected to its extraordinary ability to bring together (in one space and with astonishingly few means at its disposal) an impressive number of resources to support its effectiveness. As we shall see, these resources, which constitute a veritable grammar of curiosity, are at once fun, logical, mathematical, linguistic, semiological, anthropological... and even physiological, mechanical, pragmatic, humorous, and magical!

With *Myriam* we once again encounter a dimension of the game that we discovered in the window display, although here divination is replaced by the riddle.[10] The game draws together charades and logical inference. As we know, charades involve setting two riddles, one concerning the whole, the other concerning each of the elements intended to lead to that whole. Here, the mechanism is similar: the context of city billboards invites passers-by to assume an overall meaning – if it is an advertising campaign, it must be trying to sell us something, but what? – and thus invites them to consider each of the posters as a clue to the whole they have to find.

It is here that logic intervenes. Everyone understands from the outset that the game's outcome is based neither on chance, nor, as in a competition, on a personal appraisal, but rather on producing endogenous knowledge, whose elaboration the messages suggest bit by bit. This 'involves' passers-by in the co-production of meaning over the course of a real experiment, which consists of the posters' successive proposals and the hypotheses and the verifications made by the reader. The logic at work is very similar to that of a recursive mathematical series; that is, a calculative rule in which each natural number n is associated with a specific real number, whose value is determined by those previous occurrences. Conversely, when we know the successive values in a series, we are quickly led both to work out the underlying calculative rule and to anticipate the elements that will follow according to this rule. Therefore, when I see a series of images, each of which represents a body adorned with a set of items but each time stripped of one once compared to the previous image, I am logically led to anticipate, at least as a mental hypothesis, the third stage, the naked body that is, since it is all that is left after the removal of the solitary remaining element. And I am all the more likely to follow the series given that each image provides me not only with a succession of values, but also a calculative rule, allowing me to predict their succession: 'every two days the image will be the same as the previous, minus an item of clothing' or, to put it in mathematical terms, 'for the series of a number of garments, U, for every U of rank *n*, the value of U_n equals U_{n-1}-1'.

This logical-mathematical device is reinforced by another device, this time linguistic. In a sense, this should not be surprising: all things considered, the traditional opposition we usually establish between the 'literary' and 'mathematical' worlds does not hold, given that mathematics is purely a language, and that language, on the other hand, only has meaning by virtue of meaning, in other words because of the logic it is responsible for establishing and conveying. Nonetheless, the interweaving of the games of series and language at work in *Myriam* is rather unusual. This advert is based on a succession of promises that are each either followed or accompanied by the realisation of the precedent. Now, we know that in linguistics, a promise is a pure example of what can be termed a performative utterance, as opposed to a so-called constative one (Austin 1961). Whereas the latter establishes a link between itself and the world that is either correct or incorrect (for example, 'I am wearing a bikini'), the performative utterance refers to a world that is neither right nor wrong, but which it contributes towards realising ('I promise that on 2 September, I'll take off my bikini top'). Utterances of this kind – called 'speech acts' because of their ability to have an impact on the world rather than describing it – have two dimensions. The first, termed 'illocutionary', is inclined towards the utterance itself, given that it specifies the intention (in this case, a promise; in others an order, a threat, and so on.). The second, termed 'perloctionary', is by contrast inclined towards the effect produced by the utterance (for example, the belief in the promise, or its actual delivery). What is particular about the pattern in *Myriam* is that, after the second poster, each promise is accompanied by the previous one being realised: if, for each promise P, of rank *n*, in which * marks a promise delivered, the resulting sequence is P_1 ; $P_1^* + P_2$; $P_2^* + P_3$, a sequence which refers to a more general structure that we can write as $P_{(n-1)^*} + P_n$. Roland Canu, in the conclusion of a study demonstrating the importance of decisions and prior constraints in the development of an environmental labelling device, noted that 'certainly, *saying is doing*, however just as often it is *having done*' (Canu 2011a). In our case, on each occasion, saying means having done but also doing, and it is doing with all the more certainty given that we have shown that we have done so before. In other words, with *Myriam*, what *was* said plays a role in what *is* said: for every event that follows, the fulfilment (*performation*) of the previous promise increases the performativity of the next. The method is all the more effective as the statement involves both the anaphoric repetition of a strictly identical structure – 'on (date X) I will take off (clothing Y)', reinforced by the visual anaphora of an unchanged scenario, and the variation of its referent – on each occasion, the date and clothes change.[11] Here we find two conditions that are essential for the performativity of certain language acts. The first is their continuous reiteration, allowing the words to 'take shape' and the 'bodies' to exist through these words, without which they would amount to very little (Butler 1988). The second is the language's ability to act as the world's 'ventriloquist', making it speak and express its power not only through its words (Cooren 2010), but also through the intervention of 'wordjects'; that is to say, objects that are articulated like words (Cochoy 2010a).[12]

Nevertheless, the playing of the game, the use of logic, and the reception of performative language together produce a disturbing result, given that, rather than bringing us closer to the product, they lead us to anticipate the model stripping completely, without being able either to discern the intention or to believe it possible, 'all moral standards and advertising logics being equal'. In fact, as the campaign progresses, social conventions, the rules applicable to advertising, and, more generally, the laws penalising indecency, render each promise more unlikely than the previous.[13] Undoubtedly, showing bare breasts is not without scandal, but, as an act, it does seem to have reached the pinnacle of possible licentiousness, to the extent of making further transgressions simply unthinkable. This was 1981, that is to say a time when the topless trend, while widespread (Kaufmann 1998), was also far from the 'porno chic' that was to follow (Heilbrunn 2002), and a period in which feminist criticism seized on advertising and when the law governing it underwent significant development (Parasie 2010).

Furthermore, advertising cannot, by definition, be anonymous and free: the person bearing the cost of the campaign has a brand to promote and a product to sell, so displaying nudity for free hardly seems compatible with the rationality of advertising inherent to urban billboards. That said, the three stages of undress are compensated for by three other layers that act to minimise the scandal: firstly, the era of bare breasts bolstered public tolerance for such displays; secondly, the beach featured in the background places the foreground (the naked breasts) in an everyday accepted context (Kaufmann 1998); lastly, the contextual framework of the billboard isolates the message within a space of expression which, because it appears in the public space of the street, enjoys the licence afforded to advertising professionals. Nevertheless, this licence remains subordinate to forms of legal regulation that remain vague and unstable, largely contingent on complaints and case law (Iacub 2008; Cochoy and Canu 2006). Because of this (given the time, place, and the way the act of viewing is framed), everyone understands that the second poster takes the exhibition of the body to the limit of acceptability;[14] beyond which it would almost certainly tip over into scandal and transgression, especially for the person who remains stubbornly and determinedly stood in front of us, and whose legs are also slightly apart,[15] according to a staging that was accurate to the millimetre:

> It was very easy, but very precise, so he [the photographer] already knew exactly where I should place myself [...] there was a picture that had been done beforehand, and we just copied the picture exactly (Author's interview with Myriam).

In other words, what is logical when inside the frame is not logical when outside it, or when trying to deduce the next phase: the performative virtues of the successive statements, at least from the second poster onwards, come up against the 'infelicitous conditions' surrounding them, which cast doubts on the performance that is promised. It is precisely this blurring of mathematical logic, linguistic performativity, and social routine that makes the campaign either so attractive or so disturbing, by taking curiosity to its limit. The cognitive dissonance between performative logic and the social-legal-economic conditions that limit the campaign plunge the passer-by into a whirlwind of calculations: They wouldn't really dare? Who are they? What are they looking for? What is the meaning of all this? Where are we going? Is it tolerable? There must be a trick, but which one? Gradually curiosity becomes a *plot*, both in the sense of a story and an enigma. As the plot proceeds, a hypothesis of humour germinates as something of a saving grace. Tinged with both anxiety and pleasure, it is the small act of complicity often associated with advertising (Parasie 2010), consisting of joining in the game of co-producing the message, both in order to understand it and to be reassured (Cochoy 2011b).[16]

One of the remarkable aspects of the plot lies in its particularly distended and discontinuous nature. We find here a mode we had come across in *Bluebeard,* in which certain passages stretched time with the help of remote dialogues, delays, anaphora (Anne, sister Anne...'), and others (see above, chapter 1). However, with *Myriam,* the method becomes exaggerated. With every poster being replaced every two days, it is as if the story had been divided into a corresponding number of sequences and was delivered across a number of episodes as a soap opera. This way of working introduces a radical alternation between statement and reception. The method first requires personal and emotional involvement. As successive posters each 'press pause' for two days, it becomes possible for passers-by to come across them in several different places, to pass in front of them several times and thus to experience the message, and be moved and/or made to think about it before the next is discovered. Above all, this 'pause mechanism' enables a move beyond the bilateral relationship between transmitter and receiver that is characteristic of advertising. The sequence and the emotional charge, doubled by the suspension of time, provide the opportunity for the activation of a multilateral relationship: each person, confronted by his or her own perplexity and feelings (curiosity but also rejection, incredulity, disapproval, amusement, excitement...) has the possibility of sharing these with their loved ones and thus becoming involved in the creation of collective interpretation and judgement through their shared curiosity.[17] To put it in Durkheimian terms, the unfolding proliferation and suspension of the campaign puts to the test a strong and definite state of collective emotion. Rather than being only commercial, the production of advertising is also (above all?) social. Perhaps more than other consumption practices (Gaglio 2008), this type of media in fact has an astonishing ability to test social norms on a large scale; it allows limits to be explored, for their basis to be expressed, and for experimentation with future potential developments. Advertising works on the relationship to/with values; it excites its audience and at the same time triggers conversation, indignation, and a desire for reassurance. By creating the conditions that encourage debate, the *Myriam* soap opera, both in terms of its content and the time available, is the forerunner of today's 'buzz' and 'viral marketing' (Mellet 2009). In fact, the campaign's scandalous and mysterious nature – each time giving the public and the media two days for emotions to be stirred up – also brought considerable press coverage. This spread the message free of charge and maximised public attention as both a positive externality and an echo chamber, resulting in the transformation of a private, individual curiosity into a curiosity that was public and collective:

> The irony of the story is that the campaign only ran for ten days. Everyone felt sure they had seen it... whereas most people only learnt about it when they saw the pictures in the papers! (Mantoux 2010).

Some people discerned that behind *Myriam* becoming a 'social event' lay advertising's pretension or ability to establish itself as a cultural phenomenon. There are many works that refer to advertising as a matter of 'culture', both negatively, when criticising the medium for commercialising artistic codes, for contributing to the political economy of symbols (Baudrillard 1981), and for promoting 'marketing ideology' (Marion 2004); and more positively, when highlighting the creative contribution of advertisers (Gaertner 2010), and when bringing to light the important cultural role played by advertisers, on the sides of both supply and demand (Marchand 1986; Sauvageot 1987). This said, the 'ad culture' should be understood as they do in the French-speaking life sciences: rather than a cause that produces an effect, the 'cultural' dimension of *Myriam* is rather the result of 'cultivating' the public, analogous to the 'cultivation' of yeast in a petri dish (Brives 2010); advertising is like a lab bench; agencies are 'laboratories' where 'desires' are cultivated (Hennion and Méadel 1993). More specifically, in the case that interests us, this cultivation consists in immersing those receiving the message in one of those good old stimulus-response-reinforcement loops so dear to historical behaviourism – loops that Daniel Berlyne, a behaviourist specialising in curiosity (Berlyne 1950; 1960), presented as essential drivers of this motive:

> We have therefore arrived at the hypothesis that curiosity is aroused in a subject when a question is put to him, whether by himself or by an external agent. Some component (S_{mD}) of the response-produced stimulation resulting from the meaning of the question (r_m) is assumed to act as a drive-stimulus. And we can see that the intensity of this drive-stimulus, which will in turn depend on the amplitude of the response (r_{mH}) that produces it, will be one of the most important variables affecting the drive strength of the curiosity (Berlyne 1954: 184).

What else do *Myriam*'s successive promises do, other than to activate an alternation between the stimuli of the questions and the responses of the subject, which Berlyne seeks to describe in purest Pavlovian-Skinnerian style?[18] From *Bluebeard* to Berlyne, from Berlyne to *Myriam*, the process is always the same: being proposed a series of enigmatic stimuli (doors, questions, promises), being enticed into anticipating a response, and the latter's encouragement through instances of confirmation (riches, the solution, the promised body part), so that after each stimulus and each correct answer, the desire to give into giddy curiosity is heightened. It is no coincidence that the B-A BA of behaviourism remains just as relevant and powerful in the contemporary world of advertising (Menon and Soman 2002; Hung 2001), despite the disciplinary tradition having long fallen into academic disuse (Péninou 2003). It might be noted, in passing, that the same can be said of functionalism. Are there not many of us who have experienced this? The contemporary sociologist, who, through inattention, allows a 'function' to slip into a sentence or line of reasoning, will soon be called to order by colleagues who will inform him or her about the costs of being caught in an act of analytical weakness.[19] The police charged with hunting down outbursts of functionalism are now an integral part of the institutions many people deem necessary for the exercise of proper sociological professionalism. However, the very functions suppressed by the social sciences continue to obsess those on the ground: the engineers, traders, politicians, and above all, consumers, who want things to 'work', who want to fulfil their 'role', to serve a 'purpose', and who, despite function being considered a dirty word by specialists of the social, achieve this rather well. The same applies to advertising, whose manifest function is to sell and whose latent function is, as we saw, to test social norms. The world is full of behaviours and behaviouralities, and of functions and functionalities; since sociologists buried Pavlov and Parson, the world has never been as functionalist and behaviourist (I will come back to this). We are thus witnessing an astonishing over-performativity within markets of certain social sciences that continue to 'operate', even after becoming silent (or having been 'silenced').

At this point in my investigation, although I have carefully outlined some of the forces that inform the campaign, I have not yet broached that which is essential, the most important and the most profound. Was it the erotic charge of the posters that struck – seduced? shocked? – everyone from the outset? Yes and no. Certainly, the campaign's erotic dimension is as significant and powerful as it is evident, given that the series of posters, far from simply representing a woman's body, multiplies it and sets in it motion through a striptease and by gradually increasing the stimulation of the senses. In this respect at least, no one would judge the campaign as being unremarkable or even disappointing, even while it is somewhat 'easy', demagogical, and vulgar – indeed, inappropriate. The tendency to play on the metonymy of desires, to display a body in order to sell a product, and to hook a consumer by leading a detour via the emotions, has for a long time been one of the most basic forms of market seduction. The use of sexist representations, including the commercialisation of 'pretty girls' in a sales pitch, is now generally considered to be the most basic form of advertising.

Moreover, it is not that clear-cut whether or not the campaign does succeed in approaching the very limit of acceptability without tipping over into the scandalous. As Aymeric Mantoux reminds us in his fascinating column on the history of this advert, the collective emotion generated by the promises of the *Myriam* campaign was not limited to incredulous curiosity when confronted with the degree of audacity outlined above; among some people it also caused fierce indignation. In Lille, the association *Du côté des femmes* (On the Side of Women) filed an injunction for 'gross indecency', calling it 'a violation of the dignity of women' and 'an incitement to voyeurism'. On 5 September, the Lille court responded favourably to the complaint. In accordance with Articles 283 to 290 of the former Penal Code relating to 'gross indecency committed in particular through the press and books', the court ordered the billboard company to 'partially or totally' conceal the visible posterior (despite the injunction, it was clearly too late to deal with the breasts as Tartuffe once had, given both the changes in traditions and date!). In Paris, the association Choisir (Choose), led at the time by the socialist Member of Parliament, Gisèle Halimi (involved in advocating for women's rights), attempted to bring the matter before the National Assembly in order to have an anti-sexist law passed. Finally, Yvette Roudy, the then socialist Minister for the Rights of Women, intervened in the press against what she believed to be an exploitation of the female body and a violation of women's dignity (Mantoux 2010).

That said, in hindsight, and despite the censors, it appears that *Myriam* worked more to legitimise than suppress the unashamed commercial representation of female models; alongside the prominent political campaign featuring Mitterrand's 'quiet strength' that appeared a few months earlier, it might even have contributed to turning the French into ad-lovers (Maillet 2010). As Jean-Claude Kaufmann clearly highlighted, the campaign's primary characteristic is its indomitable ambiguity:

> What is one to make of [...] Myriam, who in 1981 appeared throughout France, taking off the top before promising the bottom? Feminist movements rose up, believing they had detected the image of a woman in her traditional role as sex object [...]. The people interviewed for a survey focused more on the trivialisation of female nudity. The campaign's success came specifically from the ambiguity (Kaufmann 1998: 60).

Here we find a Durkheimian schema but also its counterpart. In the same way that, in Durkheim, the deviant's behaviour both underlines and questions a shared norm in preparation for future developments (Durkheim 1986), *Myriam*'s audacity tests public morals and their potential shifts. However, one must not forget that addressing a shared norm and testing a collective conscience inevitably means there is an effect on those who differ from it, ranging from criminals to paragons of virtue. By appealing to an 'average' public sensibility, *Myriam* could only either enthuse or shock those on either side of this general sensibility: a sexist public, advert lovers, those with an interest in humour or sensuality on one side, and, on the other, adherents to specific religious views, the very prudish, or defenders of the status of women. The scandal was therefore inevitable, but it is also important to note its limited and clearly defined scope and a resulting disapproval which was thus far from general. *Myriam*'s immodesty is at once passé and persistent and this makes it possible to say that, despite a specific sentence being passed, confined to a particular local context, this campaign managed to go as far as it could in search of a limit, without reaching a breaking point and the risk of public opinion turning against it. This is underscored by the designer of the poster:

> We would not have been able to do this campaign five years earlier. At that time we were both at the apogee of feminist movements and in a period of calm: there had finally been a de-escalation, a reconciliation of women with their bodies, with the idea of seduction (Pierre Berville, quoted in Mantoux 2010).

Moreover, ever since *Myriam*, the advertising industry has continued to use female models, sometimes in far more outrageous ways than in *Myriam* (Parasie 2010; Heilbrunn 2002). Recently, the French internet service provider Alice even took to the extreme the tried and tested method of associating a product and a female figure, unafraid of completely identifying its brand with the image of a ravishing blonde. However, Alice's competitor, Neuf Cegetel, immediately ridiculed this approach in a caustic TV advert in which we see two advertising executives arguing with one another during a telephone call about what strategy to use when selling their product. The camera films one of them in his living room, in front of a bay window, with a beach in the background:

> — Martin? I've read the draft for the Neuf Box ad... What's with the horse? – Well, you have to make people dream, a beach, a beautiful chick... add a small, fat logo in the corner and you've got it... [A blonde in a bikini on horseback crosses the beach in the background] – Yes, but the subject

is unlimited calls in France and in 30 other countries. – If that's the only problem we'll give her a phone [The same blonde on horseback passes in the background, this time with a phone glued to her ear] – Yeah… – Then, we add comedy… [The blonde in the frame of the bay window falls off the horse] People like comedy… [The offer's conditions are overlaid and scroll past] – Hey Martin, this ad has got to say that it's all in the Neuf Box, as well as unlimited calls, all for less than thirty Euros… – Well, that's what's written, we even tell people to go to neuf.fr – And we have to show a blonde for that? – Do you prefer brunettes?[20]

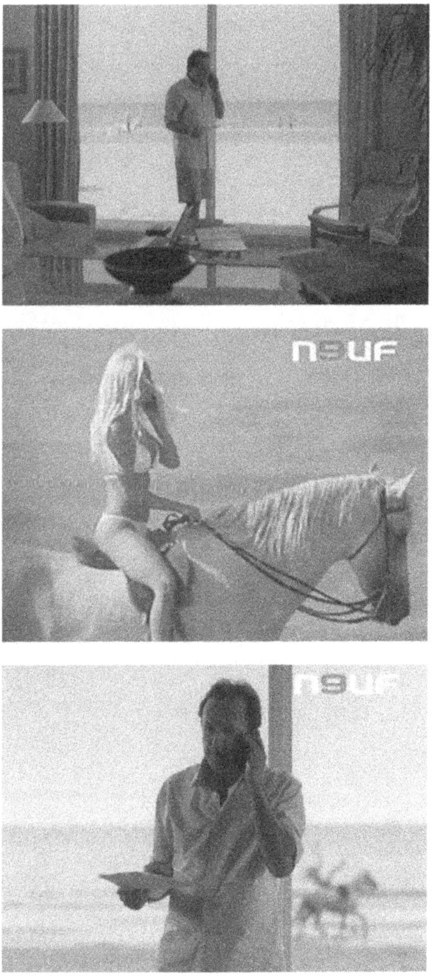

FIG. 10. Neuf Ad: Do you Prefer Brunettes?

Connoisseurs will have noticed in passing the highly exaggerated (subconscious?) homage to the skilled scenography of *Myriam*, with the beach, the bikini, the three appearances – the addition of an accessory (the phone) replacing the subtraction of another (the bikini top) – and the final punchline when the model falls ('this time, I'm removing Alice!'), not forgetting the reflexive reference to the work of advertising, using teasing (the logo 'N9UF', that reveals the identity of the advertiser, is not visible at the start of the clip) and the affectionate wink in the direction of a historical preference for brunettes.[21] However, this homage to a golden age of advertising know-how that has perhaps passed, achieved on the back of Alice,[22] does not wholly do justice to the genius of *Myriam,* as the latter goes well beyond using the female body for the purposes of marketing. *Myriam* – by taking excitement and curiosity to their limit, by playing with the three forms of promise, the desire to know, and the revelation of something intimate – does not simply limit itself to the clever use of commercial sexism. It also establishes a highly particular link to the anthropological foundations of curiosity. What is most important therefore lies beyond the body game. In order to demonstrate this, I would like this time to echo the 'how far can we go' approach by attempting a rather scandalous exegesis that I am only risking as it is well suited to an advert which, after all, adopted this approach. As we shall see, Myriam echoes the intellectual and sexual burden of Genesis (whose components it mimics), but of course to show them differently, and for an entirely different purpose.

Firstly, *Myriam* operates a double reversal of the sacred story (and therefore of its profane version, *Bluebeard*). In the Bible, as in the tale, keeping one's promises and being curious are completely contradictory: in the Garden of Eden, as in *Bluebeard,* breaking one's promise is harshly punished. Conversely, with *Myriam,* curiosity is needed for the promises to be fulfilled. Furthermore, it leads to them being kept: contrary to Eve and Bluebeard's wife, Myriam fulfils her commitments, twice over. On the one hand, she maintains the consumer's involvement in the game; on the other, she honours the advertiser's word. Every time, the promise that an item of clothing will disappear is scrupulously fulfilled. The second reversal concerns Genesis more specifically.

The excitement of curiosity is a sin connected to the Fall; striptease and curiosity are inseparable. In Genesis, the 'strip' (the sequence) involves dressing: the move is from a state of innocent nudity to an awareness of modesty, as Saint Augustine also noted:

> Augustine adds a detail [...].[23] In summary, he claims that Adam and Eve did not just become aware that they were naked but also noticed that lust, about which they knew nothing before the sin, provoked a certain stirring in their bodies. And it was precisely because of this that, albeit too late, they quickly prepared a *cache-sexe* (*From civ. Dei,* XIV, 17). However, when this 'rebellion of the flesh' occurred, before the concealment of their

> modesty, that is, Adam and Eve (continues Augustine imperturbably) began to look at their own respectively shameful parts *curiosius* (XIII, 24, 7). And in this *curiosius* is a mixture of heightened attention (let us not forget the comparative dimension) and dawning embarrassment, and even, in the persistence of the gaze, and before modesty comes into play, brazen shamelessness. [...] after the fall of Adam and Eve and, more specifically, as soon as they look *curiosius* at each other's nudity, the life of man on earth would become one of continuous temptation. In sum, man would always have a natural penchant for *curiositas* (Conf, XIII, 20–28) (Tasitano 1989: 31–32).

What Maria Tasitano is saying (and in particular what Saint Augustine says through her) warrants attention because this argument reminds us that the vine leaves are there to cover the birth of modesty, the awakening of lust, and the guilt inherent to the loss of original innocence. In the Garden of Eden, the curiosity aroused by the forbidden fruit leads to another curiosity, this time spontaneous, concerning bodies. We are therefore better able to understand the reversal operative in *Myriam* as well as its formidable, yet troubling, ambiguity. On the one hand, her striptease is scandalous because it moves in the opposite direction to Genesis. By activating a curiosity regarding the hidden body, the undressing of Myriam ruins the effort made by Adam and Eve to minimise the consequences of their Fall; it once again exposes the now shameful parts they were trying to conceal. From this perspective, the campaign lies on the side of sin and it is possible to understand how it would have generated criticism. However, from another point of view, it is equally possible to interpret Myriam's striptease as a backwards movement. It is as if, by lasciviously removing one by one the fig leaves used by our ancestors, after a fashion, to counteract their guilty sexual curiosity, we were – rather than exacerbating the Fall and its disastrous consequences – rewinding the film of Genesis step by step so as to return to the state of original innocent nudity, to a time before the Fall when Adam and Eve were naked,[24] *when they kept their promises*, just like the (still to come) Avenir poster, and when they were not aware of their sensuality,[25] as suggested by its creators:

> [The controversy] was a heresy. *Myriam* was a pure product of 1968, she had a perfectly healthy relationship with her body, with nature, a completely *guilt-free* relationship with nudity (Comments made by Pierre Berville, poster designer, quoted in Mantoux 2010; my italics).

According to this point of view, there was a lucky, innocent coincidence: because two scheduled professional models failed to show up a few days before a photography session that had been organised in the Bahamas, the photographer Jean-François Jonvelle (who specialised, admittedly, in glamour photography![26]) suggested one of his friends to the agency, whose real name was actually Myriam. Myriam was therefore not a professional model but an ordinary person, without a tiny waist or overly pronounced features; 'natural', in other words, far removed from the oneiric-artificial creatures that tend to populate the world of advertising:

> I had quite a natural look and I also had a very natural relationship with my body, and he didn't want to get too into the female vamp, the enticing woman, that wasn't really the idea and I think they wanted someone fresh [...] Funnily enough, I was 19 at the time and I refused Playboy and that kind of thing but being naked didn't bother me, in the context a nudity that was natural I was completely at ease. But I had never wanted to associate myself with an image that could be considered even slightly sexual. I didn't want to do that but the poster was clear because I had seen the drawings, it was...well, I thought it was a good idea... Of course, no one knew that it would be so successful, not me or anyone [...] A year later I went on a retreat in a forest, no one saw me any more. [It wasn't because of the campaign]. When the campaign had so many repercussions I wasn't really that concerned. I had done it just to earn a bit of money, to pay my rent while I was away, so I wanted to pay for my rent in Paris whilst I was on that retreat. So that is what the campaign did and that was the only purpose of my job as a model, I didn't want to make a career out of it (Author's interview with Myriam).

Reading the Avenir poster in this way also means returning to the difficulties within *Bluebeard,* this tale torn between a moral that is both repressive and permissive, marking the transition between a sacred curiosity (suppressed completely) and a market curiosity (often encouraged). Both of these morals are as entrenched in the posters as they are in the collective subconscious: the ambiguity of *Myriam* works both through the ever-present discourse of Scripture, in simultaneously referencing the original innocence and the feeling of guilt, and through advertising culture, in oscillating between condemning the commercialisation of the female form and variously accepting it in the name of the candour of humour, a certain emancipation, and a new language (Parasie 2010). On the one hand, just as Jupiter adopted the appearance of Amphitrion to seduce Alcmena, the advertiser borrows Myriam's body and voice to capture its audience. On the other hand, the discourse of *Myriam* particularly mischievously revives the two inseparable sides of virtue: the promises made, and the primitive innocence of the undressed body. These virtuous elements are emphasised through the extreme simplicity and starkness of its presentation. 'Thanks to the naked Eve ('Ève nue') coming ('à venir': forthcoming) soon, Avenir has arrived ('est venu' or, literally, 'has come'). This subtle pun (in French at least!), at once involuntary and somewhat juvenile, at least has the advantage of folding into a spectacular chiasmus; the entire anthropological background that, whether we like it or not, informs the story.

Of course, the mobilisation of myth is a means for *Myriam,* not an end. The advert's anthropological background is directed entirely towards the pragmatic efficacy that is disclosed in the final revelation: 'Avenir, the billboard company that keeps its promises'. Just as with modern packaging, part of the surprise is, to some extent at least, the lack of surprise, given that the bikini bottom has clearly been removed and the body exposed, despite the model rotating 180°. The 'reveal' (from the waist down), seen 'from behind' and thus far more acceptable than representing the pubis that is either expected or dreaded – the 'front' view – as well as the surprise revelation of the message's meaning – which consists of promoting, with dizzying reflexivity, the dependability and know-how of advertising professionals – are an occasion for a moment of clarification, for relaxation, and even mutual communion, taking the form of an implicit dialogue between the

BOX 3. VOLVO'S TENTATION (TEMPTATION) OFFERS

For those not satisfied with the mirror-image inverted stripteases of Myriam and Genesis, and for those who still doubt the underlying links between advertising teasing and Biblical temptation (because they observe either, at best, the hare-brained ideas of an analyst blinded by his subject or, at worst, a sacrilegious comparison), it is worth taking a detour via the following leaflet by the carmaker Volvo:

FIG. 11. Volvo Tentation Offers

This leaflet (almost! See insert 3 below) brings full circle my own stripping of the layers of the history and forces of teasing, given that it manages to draw together across three pages the highly carnal strip-tease-removal of the Kellogg's example, the triple teasing of *Myriam* (hooking, unveiling, revelation), and the symbolism of Genesis,[27] including the apple, temptation, and not forgetting the fig leaf that discreetly features in the bottom left-hand corner of the far left panel; and, of course, the Fall ('choose… succumb' – '*choisissez… succombez*').[28]

partners of the exchange: the amused 'admit that you did not guess the point and that I really scared you!' by the advertiser is followed by the 'ah, that's what it was all about then; I get it now', which is undoubtedly experienced by the majority of passers-by through registers of admiration, complicity, and relief (tainted for some by slight disappointment or, for others, frank indignation?), through a knowing smile at the corner of their mouths (or pursed lips). The promise was kept perfectly in return for a little moral hazard,[29] subtly played on the side of virtue: given that the advertiser scrupulously maintained the model's initial pose and accomplished the removal of the bottom item of clothing, it was in fact justified, in order to keep its promise, in making the most of the absence of any prior commitment about the viewing angle, at the cost of a whiff of scandal but without risking an outcry. Above all, this final 'pirouette', in the true sense of the word, gives the advertiser the opportunity to share with its public Myriam's point of view, to look with her – and if possible, with it – towards the horizon of advertising territories yet to be conquered.

The structure $P_{n-1}{}^{*} + P_{n}$ continues at least to rank 3, while secretly hoping to retain its validity until rank *n*, to infinity. Keeping the promise P_2 is accompanied by a new promise, P_3. Although implicit, the latter is paradoxically the most well understood, the most important, and the most significant of the three, given that the entire campaign is directed towards its performative potential: 'from this point and from now on "it's going to be mind-blowing": If you hire me, I promise to remove all the obstacles you would never have thought able to remove from your path; I will grant your wildest wishes'. Roland Canu (2011b) demonstrated magnificently the extent to which the effectiveness of advertising relies perhaps less on the mysterious power we assign to it than on ploys similar to those employed by the Wizard of Oz, the legendary character who succeeded in making all his companions' wishes come true by using what were in fact, quite prosaic forms of subterfuge. Avenir's advertising campaign uses at least four tricks of this kind.

The first involves linguistic confusion. Normally, 'keeping your promises' means 'realising announced objectives'. With *Myriam*, this ordinary meaning is put forward, while the promise's actual meaning is more literal, or even literary, given that it limits its respect for commitments to the linguistic scope of the statement: we say what we will do and will do what we say, but we only say and do so in within the closely circumscribed area of the billboard – to the exclusion of everywhere else. In doing so, the campaign undertakes a double substitution of the forms of effectiveness we ascribe to advertising media. On the one hand, the (discursive) fulfilment of a sequence of (still discursive) promises is presented as an (illusory) demonstration of a desired commercial effectiveness; on the other, getting yourself talked about is offered as (false) proof of commercial power, given the distance between notoriety and actual sales.

The Wizard of Oz's second trick involves a 'public illusion', to paraphrase the title and spirit of the famous play by Corneille. In the play, Clindor captivates his father Pridamant by making him believe, thanks to a magician's tricks, that he was now able to view the life of his son, who he believed had disappeared. In fact, Clindor and his accomplices are themselves acting out his life before Pridamant to convince him of the power of theatre and the nobleness of the acting profession they had embraced. Similarly, *Myriam* organises a spectacle for the captation of the general public so as to captivate the captors. Now, this strategy reminds us of the conclusion to the second of the morals in *Bluebeard*: 'No husband of our age would be so terrible as to demand the impossible of his wife, even if he be such a jealous malcontent; he is meek and mild with his wife. For, whatever the colour of her husband's beard, the wife of today will let him know who the master is'. Perrault did not know how true that was: with *Myriam*, it is as if a thousand curious wives had already been recruited to demonstrate to contemporary Bluebeards[30] – who now go by the names of Big Blue, Racing Green, the Yellow Pages, Orange, Red Bull, among others! – their ancestor's system, in order to sell them both the rooms and the keys, to the extent that they are made to fall, quite literally, into a trap of their own making. In so doing, they also validate the irony of behaviourism, according to which the effectiveness of conditioning can be greater for the conditioner than for those being conditioned (with the notable exception, as we shall see, of the conditioner of the conditioners):

> In a wealthy economy in which consumers have great latitude of action, suggestion plays a role. There is also manipulation. But who manipulates whom?

> There can be no doubt that the consumer also manipulates the advertiser, the retailer, and the manufacturer, who all carefully watch for any slight change in consumer tastes and buying inclinations. The often told story of the animal psychologist who spent years training his rats to respond to various stimuli only to realize ultimately his rats regulated his life contains a grain of truth. Among consumer and advertiser, as in all interpersonal relationships, there is interaction (Katona 1960: 242).

However, there is something even more subtle going on. The Wizard of Oz's third trick consists in initiating and then coming back to a game of masks. The *Myriam* campaign is not simply any old campaign for any old product. It is indeed an advert, but above all it is an advert about and for advertising. As such, the series of posters possesses a dizzyingly reflexive power: it appears both as a masterful exercise in advertising and as a skilful theorisation of the same; it explores how far it can push its own logic; it theorises and spells out a way of acting whilst simultaneously putting to the test its own exploration and modus operandi. To use a form dear to Roland Barthes,[31] the Avenir advert adopts a '*Larvatus Prodeo*' approach: it wears a mask as it proceeds, adopting Myriam's features while at the same time (almost) pointing to the mask. The message is: 'experience the power of the mask and discover the force behind this power'. In fact, if we look closely, the last item of clothing to be removed in the poster is less the bikini bottom than Myriam's body itself, so as to reveal, through the use of contrast, the entire power of the clothing of advertising in which she has been dressed from beginning to end. In *Myriam*, the Wizard of Oz is no longer discovered by accident; on the contrary, it is as if the wizard intended to take advantage of the public exposure of his trick, by demonstrating it to be more extraordinary and powerful than the magic it is intended to simulate.

But who is the wizard here? Who is hiding behind the mask of Myriam? Avenir, of course: in the end, it is all too obvious to expose the identity of the campaign's beneficiary. However, is there not someone else, someone hiding behind Avenir? To answer the question positively means pointing to the last mask, and the fourth and most astonishing magician's trick. This trick consists in playing with the eminently likely confusion in the mind of the general public between 'billboard company' and 'poster designer', between services responsible for dealing with the urban logistics of the various messages (managing billboards and putting up posters) and advertising agencies. Just as in Genesis, the 'work of temptation' is shared between the Creator, who designs the Garden of Eden, and the snake, who draws attention to the forbidden fruit; in the world of commercial communication the task of arousing market curiosity is split between those who respectively create and display advertising. Avenir falls into the second category: it is a 'billboard company' that was bought in 1999 by the street furniture company J.C. Decaux, but whose identity and name was retained, no doubt due to the brand's reputation ever since Myriam and, of course, thanks to her. However, Avenir is closely linked to another actor, from the first category of advertising specialists: behind Avenir's mask, and also hiding in the *Myriam* posters, was the agency CLM/BBDO, of whom the billboard company was but a client. This is what is so extraordinary: the advertising magician does not just have one understudy, but two; CLM/BBDO is wearing the mask of Avenir… who is wearing the mask of Myriam.

This set of masks, whose layering redoubles the removal of layers of clothing, plays on an intoxicating ambiguity that, as we shall see, echoes the forked moral of *Bluebeard*, but which first and foremost involves the two-sided public addressed by advertising. Advertising is directed at two targets: on the one hand, it is presented to the public; on the other, it is sold or bought by professionals – the press and advertisers, respectively (Chessel 1999).[32] So far, I have adopted the public's point of view: I read the series of posters through the eyes of the everyman – in other words, employing only the skills and knowledge of someone whose eyes landed one day on the *Myriam* poster series. However, if I switch position and adopt the point of view of advertising professionals, the same campaign takes on a completely different meaning, in a kind of final dramatic twist accessible only to those with the necessary expertise to understand the real hidden agenda, as it were:

> There was no intention or desire to shock at all. We wanted to provoke people's awareness. The brief delivered to the agency by Avenir's CEO involved a business to business problem: at the time, billboard advertising was not

> considered to be a reliable media outlet given that posting dates could not be guaranteed. It was difficult to promote. Avenir was the first to develop a system to guarantee posting dates. In order to demonstrate this, we naturally suggested they prove it through billboards, by providing regular deadlines! (Comments by Pierre Berville, quoted in Mantoux 2010).

This was therefore *Myriam*'s real mission. Behind the double promise to undress – made to the public – lay another double commitment – this time made to its sponsor – involving the tempo of the striptease. *Myriam*'s mandate (the brief delivered to the agency by the chairman of Avenir) was to act as a promotion that would prove Avenir's reliability as a billboard company. From this point of view, the performativity of the message is not only self-referential, as I mentioned earlier, but also involves a 'performance' that is well and truly material, that is to say indexed to the real world, given that everyone was able to compare the poster's promises to the actual public calendar. On the other hand, what is shown is a pretext that does not refer to anything real except to its time of exposure: Myriam's body is phatic; it is only there to say there is nothing to sell or convey except for a coded message aimed at professionals. The real promises kept are in fact less concerned with bodily revelation than with respecting the dates and intervals that ensure the scansion! The original, professional meaning of the messages is in fact as follows:

> It is indeed on September 2nd, and no earlier or later, that Avenir will put up the second poster for you; it is indeed on September 4th, and no earlier or later, that Avenir will put up the third poster for you... whatever its content, for better... or worse (a woman, breasts, buttocks, a product... it doesn't matter: each to their own).

This is what is so essential: 'unlike its competitors, Avenir is a billboard company that keeps its promises, and these promises are inevitably limited to the logistical management of billboard posting operations, regardless of what is on the billboards themselves'. Therefore, behind *Myriam*'s 'generic' campaign directed towards the general public lay an extraordinary hidden private joke between advertising professionals. There was, in other words, a message that was even more enjoyable for these private addressees given that it involved a double meaning, one intended exclusively for insiders (here, advertising and billposting professionals), the other for a general public incapable of perceiving the first.

In light of this last 'revelation', which limits the meaning of *Myriam* to a business-to-business publicity campaign for a billboard company, must we conclude that the public misinterpreted the campaign, which delivered significant promises in order to benefit a generic and reflexive advert for the advertising industry? Not at all! The 'private joke' maintains the possibility of two interpretations. The message varies depending on whether it is the candid Myriam or the astute Avenir who is speaking, or whether Avenir is considered as an 'advertiser' or simply as a 'billboard company'. This discursive virtuosity could not but impress professionals well beyond the limited circle of billboard companies, to the extent that a third kind of performativity can be added to the two others we have already come across. The first, it should be remembered, is a linguistic performativity addressed to customers which consists of making the keeping of promises within the confined space of the posters seem like the fulfilment of real promises. The second is a performativity addressed to advertisers themselves, consisting in linking the timeframe of the promises to the rhythm of the calendar. By combining their powers of impression (both illocutionary and perlocutionary), the effects of these two types of performativity became magnified in the performance of an economic outcome. The result of the campaign in fact far exceeded its initial objectives. By reaching not just the restricted circle of billboard companies at which it was originally aimed, but also the 4,500 French publicists and their advertisers, as well as the media and the general public, the campaign has earned Avenir Publicité two million francs' worth of advertising revenue since September 1981 (Mantoux 2010).

To the ambiguity of the two-sided public can be added the campaign's moral ambivalence. Just like the tale of *Bluebeard*, the story of the girl in the green bikini is open to two interpretations, as we are led to draw conclusions about either the worrying power of the creators of curiosity or their radical innocuousness.

On the one hand, the impressive set of levers for action in the poster leads us to conclude that we can never be too careful about advertising:

> Be even more careful of commercial curiosity and advertising teasing: you are being had. Look at how duplicitous it all is, how effective this device is, how the promises of advertising achieve their goals, how the surface of advertising hides deeper layers, or even tricks that you will sooner or later fall victim to!

However, the very fact that we are able to experience this kind of mistrust points, paradoxically, to another lesson. If we get the feeling that advertising has a certain influence upon us, it is only because Myriam, Avenir, and, ultimately, the agency CLM/BBDO are pointing at the mask they are wearing and, in doing so, revealing their power as much as boasting about it. 'From now on we are giving you all the keys, full access; there is nothing to hide: neither upon Myriam's body, nor beneath the surface. You therefore have nothing to fear; you can no longer complain about what is going on behind the scenes; it is all completely transparent. Those arousers of curiosity are no longer so terrible; do not distrust advertising:

> It's humorous, risk-free, inoffensive, no one is forcing you to buy anything in fact, look: today we are even putting on a thoroughly delightful free show for you which is not trying to sell you anything except for an enjoyable presentation of advertising industry know-how.

Once again, the advert is not necessarily effective in the way we were expecting it to be; its social contribution is perhaps stronger than its market contribution... even if, of course, the advertisers' whole trick consists of selling one in order to prove the other. The final manipulation lies perhaps in this act of disengagement: the best way of seducing everyone, including the professionals, would be to show them that they are under no obligation – 'They must have many other tricks up their sleeve, say the suddenly curious passer-by and advertiser, if they are giving away the secret of a feat as impressive at that'.

BOX 4. 'ADVERTEASING': A TECHNIQUE THAT IS OLDER THAN WE MIGHT THINK

I took the decision to illustrate the forces of advertising teasing with the campaign that seems to me to bring them together in the most complete, spectacular, and effective manner. However, it would be wrong to think that we owe the invention of this technique to *Myriam*. The use of teasing is in fact virtually inherent to the history of advertising, and demonstrates, incidentally, the extent to which the arousal and maintenance of curiosity is at the heart of attempts to establish commercial relations.

The appearance of advertising teasing is inseparable from the difficulties advertising has experienced, from the very outset, in getting itself accepted and noticed. The first issue, concerning the acceptance of advertising, goes back as far as early product features (which incidentally shows that this practice, usually presented as an archaic form of modern advertising, should rather be considered as a prescient representation of its more effective contemporary versions). Recall that these product features appeared in the form of short articles that introduced products using non-advertising arguments, as though about current affairs items or breaking news, similar to what are nowadays called 'advertorials'. However, if we concern ourselves less with the content of these adverts than their position in the publication, their meaning changes completely: placed on the second or third page of four-page newspapers in the first half of the nineteenth century, product features were followed, on the fourth and final page, by a more conventional advert that spelt out the underlying commercial meaning. The idea was less to arouse curiosity than to discreetly awaken a reader's initial interest in the product and then to provide him with the means of obtaining it. However, the use of a process of attracting attention that was sequential clearly set up the teasing devices that would follow (Thérenty and Vaillant 2001).

The second issue concerns the difficulties long experienced by advertisers in drawing attention to their messages. In the United States, advertising expression was, until the 1860s, severely hampered by the typographic standards imposed by the newspapers responsible for relaying it. Newspapers – convinced it was in their best interest to fit the greatest number of commercial announcements into the available space and jealous of the technical mastery of printing – obliged advertisers to write adverts that were no more than a few lines, to fit them into a single column, and to use a single font, called 'Agate'. This all changed thanks in particular to Robert Bonner, a brilliant pressman who published the *New York Ledger*, a family magazine whose increasing success was due to the appearance of stories commissioned from well-known writers – including, for example, Charles Dickens! To promote his magazine, Bonner found a way of simultaneously freeing himself from the prevailing typographic constraints whilst obeying them, given he had no choice. During a trip to England, he had noticed that English auctioneers advertised their lots as a series of separate adverts, published in a single column, all starting with the same two first lines 'DANIEL SMITH & SON WILL AUCTION'. Bonner immediately understood the extent to which this anaphoric method could, in his market, introduce a clean break with other adverts. When he was back in the United States, he expanded the method first to two columns, then to the entire page, and was not afraid to repeat the same message – for example: 'Read the New York Ledger and a new story by Cobb' – up to 600 times! Driven by the momentum of this, he found other tricks to make his own messages noticeable among the sea of monotonous, individual small ads, for example, by using vertical acrostics to highlight the publication's name: 'L-E-D-G-E-R' (Presbey 1929: 237–238). By demonstrating the absurdity and inefficiency of such typographic constraints, Bonner's tricks contributed to their abandonment. More importantly for us, such tricks introduced a highly rudimentary form of teasing, involving recognising the lack of raw and immediately available information, creating a 'hook', while also, in anticipation of the logic to come, finding a way to be noticed in stages, initially by attracting the customer's visual and cognitive attention and then, once alerted and intrigued, by revealing the meaning of the message.

Much later, by contrast, during a time in which advertising space had become saturated, other professionals logically adopted the opposite strategy, consisting in capturing the customers' attention by spectacularly shrinking the visual space, as shown in the example below.

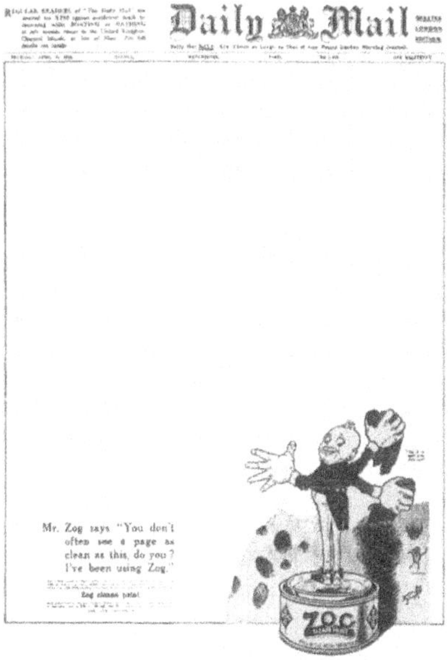

FIG. 12. *Daily Mail*, 30 April 1914 (quoted in Field, 1959)

Obviously, here we have a single image rather than a series of posters (as with *Myriam*) and there is thus immediately some distance from the sequential approach inherent to teasing. However, we soon see that this image is skilfully designed to be read as a series of boxes that are successive and superimposed on top of one another. First the eye is intrigued by the empty space, which provides a stark contrast to the usual graphical saturation of newspapers. The reader is thus led to seek the reason for this anomaly and stumbles upon the curious little three-handed figure. By continuing the exploration, the reader understands, thanks to a few carefully staged instructive indicators – the left hand stationary to help with balance, the right hand mobile, holding the same rag – that this is not about a physical monstrosity but an almost cinematographic method, designed to suggest the frantic rubbing out of what was on the page, of which just a trace remains in the bottom right-hand corner.[33] In a third stage, the gaze is then led to swerve to the left, to read the caption that sheds light on the whole scenario: 'Mr Zog says: "You don't often see a page as clean as this, do you?" [To get this result] I've been using Zog'. In a spectacular fashion, the poster links substance and form to sell a cleaning product: it 'simulates' its power by artfully substituting the cleaning product's actual performance for the performative and self-referential cleaning of the page, in keeping with an approach we will come across in *Myriam*. The scenario has a manifestly playful dimension that activates the meaning of teasing as 'seduction': the situation of reading involves a call for an interactive relationship with the reader, from whom are requested complicity, sagacity, and a sense of humour. It is nevertheless interesting to note, as suggested by Field (1959), to whom we also owe the poster, that printers did not like this genre of posters, no doubt because it rendered their know-how secondary, and thus far from those former blessed times of typographic control, but without giving them the slightest possibility of once again reversing the trend.

Despite the typographers, the same kind of approach reappeared in an even more spectacular fashion in British newspapers during the 1930s, in an astonishing advertising campaign aimed at supporting advertising. As demonstrated by Stefan Schwarzkopf (2004), British advertisers at the time intended not only to counter the effects of the Great Depression that had lost them important clients, but also to prevent consumer organisations from taking off and the growing indictment of advertising as a waste of money, both of which they had witnessed in the United States. Thus, from the first signs of economic recovery in around 1934, the British Advertising Association launched a colossal 'campaign aimed at the Consumer', that for six years mobilised hundreds of papers and thousands of adverts, with slogans such as 'you can put your trust in goods that are advertised' or 'it is the GOOD products that have a brand name'. Whereas the campaign's first adverts conventionally took the form of a slogan followed by explanatory text, a new type of poster appeared in 1936. For example, a blank page, introduced by an enormous question mark in the top left-hand corner, drew the reader's attention and confusion, who was then led towards discovering, in the diagonally opposite bottom right-hand corner, the meaning of this mysterious empty space: 'without advertisements you do not know about things you should buy'. Here again we are confronted with a prescient anticipation of the discourse of *Myriam*, in which the power of teasing is put entirely to the service of a reflexive advert for advertising.

In between the two – teasing through the saturation of the graphic space as invented by Bonner and teasing through the reflexive reduction of advertising discourse – a series of one-off, unconnected innovations were introduced of which it would be impossible to create a complete collection or chronology, but which show that the technique of teasing is inherent to the language of advertising, to all its efforts to arouse the customer's curiosity in order to attract his or her attention. This, for example, is how Knox, a milliner from New York, invented a new kind of advertising, consisting of establishing a connection to the day's news: 'Although Queen Isabelle has lost her crown, the crowns of Knox hats never come loose, as everyone who buys them at Broadway, corner of Fulton Street can testify' (Presbey 1929: 256). However, the method was risky: a pet shop owner, who used the message 'I lost my dog, I lost my dog', with the intention of subsequently showing off his products, was beaten to it and taken advantage of by a competitor: 'You'll find your dog where you can also find all the best overcoats: at Blank's' (Ibid: 258)!

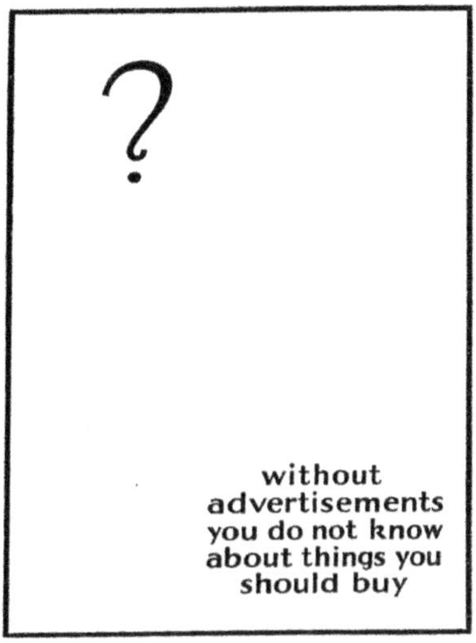
?
without advertisements you do not know about things you should buy

The new poster to be used in the present campaign to supplement the Association's Press Advertisements to the Consumer. Ten thousand of these posters will be displayed by members of the British and the London Poster Advertising Associations.

FIG. 13. Advertising Association Campaign, 1936[34]

The interest in 'teaser ads' was even clearly identified, formalised, and 'sold' for use by professionals, as shown by this short item in the *Progressive Grocer* magazine:

"Teaser" Ads Arouse Curiosity

STANDS GROCERY
FREE SUGAR
SURE!
Watch for STANDS GROCERY
EVERYBODY
STAND'S GROCERY
SATURDAY
WHY
AH!

Curiosity is a powerful instinct. The Stands grocery made it work for them with these three "teaser" ads, which they ran in advance of a large advertisement

Making the public curious pays. At least that is the experience of the E. C. Stands Grocery of Huntington, Indiana.

Recently, when they had a large newspaper ad scheduled for Friday, they ran small "teaser" ads for the three days previous. And the extra response they got from the big ad as a result more than covered the small additional expense.

"The teasers," explained a store executive, "started people thinking and wondering when we might be going to announce. It raised curiosity to such an extent that many thought first of the Stands ad when the Friday papers were delivered, and read all of it so as not to miss any special part."

The ad, headed, "Big Anniversary Sale Saturday," was four columns wide by 16 inches. It featured special prices on some foods, and in addition, announced an offer of 5 pounds of sugar with every $4 purchase, and a grand prize of a bridge lamp to the one buying the largest order.

FIG. 14. *The Progressive Grocer*, September 1929, p. 56

As can be seen, this short – in fact very short – article[35] is a perfectly illustrated manual about teaser advertising.[36] Behind the particular case described in the above text, the teasing technique is itself exposed via a communicative sequence, introduced by a message that is as appealing as it is enigmatic (see, for example, the illustration: 'Free sugar? Certainly! Watch for STANDS GROCERY Announcement Friday'), followed by a second message, shedding light on the first and attracting the reader to read it all the more because it provides the solution to the original enigma.

The same technique (amongst others?) was used a few years later by Sylvan N. Goldman, one of the inventors of the supermarket trolley (Grandclément 2006; Cochoy 2009; Wilson 1978) to promote his innovation. On Friday, 4 June 1937 – in other words, the day before Saturday, a busy day – regular readers of the local newspaper would have seen an advert that featured a woman, burdened with the weight of an overflowing shopping basket, and the caption: 'No more of this at your Standard Stores'. The text went on to explain: 'Just pick up your items from the shelves. They will be checked and placed in your car without having to carry a single item'. The effect of the recourse to a negative definition (what the consumers will no longer suffer) and the passive voice (what 'will be done' with their products) was amplified by the total lack of an illustration that might allow people to understand what this wonderful device was that would supposedly enable them to not have to carry a single item without abandoning the system of self-service. A week later, a second mysterious advert in the same newspaper struck, proudly proclaiming: 'Last weekend, the Anti-Basket-Carrying Plan was approved on the spot' – still, of course, without mentioning or showing the chosen solution… and without specifying that attracting curious people was far from enough to convince them: the introduction of supermarket trolleys was actually rejected twice, both by men who were proud of their muscles and women tired of pushing pushchairs! They were only 'adopted' following an additional ploy, consisting in hiring extras to make their use commonplace and to persuade perplexed but 'genuine' customers to try them out (Wilson 1978: 87–88).

FIG. 15. No More of This at Your Standard Stores (Wilson 1978)

CONTINUALLY AGITATING CURIOSITY, OR HOW TO LEAD A CONSUMER TOWARDS WONDERLAND

FIG. 16. Fnac, Curiosity Agitator (v. 1)

In the different layers of the display window, packaging and teaser ads, we are beginning to understand just how broad and irreversible the movement of commercialising curiosity is. In 2007, this movement was magnificently captured by the entertainment retailer, Fnac, with the slogan 'Fnac: agitator of curiosity'. This superb advertising motif sums up in two of these words the shop's entire history and its ambiguity, as well as all the know-how involved in organising curiosity to benefit the market.

We know that this entertainment retailer was founded in 1954 by André Essel and Max Théret (Chabault 2010), two people whose Trotskyist origins had connotations of 'agitprop' and political radicalism, but whose commercial orientation appeared more inclined towards 'propaganda' in the Italian and Portuguese sense of the term, in other words something synonymous with 'advertising' (Iulio and Vinti 2009). On the other hand, we are also aware of the role played in the social unrest at the end of the 1960s by advertisers and the world of consumption – as considered in *Things: A Story of the Sixties* by Pérec (1990 [1965]), *The Society of Spectacle* by Debord (1983

[1967]), *One Dimensional Man* by Marcuse (1964) or *Consumer Society* by Baudrillard (1998 [1970]). Hence the formidable ambiguity of this company that combines, to an extreme degree, culture and market, 'artistic' values and 'managerial' logic (Chiapello 1998). Beyond this history, Fnac's slogan also transformed the shop into the equivalent of the 'agitator' in the laboratory – in other words, into a piece of equipment designed to shake test tubes in order to accelerate chemical processes, as if it were a matter of promoting the sale of cultural curiosities through the 'cultivation' of curiosity.

How does this latter form of agitation operate? Part of the answer is provided by the series of TV commercials used to reinforce the slogan.[37] Each of these commercials uses a variation of the same narrative framework.[38] First we are shown a young man leaning against a bus shelter, gently sighing with boredom. Suddenly his attention is drawn by a ticking sound coming from the right-hand panel of the billboard, of which we can only see the external side: 'fnac.com'. His face lights up when he realises that the poster has in fact just opened like a door. The young man immediately enters and stumbles into a magical world where he chases hundreds of books that flutter about like butterflies, dives into an audiophile universe in which flowers and rocks act as loudspeakers, and drives a car with a computer game joystick on a circuit studded with screens… that suddenly takes him towards the exit, towards his bus shelter (now slightly dishevelled from his exciting experience), whilst the camera once again zooms in on the outside of the magic door, where the message 'fnac.com' has mysteriously turned red and has been enhanced by the addition 'Agitator of curiosity'. The entire scene is mute, simply accompanied by a very rousing song, 'Where do we go?' by the Australian artist Sandrine.[39] As we shall see, throughout its brief run this advert effortlessly employs the three key forces for those wishing to agitate curiosity: boredom, serendipity, and wonderment.

First, the Fnac advert uses an approach common to outdoor advertising: that of making the city one of the privileged sites for commercial communication (Cochran 1972, McFall 2004). However, the chosen location is not unimportant: it is neither an immobile wall, on which there are posters that attempt to make passers-by stop, nor a bus, or taxi, with attached messages that aspire to catch a pedestrian's eye, but a bus shelter – that is to say, a place for stopping and changing – that possesses aspects of both the wall, because of the shelter, and transportation, because of its horizon. The bus shelter is an empty place with no purpose of its own, other than waiting and boredom. However, this vacuity, this boredom and waiting, create precisely the right conditions for expressing/arousing curiosity. Unlike the wall, that is too immobile to arrest the moving passer-by, and unlike the vehicle that, by contrast, is travelling too fast to be read from the pavement, the bus shelter offers a moment of suspension – a vacuum, a parenthesis – and it offers particularly favourable conditions for being temporarily diverted from one's path, for a little digressive reading – it is as if the bus stop, by making city dwellers available for something else for a second, were itself the condition for an advert to begin. In other words, at the threshold of the bus shelter/advert shelter, boredom and curiosity each support the other.

According to Kierkegaard, boredom cannot be considered a mundane or fleeting feeling: the Danish philosopher in fact does not hesitate to depend on Genesis when turning boredom into an anthropological force as fatal as it is ancient...

> Since boredom advances and boredom is the root of all evil, no wonder, then, that the world goes backwards, that evil spreads. This can be traced back to the very beginning of the world. The gods were bored; therefore they created human beings. Adam was bored because he was alone; therefore Eve was created. Since that moment, boredom entered the world and grew in quantity in exact proportion to the growth of population. Adam was bored alone; then Adam and Eve were bored *en famille*. After that, the population of the world increased and the nations were bored *en masse*. To amuse themselves, they hit upon the notion of building a tower so high that it would reach the sky. This notion is just as boring as the tower was high and is a terrible demonstration of how boredom had gained the upper hand. Then they were dispersed around the world, just as people now travel abroad, but they continued to be bored. And what consequences this boredom had: humankind stood tall and fell far, first through Eve, then from the Babylonian tower.[40]

Now, we have seen that the same sacred tale also transforms curiosity into one of the key human motives for action. This rapprochement, in which boredom and curiosity are located at the beginning and at the core of the human condition,[41] is hardly coincidental: as Kierkegaard briefly yet clearly suggests at the end, it is because of her boredom that Eve paid attention to the Serpent and gave into the temptation of curiosity, just as much later her descendants built the Tower of Babel in order to once more escape the vacuity of their existence. Boredom provides one of the most favourable conditions for the expression of curiosity, as if stasis, stopping, and immobility were, paradoxically, the condition for being enraptured, carried away, for *agitation*.[42]

This enchantment occurs *along the way*. This is an important point. In the Fnac advert, curious agitation, far from being the expression of an existing inclination, occurs rather as if at a turn in the road, in the manner of a meeting, a distraction, or an opportunity. This is the second force for agitating curiosity: serendipity.

The concept of serendipity has a fabulous history, whose many facets cannot be captured in the following brief presentation. It is a word derived from a tale from the orient about the three sons of King of Serendip, the ancient medieval name given to Sri Lanka. On one of the days of their journey, the sons, who had been sent by their father to discover the world, came across traces of a camel. The eldest son saw that the grass on the left-hand side was short, but it had not been touched on the right. He concluded that the camel was blind in his right eye. The second brother noticed many chewed balls of grass only on the left-hand verge and concluded that the camel had undoubtedly lost a tooth. The youngest son inferred, from one footprint being lighter than the others, that the camel was lame. Further on, the eldest noticed, on one side of the road, an uninterrupted line of ants busy with something, and, on the other, many bees, flies, and wasps stuck to a translucent, sticky substance. He deduced that the camel was covered in butter on one side and honey on the other. The second son discovered traces indicating that the camel had knelt down, but also a small human footprint and a wet patch. He touched it, and, before even smelling his fingers, he felt a carnal temptation. He concluded that a woman rather than a child had sat on the camel. The youngest noticed handprints on each side of the area she had wet. He thought the woman had probably lifted up her body because she was pregnant. Later on, the three brothers came across a camel driver who had lost one of his animals. Based on everything they had seen, the three brothers jokingly said they had seen the camel, and to substantiate their claims, asked if the camel was blind in one eye, toothless, and lame, covered in butter and honey, and carrying a pregnant woman – all details that turned out to be correct. The three brothers were accused of theft and thrown in prison. However, the camel was found safe and sound and they were freed. After many more adventures, they succeeded their father as leader of Serendip (according to Merton and Barber 2004; and Andel 1994).[43]

The term 'Serendipity' was coined, with reference to this tale, by the celebrated man of letters Horace Walpole, in correspondence with his friend Horace Mann:

> This discovery, indeed, is almost of that kind which I call Serendipity, a very expressive word, which, as I have nothing better to tell you, I shall endeavour to explain to you: you will understand it better by the derivation than by the definition. I once read a silly fairy tale, called the three Princes of Serendip: as their Highnesses travelled, they were always making discoveries, by accidents and sagacity, of things which they were not in quest of: for instance, one of them discovered that a mule blind of the right eye had travelled the same road lately, because the grass was eaten only on the left side, where it was worse than on the right – now do you understand Serendipity? (Horace Walpole, quoted in Merton and Barber 2004:1–2).

In their fabulous chronicle, *The Travels and Adventures of Serendipity*, Robert Merton and Elinor Barber highlight all the ambiguity of this definitional derivation, based on a rough memory of the tale – the camel becomes a mule; the grass becomes better on one side than the other – hesitating (without really paying attention) between seeing serendipity as an inner faculty that gives meaning (through 'sagacity') to the world, or as an external event of discovery (by 'accident'), using the word 'discovery' to mean both an intellectual construction and a 'treasure' found along the way. They show, through an exploration of serendipity that is staggeringly reflexive,[44] how the word that was invented by

Walpole has travelled from the literary world to the scientific, and has changed continuously with them, oscillating, for example, between a particular type of intelligence, a specific genre of discovery, or, in the sense employed by Merton, the skill of taking into account unforeseen information so as to invent a new theory. It is precisely this ambiguity, inherent both to the word and to its history that we will retain: serendipity refers to both a certain cognitive receptiveness to what occurs (that is, an ability to give meaning to unforeseen events), and a disposition/event favourable to the expression of curiosity.

Serendipity activates our twin abilities; on the one hand, to be detached, indifferent, and distracted (in other words, what Albert Piette (2009) calls the 'minor mode' of action) and, on the other, to pay attention, focus, and to be able to make good use of those overflows that cognitive relaxation allows us to encounter: to consider them, to take them on board, and, eventually, to give them meaning, and integrate them into our logics of action. As such, commercial forms of serendipity combine two ways of acting, as analysts of commercial behaviour and theory have clearly identified but have tended to distinguish from one another: 'hunting' and 'foraging', when it comes to browsing the internet; 'provisioning' (Perrot 2009) and 'shopping' (Miller 1998) in urban commercial spaces; or even inside shops, the figures of the 'pacer' and the 'sleepwalker' (Floch 1990) (or even 'instrumentalists' and 'bargain-hunters', 'technicians' and 'flaneurs' (Bonnin 2002)). In the Fnac commercial, the young man simultaneously expresses and adopts these two modes of action: he happens to come across a poster that appears in his path and shows he is able to grab the invitation and therefore to fall, even if for just a moment, into a wonderful other world.

Wonderment is thus the third way to agitate curiosity. If the commercial makes explicit reference to any tale at all, it is to *Alice in Wonderland* rather than the *Princes of Serendip*. In fact, I could have begun there, given that the former is a story that, far from confining itself to wonderment, also encompasses the two previous forces – boredom and serendipity, in other words. As the Fnac advert uses the story of Alice as its main source of inspiration, it is not surprising to find both elements there. The commercial begins with the boring wait for a bus and the sideways glance towards the advert, modelled on Lewis Carroll's story, which begins with the following lines: 'Alice was beginning to get very tired of sitting by her sister on the bank, and of having nothing to do'... other than to glance at the very boring book her neighbour is reading ('once or twice she had peeped into the book her sister was reading, but it had no pictures or conversations in it, 'and what is the use of a book', thought Alice, 'without pictures or conversation?'). This is when a pure episode of serendipity occurs, when a plan Alice has just come up with to stave off her boredom – making a 'daisy-chain' – is interrupted by the appearance of a strange, white rabbit with pink eyes, who, afraid of being late, pulls a watch out of his waistcoat and hurries immediately into somewhere unknown:

> [Having seen this] Alice started to her feet, for it flashed across her mind that she had never before seen a rabbit with either a waistcoat-pocket, or a watch to take out of it, and burning with curiosity, she ran across the field after it, and fortunately was just in time to see it pop down a large rabbit-hole under the hedge. In another moment down went Alice after it, never once considering how in the world she was to get out again (Carroll 1916 [1865]).

This tale is fascinating, as it allows us to specify, perhaps despite itself, the way in which serendipity and curiosity differ from one another whilst being mutually reinforcing. On the one hand, the rabbit's appearance suspends Alice's (in)action and leads her to attempt to give meaning to the interruption, in line with the logic of serendipity. On the other, however, it is precisely both because the rabbit is curious ('she had never before seen [such] a rabbit') and because Alice is/becomes curious ('burning with curiosity') that she strays from her path (here, of immobility) and embarks on the 'serendipitous' quest for the meaning, which commands her to track after the intriguing object to solve the mystery. The same scheme appears in the Fnac commercial, where the act of waiting for the bus is disturbed by the appearance of the poster, which leads the customer towards different horizons – it is as if Alice's sister had not been reading a boring book, but Carroll's story, thereby allowing Alice to delve simultaneously into both book and rabbit-hole.

From then on, in both the story and the commercial, agitating curiosity involves enticing the subject into wonderland by drawing wonders before the subject's eyes. Certainly, the sequence of wonders in each case is very different: following the tendency of bowdlerising classic tales in advertising (Iulio 2004); the avalanche of sometimes troubling dialogues and characters in Alice, compared to a flood of images and objects that all appeal to the male consumer. However, in both the subject is caught in a strangely similar whirlwind in which the agitation affects the subject as much as the objects which surround him/her: Alice and the consumer are drawn into a succession of visions and experiences that are both profuse and disjointed, allowing no respite until they return 'to the surface', a return that is as unforeseen for the one as it is for the other. Wonderment arises precisely from these juxtapositions and ruptures, that is to say from the accelerated renewal of the new that occurs without transition. The whirlwind of wonders, rather than leading the two characters to passively abandon themselves to it, instead paradoxically pulls them toward their active involvement: Alice does a lot, she converses, she asks a lot of questions; the character in the commercial leaps towards the butterfly-books, dives into a river of sounds, and drives a car on a computer game circuit. The paradoxical involvement of subjects in the whirlwinds that carry them is associated with the 'exploration mode', the characteristics and mechanisms of which are explained very clearly by Nicolas Auray:

> Exploration is inscribed within [...] a logic of feeling one's way forward step by step; it happens through a dependence on the chosen path and a suspension of judgement. It involves an inability to extract oneself from a curious fascination that exercises a veritable tyranny and subjects one to dependence [...]. The behaviours grounded in exploration involve a concern for the maintenance of the state of excitement and the constant delaying of the moment of satisfaction through repeated stimulation (Auray 2006).

It is actually the manipulation of objects which, in both Carroll and the Fnac commercial, arouses excitement for the new and the desire to give it meaning, even if the constant appearance of new attractions continually suspends the search for the meaning of a previous object, transferring it instead to the next. Ultimately, the triple 'curiosity agitator' mechanism, based on activating and relating boredom, serendipity, and wonderment (or, in Auray's words, the 'excitement for what is new'), introduces a generalised form of teasing as no content is provided, apart from the promise that the contents will be infinitely refreshed. Curiosity remains, its objects change, and it is because the objects change that curiosity can remain as the memory of an enchantment: a form of excitement that has become a habit, even an addiction. Note that the entertainment products marketed by Fnac lend themselves to this game particularly well: the distinctive feature of the books, CDs, and computer games the shop sells is that in each case their form remains the same while their content is constantly renewed. This mechanism of the 'renewal of the same' – that Roland Barthes so clearly identified and formalised in the metaphor of the vessel Argo, the mythical ship whose permanence depended on the incessant replacement of its constituent parts (Barthes 1977) – tends to become exacerbated nowadays in the renewal of the material objects charged with carrying updated cultural content: as we can see with digital books, the players of dematerialised music, or the development of computer game download platforms. In fact, this mechanism is inherent to Fnac's identity and slogan: it is because I know that every time I go through the looking glass of posters I will discover new objects, that Fnac is now able to identify itself as a perennial agitator of curiosity. That which we see in Fnac's commercials no longer exists, although paradoxically it is this very disappearance that reinforces the relevance and permanence of a slogan that has become their hallmark; a message, in other words, that is no longer ephemeral, but rather a motif that is part and parcel of the brand and its identity.

DATA MATRIX

On the permanent carousel of new releases that can be found at Fnac, we now come across strange telephones that themselves work like a multitude of rabbit holes, each capable of transporting talking Alices ever onward towards new wonderlands. Choosing one of these phones suggests our belief that one product among others in the telephony market is being selected; however, when we use it we realise – a little late – that we have actually been sucked into a market in its own right, into a world that is both very closed, underground, and controlled, and at the same time infinite, open to a thousand possibilities, and which cannot be explored to our satisfaction. The paradox of these new objects and markets is not only that they excite curiosity, but also that they multiply the number of tools able to maintain this excitement. There are a great number of such tools – for instance, software that makes it possible to automatically identify objects (like the title of the song we are listening to[45]), to 'geolocate' a set of resources within reach (for example, restaurants, banks, or other services located within the user's immediate vicinity[46]), or to 'augment' a perceived reality by superimposing a certain amount of additional information onto the image we are filming, such as the names of stars, mountains, or more prosaically, metro or bike stations.[47] The distinctive characteristic of each of these devices is that they accompany the world and enable its serendipitous exploration, thereby sustaining the expression of curiosity.

To conclude, I would like to turn to the introduction of one such device that, to me, seems to have the advantage not only of mobilising and pulling together, quite successfully, the various capacities that I have just outlined, but also, above all, of providing an insight into the potential development of teasing practices and their associated devices. For some time now, we have seen enigmatic barcodes that look like small, quadrangular labyrinths effectively sprouting up on display windows, bus shelters, and now on an increasing number of products.

FIG. 17. Data Matrix

These types of code, termed a 'Data Matrix' (or QR code or Flashcode, depending on the standard used), are not in fact aimed at market professionals like traditional barcodes, nor specifically at consumers themselves, given that they are unable to read them, but rather at smartphones, with which an increasing number of consumers are equipped. With the help of a smartphone furnished with the relevant software, the consumer is able to decode the Data Matrix and to thus switch directly to a website containing further information about the product. By organising the sequence 'code visualisation, software decoding and activation of the corresponding link, reading the website', the Data Matrix operates, perhaps in spite of itself, as a pure teasing device – the kind of teasing where the first stage is reduced to the form of a riddle, a mystery, or a puzzle we itch to figure out, to the point of returning us to the highly archaic time of the keyholes and locks so dear to Bluebeard.

In fact, just like the keyhole in the tale, the Data Matrix only grants access to the knowledge it possesses on the condition that it is activated. Admittedly, as a keyhole it is very particular given that it is presented as a door that is freely accessible to all, as if Bluebeard had now allowed his set of keys to be copied and distributed, and had invited not only his wife but all women (and also all men) to come and visit his house, this time without attaching to the invitation the slightest restriction or threat. Nonetheless, in both cases the force urging that the door be opened remains the same: the keyhole that simultaneously deprives us of and promises us information. Because it alone will not tell us anything, the Data Matrix generates a riddle and a sense of expectation; because it is intended to mean something, it might well arouse the excitement necessary for its activation. In addition to the childish pleasure of unwrapping a present, mentioned earlier, we can now add the symmetrical pleasure of deciphering a secret message. Therefore, the entire *charm* of the device lies in its imperfection – it is illegible, and unable to grant direct access to the desired information. In its small, two-coloured, completely hermetic square, the device contains all the information that can later be revealed as long as the consumer assists. As such, the Data Matrix offers an original challenge to the classic problem of 'too much information killing information'.

This problem increased considerably with the proliferation of billposting, packaging, and labelling systems (Cochoy and Lalanne 2011), press releases (Czarniawska 2011), but also 'emails', 'alerts', 'tweets', and other 'notifications' which are taking over the world of the internet (Boullier 2009). The management of this proliferating information recently gave rise to an entire 'economy of attention' (Golhaber 1997; Kessous et al. 2010) that, on the one hand, attempts to 'economise' the attention of those involved in order to avoid saturation, and, on the other (and by doing so), to also 'economicise' a customer's attention – in other words, to convert the captured attention into economic value by selling either 'clicks', or an audience's preference for this or that newspaper, and so on (Bouiller 2009). The whole point of the Data Matrix is to (unintentionally?)

introduce a third mode in the economy of attention that lies between these two. The device in fact attempts to reduce the number of signs that might attract attention in order to spare the players' cognitive vigilance, as well as, paradoxically, to arouse and encourage it. In fact, far from being imposed upon the attention of the consumer, the additional information attached to the Data Matrix only appears as long as consumers perform a complicit gesture in order to activate it. With the Data Matrix, it is as if Bluebeard's wife was free not only to open any room she wanted without injury, but also to fine-tune the extent of her visits, or even to fashion in her own time what she wished to see displayed (according to a list of options of course deliberately framed and staged by her husband).

If consumers remain inert, then the Data Matrix refrains from pestering them; if consumers activate the Data Matrix, then they have access to the layers of commercial information into which they have been invited. In a way, it is as though the keyhole and Bluebeard's wife borrowed some of their traits from Sleeping Beauty (for the former) and the passing Prince (for the latter). In so doing, this device overturns the age-old unilaterality of commercial information in order to open it up to the game of interactivity: as each takes a step towards the other – the device as it proffers its riddles, consumers as they decode them – consumers lend themselves to a game of 'self-marketing', where, instead of struggling in the same informational space, each party freely chooses the nature and intensity of the information they intend to retain as a guide to their choice.

However, nothing guarantees that the consumer will make this small gesture of activation upon which the Data Matrix's entire capacity to inform nevertheless depends. The conditions determining the success of 'self-marketing' are as fragile as they are tiny: on the part of the device, it is the tiny, enigmatic square, stuck to the body of the product, and on the part of the actor, it is the extremely tenuous disposition created by the subject's supposed propensity towards curiosity. The chances that the device and disposition will be jointly activated are even smaller as they also depend on the availability of the smartphone and the relevant software application, without which nothing is possible, not to mention other favourable social and/or 'environmental' conditions (sufficient lighting, time, dexterity, and the available patience, etc.; see below). In order to evaluate the chances of the Data Matrix being activated, together with other colleagues I took part in a scientific and industrial project in which the Data Matrix was adopted as a means of accessing information on the 'geo-traceability' of wine (Cochoy 2011d). The idea behind making wine 'geo-traceable' is to make it possible to track very precisely the 'localised' characteristics of the grapes that go into each bottle – such as soil composition, the properties of a grape variety, meteorological and hygrometric data, plot exposure, gradient, name of owner, and more – throughout the cycle, from harvesting to production, then from production to marketing. One of the project's objectives was to grant each consumer direct access to the 'geo-indicators' corresponding to the particular bottle they had in their hands. As this information was infinitely more detailed than could be contained on the front and back labels of a bottle, the Data Matrix appeared to be the only possible way to provide access to it. In order to test the device, the project leaders designed an interactive label with two triggers: a first screen offered the internet user the choice of four options: 'authenticate your bottle' (by comparing it with an identifier on the bottle that was impossible to forge and its photograph on the website), 'discover the wine and its *terroir*' (a map of plots and a presentation of grape varieties), 'discover the wine' (a wine fact sheet and geo-indicators), 'wine-growers' story' (videos). Of course, once a choice had been made, it was still possible to navigate to one of the other options.

In order to assess how this kind of device might be received, we gave a questionnaire to 502 respondents who were representative of the French population, and conducted a series of five focus groups, two with ordinary people, two with younger and older wine-lovers, and one with technophiles.[48]

The quantitative survey results appeared to be very encouraging, given that more than 40% of respondents stated they would probably or definitely use the system (of which they were shown a photo with instructions for use) to access information they nonetheless knew nothing about. Better still, the propensity towards curiosity could even be carefully measured by distinguishing between an interest in wine and an attraction to the device: a considerable number of those who stated they were not particularly interested in information about wine thus said that they would nonetheless activate the device: 29.3% said probably and 8.6% definitely.[49] However, if taking account of the Data Matrix seems easy, based on the results of a questionnaire, when it comes to actually using it the situation changes, with the risk of people's propensity towards curiosity falling significantly.

With real bottles, smartphones, and Data Matrix in hand, the consumers in our focus groups experienced difficulties and showed very little appetite for overcoming the obstacles on the path to the wine's hidden information. Admittedly, this double complication only emerged gradually. When we invited our guinea pigs to assess two similar bottles, one of which had a Data Matrix with the caption 'To know more about the wine, scan me', quite often, as was predicted, they showed a tendency to be curious ('the "scan me", it's actually the first time I've seen this... so I would have taken [the bottle with the Data Matrix] anyway'; 'I would have scanned it out of curiosity'; 'me too'; 'maybe I would have, out of curiosity'; 'it's obviously something new so yes, I would'; 'yes, I would have scanned it'; 'just out of curiosity').

However, it proved to be during the next stage of decoding the Data Matrix when people's propensity to read the device dropped spectacularly. Even when suitably equipped, consumers do not necessarily know how to download the required application; even if they know how to proceed, the internet connection might not be good enough; even if the network is sufficiently available and the application works, people might not have a smartphone able to focus on the code (first-generation iPhones do not have a fixed focal length); even if the smartphone has the required ability to focus, people might not know how to correctly point the device; even if people know how to point their phone in the right direction, the lighting conditions might not be good enough to guarantee the operation's success; and so on and so forth! In fact, rather than being based either on the conformity of a single device or just the subject's prior dispositions, the expression of curiosity depends instead on the right configuration of a very subtle *agencement* (Callon 2015)[50] of a number of devices and a multiplicity of dispositions that the version of the device we experimented with could not achieve. If the suitable *agencement* cannot be established, the flow of curiosity is interrupted. If it is guaranteed, then the exploratory movement has some chance of being resumed. However, even when all the conditions are met and the website is accessed, people's propensity to explore it varies considerably, given the different levels of desire they have for the proposed information (some are interested in wine, others are not, and we noticed that the curiosity dynamic gives way very quickly to preferences and interests that pre-existed the intended experience).

Some of our participants did nonetheless succumb to the charm of the device. For example, a young woman stated that 'out of curiosity [she] might well go and look at the information'. She appeared to be interested in obtaining new knowledge ('things that [she doesn't] know') and in acquiring additional information on 'certain wines [she likes]'. Her openness was reinforced by her personal taste for the genre of technological devices that give access to information. In fact, she explained that she wanted the device to offer certain forms of functionality that were missing, such as the possibility of saving any choices made, of sharing discoveries with colleagues and finding them using geo-localisation. In this last example, curiosity is once again revealed as a force capable of opening Pandora's box, and an equivalent to the 'hope' that remained at the bottom of the box after all the disappointing content surrounding it had been dispersed (Latour 1999). Or, to use a more appropriate image here, we see that sometimes curiosity is the drop of wine (the desire) that can make the wine bottle overflow,[51] thus responding *in extremis* to the promises inscribed in the Data Matrix curiosity device.

The particular power of the Data Matrix as a curiosity device is that it restricts access to information in the hope of multiplying the revelation. It is certainly the case that, despite this trick, its appeal to curiosity is often unsuccessful. It appears to produce more consumers who are sceptical, disappointed, or indifferent than those who are enthusiastic. The excess of promises is jeopardised by a symmetrical excess of technical defects and a lack of interest. However, the difficulty that must be overcome is less the curiosity device and more the delicate *agencement* that needs to be established between the complex set of objects, and the human properties on which the circulation of these practices depends. Once established, this form of *agencement* leads to a flow of everyday behaviours, as the omnipresence of similar devices in Japan tends to prove.[52] In addition, even if the propensity towards curiosity within a suitable socio-technical environment remains low, the device is not necessarily condemned to failure. In order to understand why, we must not forget the presence of the very same logic in conventional forms of advertising, which is generally highly ineffective: only a ridiculously small percentage of target audiences respond positively to adverts in terms of actual purchases. If curiosity devices are therefore just as ineffective as ordinary adverts, we might wager that they have a very promising future ahead of them!

5

'CLOSER'

> As for what motivated me, it is quite simple; I would hope that in the eyes of some people it might be sufficient in itself. It was curiosity – the only kind of curiosity, in any case, that is worth acting upon with a degree of obstinacy: not the kind of curiosity that seeks to assimilate what is proper for one to know, but that which enables one to get free of oneself. After all, what would be the value of the passion for knowledge if it resulted only in a certain amount of knowledgeableness and not, in one way or another and to the extent possible, in the knower's straying afield from himself? There are times in life when the question of knowing if one can think differently than one thinks, and perceive differently than one sees, is absolutely necessary if one is to go on looking and reflecting at all. (Foucault 1985: 8–9).

CURIOSITY IS A DISPOSITION THAT INTELLECTUALS SOMETIMES ACCEPT IN or amongst themselves, but which is rarely found to be present as an operational concept in their work.[1] For them, the recognition of a personal propensity towards curiosity is tantamount to an admission, or an intimate confession, of the kind of secret we only barely dare to reveal once the investigation has been completed and in the margins of a body of research, whether in an introduction like Foucault's or a conclusion such as this one,[2] or sometimes even when it is too late, when, because of an overly long delay, curiosity can only be admitted to from beyond the grave, when one of your followers luckily lends you his pen to do justice to the burning motive that has discreetly *animated* you throughout your life:

> There is now no practice, no institution, no zone of social space, subproletariat or intelligentsia, peasant or professor, marriage or unemployment, school or church, state or market, science, art, sport, the body, the media, politics, ethics, or the relations between the genders, age groups, ethnic groups or classes, whose study was not profoundly influenced by Bourdieu. For he managed to join the rigor of the scientific method with the inventiveness of the artist, an incomparable theoretical culture wedding authors that the canonical tradition is fond of opposing – Durkheim and Weber, Marx and Mauss, Cassirer and Wittgenstein, Husserl and Lévi-Strauss, Maurice Merleau-Ponty and John Austin, Gaston Bachelard and Erwin Panofsky – with a tireless practice of research deploying the complete gamut of techniques of observation and analysis, from ethnography to prosopography to statistics, in which he invested a libido sciendi without bound or bottom. Pierre Bourdieu possessed an insatiable curiosity for all experiences, all existential games, all social universes, and he would have wanted to live a thousand lives in order to understand them all, to capture their hidden causes and their intimate reasons (Wacquant 2002).

Beyond his admission to the sin of curiosity, I would like to underline the superb definition employed by Foucault that perhaps allows us to simultaneously understand 'Bourdieu the enigma', this insatiably curious man whose focus in his work on conservative modes of action is not a priori that compatible with the expression of curiosity. Between two possible forms of curiosity, Foucault chooses if not the best, then at least the most profound; in other words, 'that which enables one to get free of oneself'. This is the paradox of the curious person: it is their detachment from themselves that reveals their identity more clearly. Curiosity is the antidote of habitus, it is a force that drives us to break from what we are; in this respect, it is a disposition that weighs against one of the central structures of sociology, not to deny it, but to set it in tension with reference both to Bourdieu's unique biography and to the far more extensive space of everyday social life. The force of habit, which roots us to what we are, can be set in opposition to the appeal of curiosity, which draws us into moving beyond ourselves. In order to better understand social action, curiosity should thus be granted its proper place, its power, and its dignity – this is Bourdieu's last lesson (in spite of himself?): as suggested by his loyal disciple Loïc Wacquant, Bourdieu's own habitus was wonderfully oxymoronic given that it was the habitus (of) curiosity ('Pierre Bourdieu possessed an insatiable curiosity').

After having visited Bluebeard's house, and having climbed from the cellar of Genesis to the attic of contemporary markets, it is now time to close the door once more, to conclude the curious destiny of curiosity, this vital disposition that was nonetheless long rejected but which appears to have rediscovered its vigour in the space of the markets. But is it really a question of concluding? Just as, given my subject matter, I preferred to use the term 'teaser' instead of 'introduction', I prefer (inevitably concerned with the 'puzzle' inherent to this very subject) to use the unusual word 'closer' rather than 'conclusion'. The word has three meanings, the first being a closing device. Admittedly, this first meaning is hardly appropriate given that its appearance is via a compound word, 'the door-closer' (Latour 1988), that is to say the technical device designed to close a door. The door-closer device is interesting because it contributes to closing the door in combination with the lock, but without being confused with the latter of the two. Whereas the lock comes into play once the door is closed by marking a distinction between those who have the key and those who do not, or, as in Bluebeard, between those who are given it and those who are refused it – hence a curiosity device – the door-closer operates further upstream by closing the open door and, most importantly, by preventing nothing and no-one from opening the door in the future.[3] Understanding a conclusion as a door-closer suggests that, after having turned each key one by one, and after having opened all the doors to allow us to explore the rooms of curiosity, we still need to find a way to avoid either leaving the doors open gaping wide or closing them again too hermetically, so as now to encourage an ordered movement between the space we have visited and other horizons to come. *Closer* is also a proper noun: it is the name of a celebrity gossip magazine that plays on curiosity, whose business is revealing celebrities' secrets (such as the recent revelation of the French President's secret girlfriend) and granting access to their private lives; in other words, arousing the passion of ordinary people for the ordinary lives of those they perceive to be extraordinary. However, after having played with the substantive (the door-closer) and in order to really understand what game is at stake in the use of the proper noun (the magazine *Closer*), we need to pass through an adjective of intensity: 'closer', meaning nearer. In order to be able to look through the keyhole one last time and to then close the door without blocking it, we must in effect come closer – for 'closer' in fact connotes proximity more than closure. Curiosity is a question of focus: it is a way of getting closer to the world that at first seems distant or foreign; it is a disposition involving if not adherence, then at least adhesion, a concern for 'making something one's own', for creating a close relationship between oneself and the world. At the same time, the curious person often wants to conduct this rapprochement asymmetrically: there is a desire to simultaneously be as close as possible to what is seen whilst trying to appear as distant as possible from the point of view of the thing or person being observed. The ideal position for a curious person is thus seeing without being seen, seeing 'closer from farther away', as it were. In order to achieve this, an asymmetrical and partial solution has to be invented, in keeping with Laurent Thévenot's 'regime of familiarity' (2001). Hence the fundamental importance of the door and its keyhole, which, when brought together, were undoubtedly one of the first devices able to allow this feat, before telescopes, spyglasses, and binoculars, and later microphones, cameras, and the various different forms of modern media that increase this possibility tenfold – the recent phone-hacking scandal involving the British tabloid *News of the World* demonstrates this rather well.[4] If the (lay or professional) curious person operates in this manner, it is because the fascination being experienced is weighed against other feelings, such as the Rousseauian shame at allowing desire to become visible, but also the fear, caution, or even disapproval aroused by the things he or she wants to see and know but does not necessarily approve of, or to which access is prohibited. By getting closer, the curious person understands the risks involved in the absence of distance. To say 'closer' is thus to state and become aware of this problem; it is at once to follow the slope and to set oneself in opposition to proximity. I would also like to adopt this ambivalent position of the curious person, partly absorbed in the fascination of what is being observed, partly remaining at a distance in the interest of watching discreetly. I therefore suggest reconsidering things from closer/further away in order to play with the effects of the door-closer's openings and closings, to explore the dynamics of proximity in the cases of both the newspaper industry and gossip magazines, and, if possible, to go 'yet further'.

DOOR-CLOSER

Let us open the door one last time, before it closes: first of all, let us move far back in order to get a better run-up for when we move closer to the curiosity of today. As we saw, the history and sociology of curiosity involve an astonishing cascade of three paradoxes. A first paradox is that the earliest of these dispositions was banned without delay by religion; a second is that science ended up killing curiosity immediately upon arousing it; the third is that this disposition, which the two morals in *Bluebeard* at once condemned and forgave, and which sociology and economics completely forgot about when respectively giving priority to habit and to interest, nonetheless proliferated within markets, through the invention and multiplication of technical devices capable of activating it.

FIG. 18. Door-closer (Nantes, August 2010)

We understand that the market multiplies the motive of desire, and thus generalises the logic that we might have thought had disappeared from the cabinets of curiosity. These cabinets underwent an initial expansion, giving rise to museums (Impey and Macgregor 1985; Findlen 1994); however, the increased access to collections was subject to two restrictions: on the one hand, although museums granted greater access to their own collections, these tended to be extremely limited and ordered according to thematic and taxonomic criteria, so that institutions lost the magical character of the curiosity cabinets' exuberant bric-a-brac. On the other, even though they were open to a wider audience, institutional collections still remain subject to a restriction of the economic order: in a museum, the triple rule in force consists of not touching anything, not taking anything, and 'paying to see' (at least in most French museums!). The market has the advantage of removing these two restrictions: on the one hand, it reintroduces the generalised bric-a-brac of the curiosity cabinet, either in the traditional form of the bazaar (Geertz 1978), or, in more contemporary forms, in the mosaic of shops that displaces the disorder and multiplicity of the goods on offer to either a town centre or a shopping mall (Andrieu et al. 2004), or, in the fantasy of bringing together all the products of the great universal market (a concept so dear to economic theory) 'under the same roof', in the hypermarket (Grandclément 2008). On the other, and in contrast to the museum, each of these market forms are the object of paradoxically less severe forms of commercialisation and usage costs, since viewing here is always free and we only pay for what we wish to take away.

Krysztof Pomian was correct to emphasise the anthropological importance of collecting and its two distinct forces: the collection cannot be reduced to economic value, and it allows the invisible to be seen through the 'semiophores' it brings together. However, he was perhaps moving a little hastily when concluding that the essence of these objects was uselessness; that is to say that they had no use beyond the access they offered to the invisible, and that they were inalienable: removed from market logic, in other words. To begin with (and as Pomian knew better than anyone else), at the time of the first collections, certain pieces were considered eminently useful, in particular because of their medicinal properties. What is rare and curious also heals: the bezoar, the unicorn horn, and dragon's blood are each said to have curative properties. The reasoning behind the identification of these properties often stems from analogical thinking, as was skilfully identified by Foucault (1973), and involves establishing a link between the object's shape and its ability to heal: the calcifications of a snake's head are reputed to absorb poison; the eagle's stone in the shape of an egg supposedly prevents miscarriages; and so on (Schnapper 1988). Most importantly, the pieces in the collection are less inalienable than we might think. In fact, selling and choosing are merely two sides of the same coin: all collectors know that a collection is never static and must almost inevitably be linked to a corresponding market, not only for works to be acquired, but also very often for some of them to be disposed of to create the means for obtaining others. In other words, there is not a great divide between the collection and the market; there is certainly a difference, but rather than being a difference in nature, it is simply a difference in the degree, proportion, combination, and organisation of the logics of assembly and exchange.

Moreover, and thanks to the commercial uses of curiosity, we have already seen how collecting has been making a dramatic comeback for some time, on the sides of both supply and demand. In regards to demand, the market encourages the spirit of collecting by increasing the amount of potential acquisitions, but also, and paradoxically, through inviting a number of actors who, out of either boredom with (or even repulsion towards) aspects of its dominant utilitarianism, develop ways of changing it, escaping it, investing it with culture, or re-enchanting it (Belk et al. 1989). For all that, the market for its part 'recovers' these practices in order to make collections themselves a marketable product in their own right, something that we learn when we are young, from the collections of Panini or Pokémon images designed for children (Allison 2003), and, into adulthood, from magazines selling collectable items part by part (e.g. Atlas and Altaya in France) and, more generally, from the various products whose purchase makes even more sense if one already owns a set (works by an artist, a panoply of sports gear, Apple computer products, and others). In terms of supply, the market has long been feeding and intensifying the collecting spirit by playing with the multiplication and continuous variation amongst series of objects, thanks in particular to the power of fashion and its collections (Godart 2009). Even more subtle is the harmonious arrangement and presentation of 'product lines' in the distribution sector, that here involves reversing the process, so not inviting customers to assemble products that 'go together', but, by playing instead on the seductive nature of such assemblages, instead inviting these same customers to transgress them, to undo them, to consume them – this is, as we have seen, one of the principal powers of the art of the window display. This overview of the proliferation of forms inherent to devices of market curiosity helps us to finally understand that curiosity is a delicate balance between revelation and mystery; in order for it to continue, curiosity must both be satisfied yet remain frustrated. In *Bluebeard*, and following this scheme, if we do get to the end of the tale to discover what lies in the forbidden cabinet, it is perhaps because we had hoped all along, albeit in vain, to discover why the beard was blue.

The generalisation of curiosity and its devices ends up rendering irrelevant Hirschman's beautiful model (1977), by reopening the two Pandora's boxes that each contain the motives for action respectively placed there by economists and social actors: one labelled 'interest', the other 'habit'. As Hirschman suggests, Adam Smith closed the lid on his own box by channelling human passions towards interest. Interest is used as the general equivalent of passions, and thus succeeds in pacifying them by directing them towards the quest for material goods, rather than towards a desire to possess directed immediately towards others. Sociologists like Elias and Bourdieu have demonstrated that actors have themselves built their own box, by submitting the diverse motives for action to mechanisms of internalisation and social reproduction, at the price of ever more stifling self-control and routine. Hence follows the twofold idea of the domination of humankind through two forces: market and society. This view of the world certainly remains largely valid: social norms and price systems contribute considerably to the shaping and homogenisation of powerful practices. For all that, actors, and particularly those of the market, paradoxically cannot continue to be satisfied by the hegemonic reign of calculation and routine. By rendering all entities commensurable, calculation rids the world of meaning and establishes competition as an inferno that aligns all magnitudes against a single dimension and towards the lowest. The result is the emergence of an interest in moving beyond interest, in finding the means to 'cut short' calculation (Cochoy 2003), by playing not only with qualitative rupture, but also with other motives for action, amongst which curiosity features prominently.[5] Routine, by trapping practices in a circuit, eventually becomes the source of weariness and boredom. Now, these last two feelings, which sociology has curiously ignored despite them being extremely common and widespread, nonetheless prepare the expression of curiosity that then acts as the impetus for reopening the two Pandora's boxes and releasing all the motives for action locked up inside.

However, we are now confronted with a certain confusion. I was speaking about curiosity but here find myself being drawn into talking about other motives for action, such as weariness and boredom. I began with curiosity as it operates as a metonym for the key, and continued with weariness and boredom, as they serve as auxiliaries to curiosity and help in the opening of the two Pandora's boxes of habit and interest. Curiosity, encouraged by weariness and boredom, is however only the precondition for a far richer game, in that it liberates many other forces of action. This is why it was logical to begin with curiosity: it undoes habit, arouses other centres of interest, makes values discernible, opens up emotion, and finally allows a thousand other motives for action to proliferate, including pleasure, greed, desire, nostalgia, charity, fantasy, altruism, abandon, and the like: so many motives of which interest, habit, and curiosity are but three.

In this sense the market is as polychromatic as a rainbow. Indeed, and contrary to a view that has been widespread at least since Marcuse's *One-Dimensional Man* (1968), the market is not just the somewhat uniform grey drab hue of utilitarianism and interest; its appearance could not even be satisfactorily described in the bichromatic shades of interest-habit that sociology had the merit of introducing. With the help of curiosity we understand that the market possesses a palette of colours and patterns infinitely richer and more iridescent than is postulated in classical critiques of the market. The market is filled with a thousand motives for action on the sides of both supply and demand, and of course (above all?) in the social-technical mediations that invent, embody, and combine these motives in order to match them with each other. In the end we discover that the cabinet of market curiosity is not only cluttered with objects, it is also overflowing with subjective and intangible entities that only exist because of their double attachment to both people and objects. Materiality, rather than rendering subjective richness sterile, instead awakens and multiplies it. We recognised the quality of products, initially as one-dimensional and variable (good or bad, as in Akerlof 1970), then multi-dimensional (as in Lancaster 1975). Thanks to the flow of dispositions between people and through things, we ought to now rediscover the quality of people, in the old sense of people of quality(/ies) but also in the more modern sense of people who are qualified; in other words, people in whom qualities are incorporated or to whom they are attributed. The effort of qualification is twofold: whereas economics and sociology have described to the point of exhaustion the qualification of products and their surrounding social space, the symmetrical operation of the qualification of people remains to be described.[6]

The first confusion leads to another, this time lexical. The game of captation cannot be reduced to the twin pair of a disposition and *dispositif* (device). In fact, upon reflection, the initially seductive pun that grounds this dichotomy proves far too restrictive. I described curiosity as a disposition for the sake of simplicity in order to move quickly and to avoid becoming entangled in an overly theoretical discussion. However, strictly speaking, I should have specified that, although curiosity does indeed sometimes appear as a disposition – that is to say either as a naturally occurring inclination in the Aristotelian sense, or incorporated through culture in the sociological sense – in other circumstances it is also an emotion. It can thus be a sudden urge that, once activated, can in turn become either a passion – that is, an objective that is given to us or that we give ourselves (in fact, Thomas of Aquinas and tradition both deal with curiosity in terms of passion) – or a reason, a calculation of the kind we came across with the *libido sciendi*, in other words a powerful cognitive aptitude for ordering the world in correspondence with the objectives we pursue.

This inventory of the different facets of curiosity sets us on the road to a less approximate approach towards the forces of action. We now have four types of motives: dispositions, but also emotions, passions, and reasons.[7] These motives are connected in part to Weberian registers of action, given that dispositions are related to routine, emotion to affects, passions to value-rationality, and reasons to means-end rationality. A (re)turn to taking this repertoire into account begins with a redefined sociology of 'social mo(ti)bility': the expression would no longer (only) mean the movement of people between strata and social groups, but also the mobile circulation of the motives that underlie people's actions within or beyond these groups and strata. Such a sociology makes it possible, for instance, to put calculation (reason) and routine (disposition) back in their place amongst many other possible motives for action, to observe the relationships between calculation and other motives for action, to examine how these motives can be made to play with or against one another, and so on. In light of this inventory, it would be more accurate to speak of devices as relying on 'motives' rather than on dispositions.[8] The range of motives for action represents a real challenge for the provision of a social explanation, as the more I increase the number of reasons, routines, passions, and impulses for and of action, the more uncertain I make the explanatory model, and the more I undermine what we have patiently worked to distinguish and simplify. Nevertheless, the sociologist's problem is also, and above all, that of the actors who work hard to try to identify, or even imagine, motives for action that can be used to anticipate and control the actions of other people, and also to confuse forms of self-control. That said, if wanting to do the job properly, the sociologist has no other choice than to take note of the multiplication of motives and to describe the ways in which they are mobilised.

The awakening of curiosity through the 'breaking away from calculation or routine' that I have foregrounded here in fact demonstrates that dispositions are less 'buried' in subjects and more 'used' against them: innovating and managing an 'economy of surprise' is the responsibility of the supply side; even weariness and boredom, which might be thought of as appropriately interior to the subject, can be extensively cultivated and come to act as so many aids to the expression of curiosity. Thus we understand that curiosity is not always a motive that is spontaneously available, but that, on the contrary, must very often be aroused, awakened, and activated, as Bluebeard allows us to understand particularly well: the character in the tale is anything but seductive and yet he is able to seduce more effectively than anybody else. His power of seduction therefore lies somewhere other than in himself: it is grounded in the character's ability to identify a motive for action that is adapted to the situation (curiosity) and to construct a device capable of activating it (a system of rooms and keys), in order to transfer it to the target to whom it corresponds, or to awaken it in her. This manner of activating curiosity might lead us to believe that we were witnessing a mechanism of pure manipulation, including an 'activator' who has complete control over both the mechanism that activates the motive, and the action of the person being 'activated'. Fortunately, the inventory and study of curiosity devices has shown us how simplistic this kind of approach is: on many occasions we saw how the hope of activation sometimes manipulates the activator more than the person being activated, or, to use Perrault's words, 'It can be difficult to tell which of the two is the master'. Moreover, the confrontation between activator and activated only provides a very imperfect indication of the eminently plural character of the entities involved in activating curiosity; just as the actors involved in a dialogue are but the 'ventriloquists' of other elements expressed through them and influencing what they say (Cooren 2010), those caught up in playing the game of the captation of curiosity are also the expression of the logic inherent to the tools they handle and which are often beyond their control – window displays that are able to attach us to a crowd of objects and customers, advertising devices as fascinating to advertisers as to consumers, electronic tools that can pull both marketing and customers in unexpected directions. All in all, the exposition of these initial issues points towards the need to explore in greater detail the social mechanisms through which markets are animated.

From this perspective, the conclusion really is like a 'door-closer' in the manner of the mechanism described above: it is a device whose responsibility is to ensure that any closure is not definitive but temporary, and thus to simultaneously provide for the possibility of reopening the space that has been visited by anybody wishing to continue this sketched investigation of curiosity (which includes the author of these words!). In fact, from this perspective, instead of using the metaphor of the hydraulic door-closer, I ought to prefer that of the 'magic door' (another type of door-closer) that opens doors when we walk over a carpet or in front of a photoelectric cell designed for the purpose. Ever since they were invented, the miracle of these sophisticated doors that open and close 'by themselves' has *enchanted* children. However, although 'magical', these doors are no less than devices of 'control': their mission consists of practising their magic in a single direction, forward, and to the exclusion of a return. If only I were also able to discover a force that would help me achieve such progression!

FIG. 19. *The Progressive Grocer*, The Magic Door, February 1951, p. 201

CLOSER

In spite of all the religious and moral obstacles that have stood in its way, curiosity therefore truly remains a fundamental force of action; it is one of the forces that can still be used to thwart the unidimensional retailer, as we will see by closely placing this tiny little page, whose origin and status I will detail later, under the microscope:

FIG. 20. *The Progressive Grocer*, August 1940, pp. 76–77

Americans are born curious

(THANK HEAVEN!)

A CLOSED DOOR is as irresistible to an American adult as a closed box is to a baby. Americans just have to see what's inside. They hate secret sessions. Mystery. Diplomacy in whispers. And it's a good thing.

The more they dig into the dark corners, turning the flood of their curiosity on political figures, crimes, injustices, heroes, and villains alike – the better for America. For when their curiosity is satisfied, somehow the soft spots have disappeared. America is tougher and stronger.

Find the men and women who have a thirst for knowing all the facts, and knowing *neat* information, and you will find the Americans who are helping push the country forward.

For them, the *Saturday Evening Post* prints the *whole* story. Not just a fragment seen through a keyhole, but a bay window view. For them, the Post is 'America between two covers'.

And this same curiosity, this extra measure of confidence in the Post, extends to editorial and advertising pages alike. Year after year, surveys serve only to reaffirm the fact that people like to read adverts in the Post… and that they are more likely to see your advert there than anywhere else.

THAT'S ONE REASON *why food advertisers – to cite just one field – last year invested more of their advertising money in the Post than in the next 3 weekly magazines combined.*

Could I have dreamt of better material for reviewing the road we have travelled along and the lessons we have learnt? In this text, I find 'curiosity', its 'closed door', and 'keyhole', the 'bay window' of a display window, 'advertising', and 'teasing', all contained in an enigmatic message that only makes sense once you read the small print. Only the Data Matrix and smartphone from my fourth chapter are missing, but it would be inappropriate, to say the least, to reproach a text from 1940 for their absence when we could not reasonably expect them to be included! What's more, the text brings us back to the very starting point, towards the fundamental anthropology of curiosity established by Genesis, although it makes a curious inversion: whereas in Genesis, God immediately and severely punishes the emergence of curiosity, here the same Creator is instead given credit for his invention: it is 'thank heaven' that Americans are 'born curious'! It is as though with time, the discovery of America, and the development of American civilisation, divine wrath had been appeased to the point that God eventually went back on his initial condemnation and endowed humans with the very disposition that he had originally refused them. In this version, the curiosity of Aristotle and the Church are ultimately reconciled, and even merged, in the form of a disposition that has finally been incorporated into human nature – defined as universal and congenital – 'Americans are born curious'.

What is the effect of this curiosity? It is to lead all the citizens of America to irresistibly seek that which is hidden from them: 'A closed door', we are told, 'is as irresistible to an American adult as a closed box is to a baby. Americans just have to see what's inside'. This image of a closed object or door brings with it a twofold lesson. On the one hand, the metaphors of the 'door' and the 'box' highlight the crucial role of technical devices in activating curiosity, even if congenital. On the other, by distinguishing a particular device for each stage of life, from the 'baby' to the 'American adult', the text presents this disposition as being not just universal but also permanent – curiosity is present in everyone and, far from diminishing with age, it drives us throughout our life. Above all, by anchoring curiosity in childhood – an anchorage which is strongly emphasised by the photograph of the near-naked baby with its box – the text aims to turn the curious exploration of the world into the very expression of ingenuousness, and of a return to original innocence, according to a sales pitch that, while reminiscent of *Myriam*, is this time not in the slightest ambiguous,[9] as if it were Myriam as a child that was being depicted. Furthermore, our curiosity is not only excused, but is suddenly given a dignity and a moral function. Curiosity, like interest in the Smithian mythology of the market, should guarantee public virtues. More so, in fact: whereas with Smith and Mandeville interest remains a private vice whose indulgence paradoxically ensures collective virtue, curiosity itself shares this condition of virtue with the public good it enables: 'And it's a good thing. The more [Americans] [...] turn the flood of their curiosity on political figures, crimes, injustices, heroes and villains alike – the better for America. For when their curiosity is satisfied, somehow the soft spots have disappeared. America is tougher, and stronger'.[10]

Behind the assertion of the 'native' dimension of curiosity, and behind the defence of its 'positive' contribution, this text introduces a theme which we have barely touched on until now: that of the public space, the press, and the particular role that curiosity plays there. The text refers to both American politics and its ideal of transparency, inherited from the liberal tradition, and to the recent past of American journalism, to the glory days of 'muckrakers', in the wake of *The Jungle* by Upton Sinclair (2010 [1906]) and, more generally, to the 'Progressive Era' movement (Glad 1966), of which the *Progressive Grocer*, the magazine that published this text, is one incarnation, as its title very clearly shows. Praise for public curiosity functions as a call for complicity with another species of curiosity, that of the press and journalists. Journalists are inveterately curious; they are 'muckrakers' who do not believe in appearance alone and who want to know more, and, in order to do so, they hunt down scandals, track 'affairs', and tirelessly seek to break open guilty secrets in order to deliver them to the public.

In other words, it is the job of the press to exercise everyone's curiosity by proxy (an act of delegation highlighted by the anaphoric repetition of 'For them [Americans]'). As always with professional dynamics (Freidson 1988), the legitimisation of a profession is achieved by establishing a difference between experts and laypeople: after having been discreetly suggested, the distinction between the curiosity of the public and the curiosity of journalists is made the object of a subtle differentiation: whilst the former is characterised by the simple and private images of an innocent box and a more provocative keyhole, the latter, whose ambition is supposedly much broader and less questionable, is linked, significantly, to a metaphor implying transparency and a view that is unanimously accepted and collective: the window. '[That which is published by the *Saturday Evening Post* is] Not just a fragment seen through a keyhole, but a bay window view'. The text aims to show how important the difference between the devices is by emphasising, through the use of repetition accompanied by an inverted distribution of italics – 'the whole facts, *neat,* [/] the *whole* story, [...] a bay window view' – that, in contrast to the keyhole, which restricts vision to a truncated piece of information, the display window is naturally oriented towards a comprehensive, panoramic view. According to this sales pitch, seeing everything is paradoxically less reprehensible than seeing only a fragment, as the complete image is less deceptive than a detail might be. In sum, the mediation of journalism makes a strong contribution to the trivialisation of curiosity: the intervention of a specialised third party multiplies the occasions for being curious; it reduces the cost of doing so considerably, in terms of effort as much as responsibility; it increases its reliability, by palliating the risks of errors of judgement associated with the falsities of a partial view, thanks to its demand for systematic and exhaustive information. The press also makes curiosity less reprehensible and more legitimate: since the fourth chapter we have known that, by abandoning the keyhole in favour of a window that is wider, more complete, and transparent – the display window – a window that is most importantly licit, which occupies 'its rightful place', the public is encouraged to look collectively and without shame at the elements offered up to its gaze. Thanks to the display window of the press, the public discovers that curiosity, far from being a shameful and misplaced inclination, also appears to be an astonishingly important resource, possessing a powerful capacity for exploration and emancipation.

This text defends the press and, as in any case for the defence, one must of course be attentive to the role played by rhetoric. The art of oratory lies here not only at the heart of the argument, as we have just seen by studying the way in which the text supports a form of professional curiosity, although it is more discreet in the beginning and less inhibited at the end.

In the beginning, the promotion of curiosity is based on a very subtle, logical argument consisting in the assertion of the innateness of curiosity in order to better encourage its acquisition. The assertion relies on its performative virtues:

> The more 'naturally' curious you think you are, and/or that others are naturally curious, the more curious you will become, and it will thus be 'abnormal' not to be curious like other people. And if I am telling you this, it is because being curious is not enough. You will thus be more inclined to be curious if you accept you already are, that you have always been and cannot cease to be so, for being curious is as natural as breathing.

Thus the text 'ascribes' the disposition of curiosity in the way I mentioned in the introduction: it supplies it and naturalises it; it naturalises the more effectively to supply it. If Americans are indeed born curious, they cannot help being curious or admitting to being curious; their birth and their recognition of curiosity are closely connected. The fundamental point of this procedure is to remove guilt: the press needs to legitimise public curiosity in order to support its own exploratory activities. The two types of curiosity – profane and professional – support each other, and thus, in order to ensure this remains the case, in order to avoid the investigations of the press being viewed with suspicion, the guilty curiosity of the public needs to be transformed into a virtuous quest. This transformation begins with the naturalisation of the disposition, and continues with an extraordinary reversal, in which the very hatred of curiosity renders it legitimate: 'They hate secret sessions. Mystery. Diplomacy in whispers'; the paradox requires that the loathing of mystery comes to reinforce its adoration.

But what is this text, and why does it defend both the press and curiosity? What is the intention and the status of this new narrative that has the effrontery to attempt to overturn thousands of years of condemnation of curiosity, in order to do the reverse via the mediation of the press, one of the pillars of American democracy? This ambitious text that navigates between fundamental anthropology and the power of democracy is in fact a tiny text, a simple advertisement, and an ordinary publicity insert, which appears when leafing through a trade magazine for small independent grocers. It is here, and particularly at the end of the text, that the uninhibited promotion of the press as an economic object appears. We are in the presence of one achievement of copywriting among (innumerable) others, this literary form created by advertising which was often originally entrusted to professors of literature. At the beginning of the twentieth century, this consisted in accompanying a slogan, advertisement, or image with a skilful and elegantly written sales pitch (Presbrey 1929). This text thus appears as a small masterpiece of commercial rhetoric: it aims to fold an entire world within a few simple words, thanks to the *mise en abyme* of the slogan whose mission it is to promote and clarify: 'America between two covers'.

Of course, what is being promoted here is less America, its anthropology and its forces of democracy and more its 'cover/s', with the double meaning of journalistic reportage and covers made of paper. In fact, this text is advertising the *Saturday Evening Post*, or rather it is advertising both the paper and the advertising that can be placed in it. It is vaunting the dynamic that is particular to the press as a two-sided market (Rochet and Tirole 2003), that is to say, as an enterprise geared towards a double clientele – both its readers and its advertisers – 'this same curiosity, this extra measure of confidence in the Post, extends to both editorial and advertising pages alike', as our text explicitly states. The America between two covers is both the country and its public: the paper gives access to that to which, and to those to whom, it gives access. In other words, the *Post* sells the existence and profile of its readers to advertisers, places advertisements in the path of its readership, and in order to do so finally promotes the supposed effects of this double investment: 'Year after year, surveys serve only to reaffirm this fact that people like to read advertising in the Post… that they are more likely to see your advertisement there than anywhere else'.

The *Saturday Evening Post* is not just any newspaper: at the time of this advertisement, it was one of the main American popular magazines and thus, simultaneously, an enormous publicity vehicle. Between 1903 and 1928, the volume of advertising in the magazine rose from 162,319 lines to 4,108,509 lines, an increase of nearly 400% in the space of two decades! (Presbrey 1929: 443) However, even if the *Post* is not just any newspaper, it is, all the same, one paper among others in the magazine market. America is to be found not only between the two covers of the *Post*, but also between those of competing newspapers, and from this point of view, it is important to assert its specific advantage: '*food advertisers – to cite just one field* [the one that interests *Progressive Grocers* advertisers!] – *last year invested more of their advertising money in the Post than in the next 3 weekly magazines combined*'. This implies that 'between the two covers of the *Post*, you not only find America, but also investments in advertising that are as well placed as banknotes in an interest-bearing account, the proof being that advertisers rush there *en masse* and more than to anywhere else. Wouldn't you be mad not to do the same?' To the question's uncertain answer, one might as well add imitation by other suppliers, about the power of which Harrison White would much later theorise (White 1982).

But there is more. This double game of public and market spaces, far from limiting itself to the enclosure of the covers that protect the content of this newspaper and its competitors, also extends to the *mille-feuille* of information and publicity inserts: the America which is housed between the two covers of the *Post* is itself placed somewhere between the two covers of the *Progressive Grocer*, a paper which is itself placed between the dual public of its advertisers (including the *Saturday Evening Post*) and its readers (grocers). In this staggering game, in which advertising devices become enshrined within advertising devices, the organs of the press and their public echo back the image of the box, of secrets being enveloped and the hope they will be revealed: in the same way that the child seeks to know what is inside the box, readers seek to know what is inside their papers, brands seek to know what papers their customers are reading, and on and on. When all is said and done, this game functions as a new and astonishingly reflexive curiosity device: within the pages of *Progressive Grocer*, within the frame of the publicity insert, the exciting box of secret America works hard to excite an attention towards the *Saturday Evening Post*, the exciter of attention.

This insert therefore has a very clearly commercial and situated character: it is an old advertisement which appeared in August 1940, lost between two pages of an obscure trade magazine aimed towards the declining profession of small independent American grocers. However, paradoxically, it is this commercial and situated character which gives this advertisement a very general scope, enabling it to better grasp two essential forces of curiosity: curiosity as a commercial 'trick', but also curiosity as a taste for *current affairs*, the inclination that everyone has towards these curiosities of the moment, the sharing in which enables a belonging to a public (Tarde 2006). To be curious is not only to be consumed with the desire to see *what is to be found* on the other side of the door, but above all, to be consumed with the desire to know what is *currently* happening behind the door: to such a degree, in the modern world more so than in *Bluebeard,* is the flow of current affairs, news, and *events* greater than the stock of past secrets. To approach – to be nearer, closer – is thus to be closer in space as well as time, to be right up to the here and now. In this movement for getting closer, organs of the press like the *Post,* to a greater extent than the door of yesteryear, occupy a central position, insofar as it is they who allow us to ascend from Genesis not just to the most burning current affair, but also to the most timeless, if understanding current affairs as a theme and not a period. To conclude this journey I will therefore focus on the press as a general device for arousing curiosity.

The press, as the advertisement of the *Saturday Evening Post* suggests, draws its power from the revelation of secrets. Therefore, its success rests on the paradoxical connection between an inexhaustible reservoir of hidden information on the one hand, and a generalised demand for transparency on the other. Unsurprisingly, the press therefore revives the fundamental importance of the secret (so skilfully analysed by Simmel); as the sociologist notes, it plays on this delicate balance between sharing information and maintaining a domain that is reserved, both of which are necessary to social life:

> All relationships of people to each other rest [...] upon the precondition that they know something about each other. [But] the reciprocal knowledge, which is the positive condition of social relationships, is not the sole condition. On the contrary, such as those relationships are, they actually presuppose also a certain nescience, a ratio, that is immeasurably variable to be sure, of reciprocal concealment (Simmel 1906: 441–448).

However, the nature of the press is such that it goes beyond the type of reciprocal relationships that interest Simmel. The press makes a profession out of divulging secrets, and, by doing so, also emphasises their counterpart – curiosity – which becomes a tool for the public sharing of information about the world, with the result that there is a continuous shifting of the boundary between the secret and public spheres of social life. Thus, accompanying every secret is a concern about its discovery, about the act so well encapsulated by the three words 'disclosure', 'divulge', and 'revelation'. The first puts the emphasis on the disappearance of an enclosure which has to this point been hermetically sealed; the second insists upon the 'public' destination of this operation (etymologically, to divulge is to put make something available to the *vulgus*, to provide access to the crowd); the third indicates what is at stake in the first two by stressing the objective of veracity. The press is thus the location of an active curiosity which combines the forces of serendipity and enquiry: journalists seem to be as attentive to the information they seek as to that which appears incidentally. Among the latter, one finds not only the colossal wave of dispatches fed in by press agencies (Czarniawska 2011) but also, more rarely but more spectacularly, the 'leaks' which, in certain sensitive cases, feed into newspapers from the outside.

The 'leak' is a fantastic vector of curiosity because, as the term itself indicates, it suggests a hydraulic accident, a failure of a previously watertight system, and therefore a sudden outpouring of information that was if not unsuspected then at least not known about, which in itself attracts/excites attention. Over the past few years, the public exploitation of leaks so beloved of investigative journalism has been newly extended and intensified, with the appearance in 2007 of *Wikileaks* – the website whose name means, literally, 'collaborative leaks' – which presents itself as a participatory organ of the press to which anyone can bring to the attention of everyone – on a global scale! – sensitive information that they have been able to gain access to. *Wikileaks* thus became known for making public a list of members of the BNP (the extreme right-wing British party), for publishing the huge collection of private text messages sent in the United States on the day of the 11 September 2001 terrorist attacks, and for putting online the video of the blunder by the American army in Iraq in which civilians can be seen being shot like rabbits (LeMonde.fr 2010). Yet more recently, *Wikileaks* published 91,000 confidential documents concerning military action undertaken by the coalition in Afghanistan, revealing the activities of a mysterious 'Task Force 373' (responsible for numerous blunders and which takes its orders from beyond the command of NATO), the existence of a much higher number of civilian casualties than had been publicly estimated, and the double game played by Pakistan which, behind its official support of the United States, on occasion supported the Taliban rebellion (Fournier 2010). On 28 November 2010, *Wikileaks* also made public the content of 250,000 American diplomatic telegrams, considerably embarrassing not only the United States authorities, but also many other countries and foreign ministries.

It is fascinating to observe the extent to which the revelation of secrets, far from leading to their abolition, relies rather on their conversion, on their staging, and on their substitution. Concerning conversion, the *Wikileaks* model is founded on the guarantee of anonymity given to informers who can submit their documents either via a secure Internet connection or by post: when it comes to revelations, the rule is that the price of obtaining a leak of secrets is guaranteeing the secrecy of sources! Concerning staging, *Wikileaks* takes care not to reveal the information that it has at its disposal in a brutal manner but rather plans its revelations very astutely and conscientiously. Thus, when the video revealing the American blunder in Iraq was published, the site, akin to an electronic *Myriam*, had already skilfully aroused public curiosity first by announcing that it possessed an 'exceptional document', and then by declaring that it was being spied on by the CIA. In the case of the 'Afghan files', *Wikileaks* invited major international newspapers such as the *Guardian*, the *New York Times*, and *Der Spiegel* to be the first to hear its revelations, while asking them to wait until 26 July 2010 before revealing the content (LeMonde.fr 2010), a delay designed to attract attention (or heighten tension) for the benefit of its own site, the only place where the information that had been partially published by the press could be accessed in its entirety. The same strategy was used in the case of the diplomatic telegrams, which large international dailies had access to several weeks before the revelations were announced in public (Ourdan 2010). Finally, concerning substitution, one cannot forget the astonishing leaks that flowed from the leak machine itself: a few weeks after *Wikileaks* revealed the Afghan war secrets, we learnt that rape charges had been pressed against its founder and charismatic organiser, Julian Assange, which led, in the space of a few hours, to a search warrant being first issued and then retracted. Much later, on 18 November 2010, the Swedish public prosecutor's office issued a warrant for the arrest of the *Wikileaks* founder (LeMonde.fr 2010b). Behind this troubled affair, it is if the revelation of public and private secrets are mutually exclusive – symptomatically, Julian Assange himself has always maintained an air of great mystery around his own life (Thomas 2010). With *Wikileaks*, therefore, we understand the way in which the media play on the maximal differential between collective and political forms of exploration, quite distinct from the private concerns of the market, and the arousal of a desire to know that is highly personal and highly intimate.

The way in which the media arouses public curiosity about the world's secrets (of which *Wikileaks* provides such a spectacular illustration) does in fact emerge from a very general scheme in which substance is inseparable from form. To illustrate this point, I propose to use the Woerth-Bettencourt affair, which was the talk of the town in France over the summer of 2010, at the same time as the *Wikileaks* Afghan revelations, which incidentally shows that Americans are not the only ones who are '(born?) curious'!

BOX 5. THE WOERTH-BETTENCOURT AFFAIR

The Woerth-Bettencourt affair began as the Liliane Bettencourt affair, and concerned the octogenarian heiress of the L'Oréal group and the richest woman in France, before spreading to also involve Éric Woerth, Minister for Employment in the government of François Fillon. It all started as a family dispute between the mother (Liliane), and her daughter (Françoise) who filed a complaint in December 2007 for an 'abus de faiblesse' [the exploitation of a physical or psychological weakness for personal gain] of which her mother was allegedly the victim. For several years, Liliane Bettencourt had in fact shown uncommon generosity towards her photographer friend, François-Marie Banier, giving him gifts worth nearly a billion Euros. The 'affair' began on 16 June 2010, when the information website *Mediapart*, and the magazine *Le Point*, published extracts from Liliane Bettencourt's private conversations, recorded by her butler without her knowledge. These recordings brought Patrick de Maistre, the billionaire's asset manager, into the picture. He is heard not only giving a report on Swiss bank accounts and a possible transfer of funds to Singapore, but also inviting the elderly lady to make donations to associations that financed members of the UMP, the majority party of the President, including a man whom he called a 'friend', Éric Woerth, treasurer of this party and minister for the Budget at the time… and husband of Florence Woerth, an employee of Clymène, the company managing Liliane Bettencourt's assets, of which he was the director. Patrick de Maistre also mentioned that Patrick Ouart, the Elysée's legal counsel, whom he 'saw regularly on her behalf', had told him 'that the prosecutor Courroye was supposedly going to announce on the third of September that [her] daughter's request was inadmissible. The case would therefore be closed'. From then on the revelations did not stop. At the end of June, *Le Point* revealed that

Éric Woerth had personally bestowed the Legion of Honour on Patrick de Maistre, and, on 31 August, L'Express revealed that it was indeed Éric Woerth who had taken the initiative to apply for this decoration, in a letter dated March 2007. The hiring by Florence Woerth in the company directed by Patrick de Maistre in November of the same year (after the awarding of the Legion of Honour) raised suspicions of corrupt practice. But the affair did not stop there. On 7 July 2010, Claire Thibout, Liliane Bettencourt's former accountant, stated at a hearing that political figures regularly came to the billionaire's residence seeking ready cash and that Éric Woerth had received €150,000 to fund Nicolas Sarkozy's campaign (but *Le Canard enchaîné – a weekly satirical newspaper* – would reveal on 21 July that the former accountant had received €400,000 from the billionaire's daughter, raising suspicions regarding the sincerity of her declarations). The prosecutor Philippe Courroye launched three inquiries into issues of tax avoidance, laundering the results of tax evasion, and conflicts of interest, but did not refer the matter to an examining magistrate. The magistrate, Isabelle Prévost-Deprez – responsible for the inquiry into the abuse of the state of weakness and a colleague of prosecutor Courroye at the court in Nanterre, but in open conflict with him – ordered that supplementary information be provided following the revelation of the secret recordings. On 16 July, the magazine *Marianne* revealed that a cheque for €100,000 had been drawn on one of Liliane Bettencourt's accounts four months before the presidential election, and that Éric Woerth and Patrick de Maistre had met a few days after it had been paid out. The Minister announced his resignation from his post as treasurer of the UMP, and on 2 September finally admitted that he had initiated the request for the Legion of Honour for Patrick de Maistre. On 20 September, after two of its journalists had seen their telephone bills intercepted by the General Directorate of Intelligence, *Le Monde* filed a complaint against person unknown for 'violation of the secrecy of sources'. The prosecutor for his part (using the complaint for violation of investigational secrecy lodged by Liliane Bettencourt's lawyer after the publication of an article in Le Monde), requested that the police examine the telephone records of the two journalists in order to show that his colleague and rival, Mrs Prévost-Deprez, had been speaking to the press. In light of this step, on 29 October, the general prosecutor of the court of Versailles (the hierarchical superior of magistrate Courroye), ordered the latter to open an investigation into all dossiers for which he was responsible, and sought the opinion of the Court of Appeal as to whether it would be possible for all dossiers processed at the Nanterre court to be moved elsewhere (several weeks earlier, the President of the Court of Appeal, having been approached for an opinion by a political figure, had recommended that an examining magistrate should be appointed, but this was unsuccessful due to the absence of the power to issue a court order). On 17 November, the Court of Appeal decided to move all the dossiers to the Bordeaux court, while the general prosecutor's office recommended that they be moved to Paris on the very same morning.

(According to Laurent (2010) and other press articles.
See the dossiers of *Le Figaro, Libération, Le Monde, Le Journal du dimanche*,
the special issue by *Le Monde* on the affair, and others).

With regards to substance, this affair brings together, astonishingly, almost all the ingredients that might be found, usually singularly, in this social form that we call a 'scandal', and which is presented as 'something which reveals, almost in the photographic sense of the word, pre-existing relationships of power, structures, positions, or norms' (De Blic and Lemieux 2005). Indeed, the Woerth-Bettencourt affair assembles a story of troubled friendship and difficult family relationships around matters of finance; it unites political issues, suspicions of conflicts of interest, and the illegal funding of political parties, and institutional questions around the separation of judicial and executive powers, not to mention the place of the press and its freedom to provide information – all of which is grounded in social and financial relations, with the affair involving one of the jewels of the French luxury goods industry, tax issues, and problematic personal relationships between the social, financial, legal, and political elite. All these elements are echoed in the collective conscience, either because shared public issues are involved, such as the requirement for an independent judicial system, the imperative of equality of treatment by the law, the concern to guarantee the freedom of the press, the rule against using public institutions for the benefit of private interests, or because, on the contrary, it deals with issues which resonate within the private sphere, including family relationships, friendship, personal relationships, questions of dependence, and personal vulnerability – elements that, even if one cannot identify with them, then at least can be related to one's own experiences, values, and beliefs. The extraordinary marriage of this almost exhaustive collection of circumstances and issues (possibly in the collective conscience) forms a potentially explosive mixture, one likely to arouse public curiosity and/or indignation and therefore to generate a flow of attention towards the press, perhaps with the risk of a degree of saturation. Today it paradoxically seems that 'too much is too much', which can not only, as a Durkheimian theory might suggest, set in motion a major movement of disapproval, but also engender apathy, weariness, and resignation amongst some sections of the public, at least until another affair occurs – for example, the arrest of the Director of the International Monetary Fund (IMF), a possible presidential candidate, for the alleged rape of a chambermaid in a New York hotel room – and re-ignites public excitement about crimes that certain personalities of this world may (or may not) have committed or about conspiracies of which they may have been the victim (it all depends)... constantly supported by the press, in all its forms, even supported by astonishing devices for participation such as 'CoveritLive' (see below, chaper 4).

Indeed, with respect to the press and its tools, exciting curiosity depends just as much on the appeal of substance as on the seductions of form; it relies at once on attempts to fan the flames of public and democratic debate and democracy and the concern to support the very existence of the press as an economic activity, in a context where this activity has itself been weakened by the spread of the internet, the development of the free newspaper (*Metro, 20 Minutes, Direct Soir*, and others), and the proliferation of sources of information that overflow the official framework of 'old' media. To ensure its survival, the press plays on forces of formal curiosity which it has long controlled, but also draws new resources from the very internet technology that remains a threat.

The first force consists in attempting to renovate, in a manner as sophisticated as it is subtle, the teasing approach inherent to headline displays that aim to arouse the desire 'to know more', to discover the inside pages, and therefore buy the paper. Paradoxically, it is *Mediapart*, an exclusively online information source and one of the most innovative media operations in France, that uses the power of its front page and its headlines in the most traditional way.

Mediapart, as an exclusively online press operation, has chosen an economic model in which content is paid for and is presented without accompanying advertising. That is to say, the reader has to 'pay to view' or rather 'pay to view more' to be able to read entire articles. As suggested by the paper's mascot – the small old-fashioned newspaper seller in the top left of the screen – although they stick to tradition by offering free access to front page news (symbolised by the day's date in the image), it is only really possible to gain access to content by buying a copy of the paper that the little man holds so tightly and well-guarded under his arm. On the sensationalist front page, designed to launch the 'Revelations about the L'Oréal heiress [...]', the largest font size is used for high-profile figures: the President (Nicolas Sarkozy) comes first, followed by his Minister for Employment (Éric Woerth), while the ellipsis of the explanatory elements creates a brutal association (itself reinforced by the irreverent omission of titles

Mer. 16 Juin

RECHERCHER

Nos Unes de la semaine

MEDIAPART

LE JOURNAL LE CLUB

CONNECTEZ-VOUS

Identifiant

Mot de passe

Identifiant ou mot de passe oublié ?

9€ PAR MOIS

ABONNEZ-VOUS ICI

LE JOURNAL MONDE FRANCE ECONOMIE CULTURE

LE CLUB

PARTICIPER BLOGS EDITIONS

L'ESSENTIEL DE L'ACTUALITÉ

REVUE DU WEB

- Frédéric Bastiat, repère intellectuel de la droite américaine (La Vie des idées)
- Coup de feu sur un arbitre de touche en plein match (Sud Ouest)
- Chatroulette veut mettre un logiciel de reconnaissance de pénis (Popular Science)
- Neil Gaiman: la vie est plus étrange que la fiction (Prospect)
- L'abus de Coupe du Monde peut être dangereux pour la santé (Terra Eco)
- Des pistes pour réformer l'accession sociale à la propriété (localtis info)
- Comment la police compte le nombre de manifestants (20 minutes)
- Bart de Wever, l'homme qui veut faire «s'évaporer» la Belgique (Le Monde)

LA UNE

Révélations sur l'héritière de L'Oréal

Sarkozy, Woerth, fraude fiscale: les secrets volés de l'affaire Bettencourt

Par Fabrice Arfi, Fabrice Lhomme

L. Bettencourt © DR

Stupéfiant rebondissement dans l'affaire Liliane Bettencourt. La fille unique de la milliardaire, convaincue que sa mère est dépouillée de ses biens, a transmis à la police judiciaire des enregistrements pirates de conversations entre l'héritière de L'Oréal et ses principaux conseillers. Ces documents audio, dont Mediapart a pris connaissance, révèlent diverses opérations financières destinées à échapper au fisc, des relations avec le ministre Eric Woerth et son épouse, ainsi que les immixtions de l'Elysée dans la procédure judiciaire.

Lire la suite

Sur le même sujet

- Affaire Bettencourt: réactions à nos révélations

Affaire Bettencourt: réactions à nos révélations

Par Fabrice Arfi, Fabrice Lhomme

Mediapart a sollicité les personnes (ou leurs conseils) concernées par les enregistrements réalisés au domicile de Liliane Bettencourt.

Lire la suite

Petite enfance, grande démolition

Par Les invités de Mediapart

Après la parution du décret *«relatif aux établissements et services d'accueil des enfants de moins de six ans»*, **Christophe Najdovski**, adjoint (Vert) au maire de Paris chargé de la petite enfance, dénonce le choix fait par le gouvernement d'un accueil au rabais.

Lire la suite

EDITION : LES INVITÉS DE MEDIAPART

Claude Perdriel, le sanibroyeur du Net

Par François Bonnet

Il est rare de lire une telle avalanche de bêtises en une si petite poignée de phrases. Claude Perdriel s'y emploie avec succès. Et nous démontre pourquoi les patrons d'une presse papier en pleine crise n'ont décidément rien compris.

Lire la suite

FIG. 21. *Mediapart*, 16 June 2010, 'The Stolen Secrets of the Bettencourt Affair' [Headline reads: Revelations about the L'Oréal heiress: Sarkozy, Woerth, financial fraud: the stolen secrets of the Bettencourt affair]

and first names) between these two public figures and an affair concerning tax fraud. The colon (':'), which usually carries the promise of elucidation, only acts to thicken the air of mystery… and excitement. Here we are invited to penetrate an 'affair', a word which is already exciting in itself and one which is all the more so as it is presented to us not only in classical terms as a 'revelation', but in the even more titillating language of 'stolen secrets'. Only by reading the lead paragraph is a corner of the veil lifted, which rearranges the order of the names in the headline:

> An astounding new development in the Liliane Bettencourt affair. The only daughter of the billionaire, convinced that her mother has been stripped of her assets, has sent the Criminal Investigation Department clandestine recordings of conversations between the L'Oréal heiress and her chief

> advisers. These audio documents, discovered by Mediapart, reveal various financial operations designed to avoid tax, relations between the minister Eric Woerth and his wife, as well as interference in the case by the Élysée (*Mediapart* 16 June 2010).

But what exactly are these 'financial operations designed to avoid tax' which are being hatched in the secrecy of Liliane Bettencourt's private residence? How are the Minister and his wife involved? What steps has the Presidency of the Republic actually taken? To find out, one only has to click to 'Read more'; however, if this command is obeyed, a screen for subscriptions appears. It is not possible to buy separate editions; the only concession offered is a trial period of fifteen days for the special price of one Euro. One must therefore not simply pay, but pay over a considerable period of time. The same mode of contractual and monetary access to the paper's contents is also presented in the upper right-hand corner of the banner at the top of the screen, like the modern counterpart of the newspaper seller of yesteryear: to 'open the paper', to enter *Mediapart*, you either need to subscribe, or, if already a subscriber, enter a username and password. At each point of entry to the site, we are therefore confronted with a three-part scheme, reminiscent of the tricks in *Myriam*, with an eye-catching title, a lead paragraph which shows us a little more, and then a final promise, consisting here of directing us towards a subscription that will enable us to know the final part of the story.

Unlike to the newspapers of yesteryear, the subscription requirement draws a strong boundary between inside and outside, which is itself a vector of curiosity. The sense ('the meaning') and the *cens* (from the French: the fee to be paid and thus here 'the restriction') of this division are emphasised and explained by another counterpoint which, like the previous one, is found in the black banner running from left to right: the identity of 'The newspaper' (*Le journal*) is only understood in relation to 'The club' (*Le club*), this closed circle which is clearly separate from the paper itself and run only by subscribers, even though its content can be read by the public. More specifically, the *Mediapart* club is a small society which, if not secret, is at least privileged, and allows the subscribers who wish to do so to 'participate' (not only by posting opinions but also their own content), to have access to reading or writing 'blogs', and even to organise the drafting of special 'Editions'. When compared with the Club, the section of the paper reserved for professional journalists appears as an area that is even more privileged and restricted (Canu and Datchary 2010). The name *Mediapart* is a good interpretation of the paper's concern to engage readers in an exciting '*Media*-centred *part*icipation' experience (Ibid., my emphasis). However, the same name also has the inseparable connotation of the idea of a 'media apart', with the double meaning of an atypical paper but also a private paper, a medium made up of private conversations, exclusive content, and discussions, and each of which are therefore as exciting as the other because of their exclusivity and because they are shared amongst the restricted circles of subscribers and journalists.

Concerned to find a new economic model that might guarantee their survival, the old traditional papers for their part offer variants of the same strategy. Perhaps with the exception of *Le Canard Enchaîné* (literally, 'The Chained Duck', a leading satirical newspaper, whose website is more a refusal to be a website![11]), they generally combine a website with more or less restricted but free access on the one hand with the sale of conventional paper copies on the other, not only at the risk of the partial cannibalisation of the two forms of publication or their profitability, but also in the hope that the internet will provide a display window for, and a step towards, the purchase of (and ideally subscription to) conventional or online content. For example, the *Le Figaro* website offers a wide selection of articles online but also takes the opportunity to sell subscription forms and to experiment with new ways of connecting with the paper issue (see below). On the *Libération* and *Le Monde* websites, online articles (which are open to all) co-exist with others which are reserved for their subscribers (identified by a white cross in an orange rectangle for the former and by a golden 'subscribers' edition' tab for the latter), in the hope that frequenting one will arouse an interest in the other. The *Le Monde* website completes this common strategy with an intermediate solution consisting of offering two versions of the same article: a free one which is reduced to the essential elements, and the full one which you can obtain by referring to a message which reads: 'Read the full article [hyperlink] by [writer X] in the

Subscribers area or in *Le Monde* dated [date] available on news stands on [same date] from 2 pm'.

However, taken together, all these options are only hesitant variations, from one paper to another but also within the same paper over time – of one and the same teasing logic – consisting in giving partial access to information and in dazzling readers with the advantages possessed by the elected, the happy few, and the privileged readers who have access to the full articles. This technique relies on two principal devices. The first consists in playing with the sequential scheduling of information. This means 'distilling' the 'news', in the sense of scriptural alchemy, and revealing it progressively, moreover without it being necessary to make hypotheses concerning a strategic withholding and a planned revelation of the available information, given that the format of the press itself, by definition (at least until the appearance of the internet) cannot but present information in a limited way, sequentially, bit by bit. Indeed, when we talk about leaks, we would be wrong to think that this is a one-way operation, that the only effort to be made is to open the breach: as leaks are made public, access to information is often tightened; as in a good hydraulic system, this therefore means 'increasing the pressure'. This is used to maximum effect by *Mediapart*, which, since the summer of 2010, seems to have deliberately favoured the coverage of 'affairs' (for example, the Bettencourt affair, but also the Karachi affair, the Mediator affair,[12] and more), and the restrictions on their accessibility. The second journalistic teasing technique consists of ensuring that access to information is made more difficult through the creation of an 'à la carte' press, which lies somewhere between being free and subscription-based, and follows the logic of concentric circles, in which access is granted not only to information but also to a group, to a coterie, and a privileged caste, akin to the Harvard final clubs (Grousset-Charrière 2010) or to the strata which distinguish subscribers to airline frequent-flying programmes according to their air miles (Kjellberg 2010). Implementing this kind of system involves organising a 'courtyard market', as if Bluebeard had targeted not a single woman but groups of women, for example by organising a visit similar to the contemporary 'private sale'. This strategy, resembling the so-called 'shelf talkers' in supermarkets, charged with signalling the discounts made available to a shop's loyalty card holders, involves assuring members of their privileges as much as it does demonstrating to non-members the cost of remaining on the outside, and therefore, inversely, what they can gain by signing up (Cochoy 2007b). Here, amongst all the conceivable motives for action, curiosity is supported by jealousy, even vanity and a certain gregariousness, by arousing a concern for 'being one of them', to 'not feeling like a second class citizen', and for 'being in the know'.

If the first force of journalistic curiosity consists in renewing the art of teasing, the second consists in practising a twofold rapprochement. The first operates in space ('closer'), by allowing scattered and distant readers to enjoy the impression that they are 'as close as possible to events'; the second, extends into diachrony, by offering each person the possibility of 'living in the moment', and of 'following the present'. The power of this double reconciliation – this game of intimacy and reality – has increased significantly in recent years, not only, as we have seen, with the possibility of readers entering into the very heart of journalistic production, in the numerous blogs, in collaborative articles, and in the interactivity in the form of posted comments (Canu and Datchary 2010), but also through the promotion of new ways of ensuring continuous and immediate access to information, with the development of online 'chat', the continuous posting of dispatches, tweets, RSS feeds, among others; in short, the flood of all these various exciting pieces of news, which are not there because we seek them out, but paradoxically because they have come to us, and because they give us the impression of having crossed the globe, through serendipity, at the mercy of the twin movements of dispersal (Datchary 2010) and exploration (Auray 2011). Furthermore, certain devices allow these two forces to be combined, by soliciting the participation of the public in topics of the moment, such as, for example, the instant surveys offered daily on the *Le Figaro* website (Fig. 22).

The device is threefold, as the sequence of three illustrations shows. Firstly, 'I' (the internet user looking at the screen) am asked to give my thoughts on a matter of opinion – for example: 'Are you in favour of banning the burqa in public areas?' It appears as though it were less a matter of my own curiosity as a reader (I of course have, or believe I have,[13] my own beliefs on the proposal, and would not therefore a priori be curious about myself) and more the pollster's, who is trying to probe the soul of the population. However, between the question and the

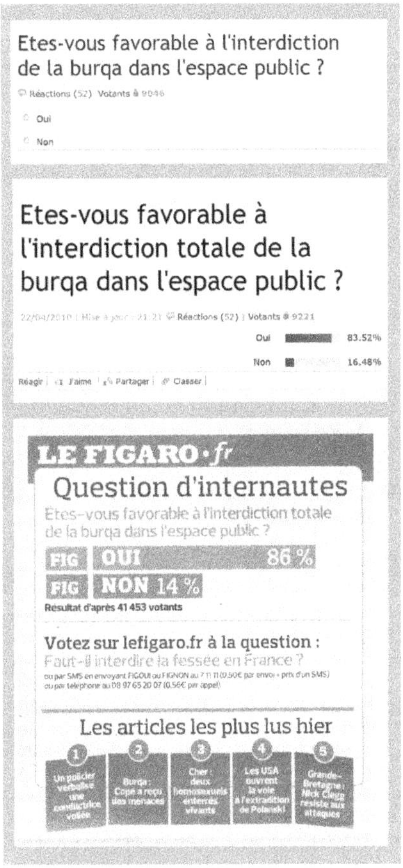
Etes-vous favorable à l'interdiction de la burqa dans l'espace public ?
Réactions (52) Votants à 9046
Oui
Non
Etes-vous favorable à l'interdiction totale de la burqa dans l'espace public ?
Réactions (52) | Votants à 9221
Oui 83.52%
Non 16.48%
Réagir | J'aime | Partager | Classer
LE FIGARO·fr
Question d'internautes
Etes-vous favorable à l'interdiction totale de la burqa dans l'espace public ?
FIG OUI 86 %
FIG NON 14 %
Résultat d'après 41 453 votants
Votez sur lefigaro.fr à la question :
Faut-il interdire la fessée en France ?
Les articles les plus lus hier
1
2
3
4
5
Les USA ouvrent la voie à l'extradition de Polanski

FIG. 22. *Le Figaro.fr* and *Le Figaro*: Are you in favour of the total ban on the burqa? (22 and 23 April 2010)

binary 'yes/no' alternative that I am offered, two separate elements intervene which change the situation: I learn that during the very instant it takes me to peruse the question, 52 people have already responded, while 9,046 have already voted. Thanks to these instantaneous indicators, as the potential 9,047th voter, I understand that in facing my screen and by clicking on either answer I will not only be able to generously share how I feel (an altruism which I, and others like me, often baulk at with conventional surveys), but above all, I will also instantly know the total breakdown of all the opinions, as well as realising that I will not be able to know where I stand without casting my own vote. This is the force of the device: this survey arouses my curiosity in relation not only to the question asked, but also the answers given. It mobilises a sense of belonging: the desire I have, or which comes to me, to know not only how the answers are distributed, but also where I stand in relation to them. Everything rests on my desire to know whether my personal feeling, which I of course have to formulate blindly and in advance, is on the side of the majority or the minority, which I will discover in the second stage, after clicking:[14] an overwhelming majority of 83.52% of those who voted declared that they were in favour of a total ban of the Islamic veil; only 16.48% were against it. I now finally know which side I am on, or almost: of course, on the one hand, the opinion of participatory internet users on the *Le Figaro* website tells me nothing about the paper's typical readers, and even less about the opinion of French people; but on the other, I have at least learnt where I stand in relation to an impressive group, which, while admittedly anonymous and whose contours are unclear, is nevertheless very much present and significant, comprising all those who have, like me, just voted. Furthermore, I am more inclined to connect with them as a series of icons allows me to 'post' comments ('React'), to show my enthusiasm ('Like'), to circulate the information ('Share'), and so on.

The device does not stop there: the next day, in the daily paper version, the full result of the previous day's Internet survey is published. The figures are roughly the same, with 86% of people in favour against 14% who are reluctant for the veil to be banned. However, the final tally of respondents has greatly increased; in the end 41,453 curious people took part: the survey's total lack of representativeness has its counterpart in the highly unusual quantity of opinions that were registered in comparison with conventional surveys, which generally only involve a thousand people (due to the law of averages according to which this sample size is sufficient to obtain sufficiently reliable results, with a margin of error of a few percentage points). What is even more interesting is that the insert finishes with two opposing elements. The previous day's results have barely been announced when the new day's question is asked: 'Should smacking be banned in France?', as serious a question as the previous one, and which one can immediately answer by returning to the website. Or why not express your opinion by other means and give in to the sadomasochistic use of premium-rate numbers (another form of 'smacking' which could perhaps benefit from being banned given the cost!), or vote by text message (for 50 Euro cents) or, worse, by telephone (56 cents). Conversely, the box ends with a retrospective ranking of 'yesterday's most-read articles', thus giving an idea of the issues that interest the participatory internet users of the *Le Figaro* website: in first place, the fine given to a veiled female driver, which was in the news and provoked the previous day's survey; this was closely followed by the threats aimed at the President of the Union for a Popular Movement (UMP) party (Jean-François Copé), after he proposed the ban on the burqa to the National Assembly; then a different story ('two homosexuals buried alive' in Cher); an American decision paving the way for the extradition of the director Roman Polanski, under house arrest in Switzerland for a historical rape charge, and finally, in last place, an item on international politics concerning the attitude of the Liberal Democrat (LDP) candidate in the elections to the House of Commons.

This last detour via England, as fortuitous as it is unexpected, sets us on the right road: it reminds us, by chance, that we should be directing our gaze across the Channel. In order to gain a better understanding of the question of the feedback between the interactive *Le Figaro* survey and the daily paper version, I intend in fact to draw a parallel between this device and an installation created by the British sociologist, Andrew Barry, and the artist Lucy Kimbell, in the context of the major exhibition 'Making Things Public', organised by Bruno Latour and Pieter Weibel at the German contemporary art centre (ZKM) in

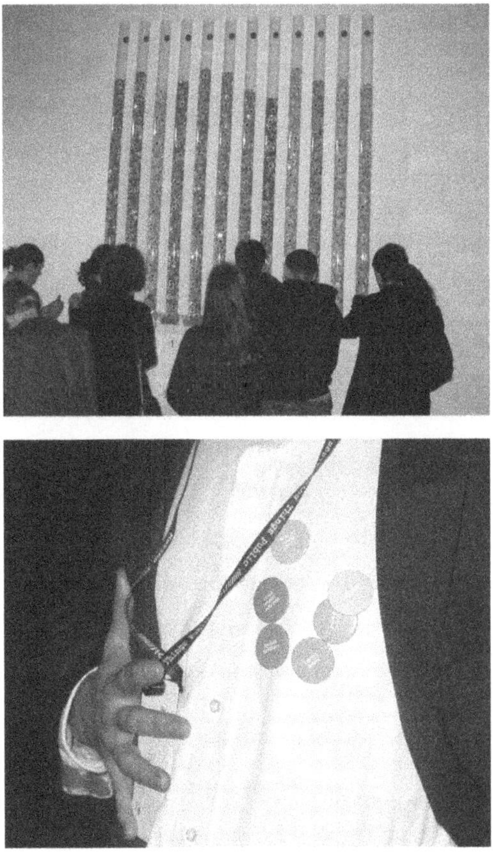

FIG. 23. Making Things Public, ZKM

Karlsruhe in 2005. The theme of this exhibition consisted in showing that there are a thousand different ways of assembling and bringing to life a public, other than those involving conventional political institutions, that include laboratories, supermarkets, financial trading screens, environmental controversies, and others (Latour and Weibel 2005). Among the various installations designed to address this proposal, the one devised by Barry and Kimbell possessed an elegance, a simplicity, and a rare efficacy (Barry and Kimbell 2005).

The two photographs make it possible to understand the function and intention of the device. In the top image, we see a series of twelve transparent tubes containing different coloured badges. Each colour, and therefore each tube, corresponds to the endorsement of a particular civic gesture. For example: 'I recycled', 'I said what I believe', 'I used public services', and so on, with each statement printed on the badges. Visitors to the exhibition were invited to choose those badges which corresponded to activities that they had recently carried out, and to pin these badges to their clothing. The immediate and participatory engagement with the work allowed visitors to break down the anonymity of the crowd to some extent, thus promoting an exercise in reciprocal curiosity – by consulting each other's badges between themselves, each person was now able to access each other person's civic identity and the degree of engagement (see the bottom picture). It also offered people the possibility of obtaining an instant measure of the distribution of the different endorsements among visitors by consulting the levels of badges in the different tubes (see the top picture).

The interactive *Le Figaro* survey and Barry and Kimbell's installation work in largely the same way. Both of them aim to measure a public, but above all, to create that public and to bring it to life. Here we find the mechanism that is so well described by Gabriel Tarde, who relates the existence of a public to the establishment of a physical or mental relationship among its members, and thus emphasises the role of curiosity towards others in a curiosity about the state of the world:

> We have dealt with the psychology of crowds; we still have to deal with the psychology of the public, as understood in this other sense, namely that of a purely spiritual group, a scattering of physically separate individuals whose

> cohesion is entirely mental. [...] The reader is generally unaware that they are being subjected to this persuasive, almost irresistible influence of the newspaper that he usually reads. As for the journalist, he will be more aware of his obligation towards his public, whose nature and tastes he never forgets. The reader is even less aware: he has absolutely no idea of the influence exerted over him by the mass of other readers. It is, nonetheless, undeniable. It affects both his curiosity, which becomes the more intense if he knows, or believes it to be, shared by a broader or more select public; and in his judgement, which strives to agree with that of the majority or of the elite, depending on the issue at hand. I open a newspaper that I believe is from that day, and I avidly read some news; then I notice that the issue is a month old, or a day old, and it immediately ceases to interest me. Where does this sudden disgust come from? Have the facts lost anything of their intrinsic interest? No, but we tell ourselves that we are the only person reading them, and that's enough. This therefore proves that our lively curiosity holds on to the unconscious illusion that our feeling was shared by a large number of minds. A paper from the day before or the day before that, when compared with today's paper, is like a speech read out in your house compared with a speech heard in the middle of a huge crowd (Tarde 2006).

Tarde tells us that each person is accordingly more curious about the world when they know that others are too. Each one of us only gives value and meaning to objects that allow us to relate to others through the same shared experience: whether it is in Tarde's example of reading the daily newspaper, or in participating in the instant survey on the press website, or in the experience of Barry and Kimbell's installation. What is new is that newspapers seize reflexively upon the social curiosity that is discreetly attached to the reading of a newspaper in order to animate their public, to arouse the public debate that is their profession to inform, and thus to position their publications more effectively.[15] We therefore have a better understanding of how significant the difference is between the classic survey and the interactive survey mentioned above – in one case a limited but representative sample, in the other a large but unrepresentative population. We would be wrong to criticise the interactive survey for its low level of representativeness, which may mask the opinion of a more significant population, but in which the law of large numbers shows little interest. The objectives of the two tools are quite different. In contrast to the ordinary survey, the participatory survey is intended less to measure current opinion and more to stimulate public participation: the device strives both to encourage circulation between the different versions of the paper and to constitute the public required for this circulation. The idea is that of a catharsis, a setting in motion, of gathering everyone around an issue which draws people out of their isolation in order to enrol them in a collective experience.

However, and once again, the orientation of this experience varies according to substance and form. Comparing the newspaper and the installation is enlightening. In Barry and Kimbell's installation, the range of the choice appears to be very broad, as there are no less than twelve options, but one may also choose to make multiple choices which are not mutually exclusive. However, upon closer inspection it becomes obvious that the choices being offered all, without exception, derive from the affirmation of a single inclination: one that is virtuous, public, and civic. In the same way that our motives for action are often communicated to us by external sources, our political choices are here narrowly framed as a list of actions which is, if not without a loophole – abstention is of course possible – then at least without an alternative. The messages which can be displayed are: 'I used public services' (salmon pink), 'I kept myself informed' (red), 'I bought ethical products' (orange), 'I supported a political organisation' (yellow), 'I protested' (green), 'I raised issues' (blue), 'I recycled' (blue), 'I signed a petition' (pink), 'I obeyed the law' (purple), 'I said what I believe' (grey), and so on. All things considered, Bluebeard's citizen wives of this installation are invited to wear the colours of a rather monochromatic rainbow, if I may risk using this oxymoron as a final nod to the subject of my book: the expression (or rather the implementation) of personal motives functions here as the projection of a discreet but genuine social normativity.

The use of the *Le Figaro* participatory survey works according to a completely different register, one midway between public and political issues and more private and differentiated practices. The questions asked are of a very particular type – here are some examples: 'Should the Catholic Church authorise the marriage of priests?' (11 March 2010); 'Should smacking be banned in France?' (12 March 2010); 'Are you in favour of a police presence in schools?' (6 May 2010), among others. These questions are usually set against a backdrop of events which are likely to generate public attention and lead to the voicing of their convictions: paedophilia scandals in the Catholic Church, the arrest of a veiled woman, incidents of violence in schools, and the like. The participatory survey calls forth events and issues which challenge the collective conscience or, more precisely, which stir up a divided conscience. Indeed, this device shows us that appealing to social conscience does not necessarily invoke Durkheim's common and unanimously shared sentiment: on the contrary, it acts to build, mobilise, and oppose binary collectives around the opposing values that are under debate, including public freedoms and secularism (the burqa), religious institutions and sexuality (the marriage of priests), children's rights and educational methods (smacking), the securitisation of schools and the safety of pupils (police in schools), and more. While Barry and Kimbell's installation animated the public, *Le Figaro* 'scolds' its readership in all senses of the word: it generates a clamour; it incites the noise of at best a debate, and, at worst, a fruitless confrontation, carried along by the emotion and passion of the moment, which is hardly conducive to the objectivity and cool-headedness required for the examination of societal issues.

A yet more sophisticated and effective way of arousing public curiosity in the emotion of the moment is offered by the extraordinary device 'CoveritLive', which, when a particularly 'hot' topic arises, allows subscribers to online papers, like *LeMonde.fr*, to experience not only the excitement not just of instantly receiving the influx of dispatches previously reserved for press agencies, but also of interactive participation in the real-time production of this very information. In fact, not only are readers able to continually read the dispatches but they can also 'Send questions or comments' (see bottom of the screen, figure 23), which will, if approved by the moderator, join the flow of dispatches and/or motivate journalists who are 'running the live feed' to respond. Both sides are thus able to feed into the furious/curious echo chamber of this public forum, hypnotised by the punctual temporality of the instant, and to enrich it by including images, videos, tweets, and hyperlinks (including to instant surveys, even if *LeMonde.fr* itself does not support this option) in the 'CoveritLive' dispatches.

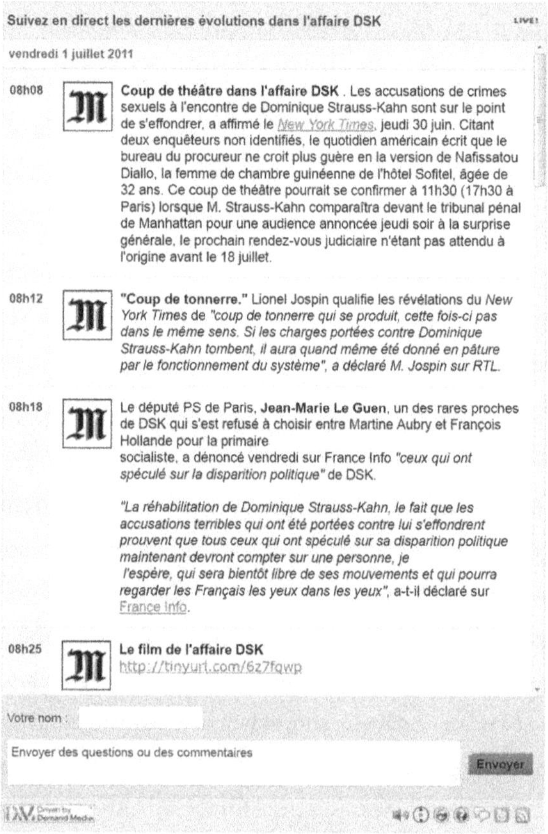

Suivez en direct les dernières évolutions dans l'affaire DSK LIVE!

vendredi 1 juillet 2011

08h08 **Coup de théâtre dans l'affaire DSK** . Les accusations de crimes sexuels à l'encontre de Dominique Strauss-Kahn sont sur le point de s'effondrer, a affirmé le *New York Times*, jeudi 30 juin. Citant deux enquêteurs non identifiés, le quotidien américain écrit que le bureau du procureur ne croit plus guère en la version de Nafissatou Diallo, la femme de chambre guinéenne de l'hôtel Sofitel, âgée de 32 ans. Ce coup de théâtre pourrait se confirmer à 11h30 (17h30 à Paris) lorsque M. Strauss-Kahn comparaîtra devant le tribunal pénal de Manhattan pour une audience annoncée jeudi soir à la surprise générale, le prochain rendez-vous judiciaire n'étant pas attendu à l'origine avant le 18 juillet.

08h12 **"Coup de tonnerre."** Lionel Jospin qualifie les révélations du *New York Times* de *"coup de tonnerre qui se produit, cette fois-ci pas dans le même sens. Si les charges portées contre Dominique Strauss-Kahn tombent, il aura quand même été donné en pâture par le fonctionnement du système"*, a déclaré M. Jospin sur RTL.

08h18 Le député PS de Paris, **Jean-Marie Le Guen**, un des rares proches de DSK qui s'est refusé à choisir entre Martine Aubry et François Hollande pour la primaire socialiste, a dénoncé vendredi sur France Info *"ceux qui ont spéculé sur la disparition politique"* de DSK.

"La réhabilitation de Dominique Strauss-Kahn, le fait que les accusations terribles qui ont été portées contre lui s'effondrent prouvent que tous ceux qui ont spéculé sur sa disparition politique maintenant devront compter sur une personne, je l'espère, qui sera bientôt libre de ses mouvements et qui pourra regarder les Français les yeux dans les yeux", a-t-il déclaré sur France Info.

08h25 **Le film de l'affaire DSK**
http://tinyurl.com/6z7fqwp

Votre nom :

Envoyer des questions ou des commentaires

Envoyer

FIG. 24. *LeMonde.fr* and *CoveritLive*, 1 July 2011

And after the first Fall comes another – or a redemption, as in the last example? The lack of perspective makes you giddy! – a double fall, in fact: on the one hand, with the press, we encounter once again the original sin of the Bible which marked the beginning of this book, as newspapers make a profession out of playing with the sin of curiosity; on the other hand, the democratic hope borne by the press risks falling back at any moment into the commercial quagmire, especially when, in a spectacular act of regression, the press reverses the course of history and abandons its hard-won status as a display window to return to the initial keyhole phase and to a form of curiosity as vain as it is voyeuristic – the 'lusty gaze' that was denounced by Saint Augustine. It is, of course, with the 'celebrity' press that this regression reaches its peak.

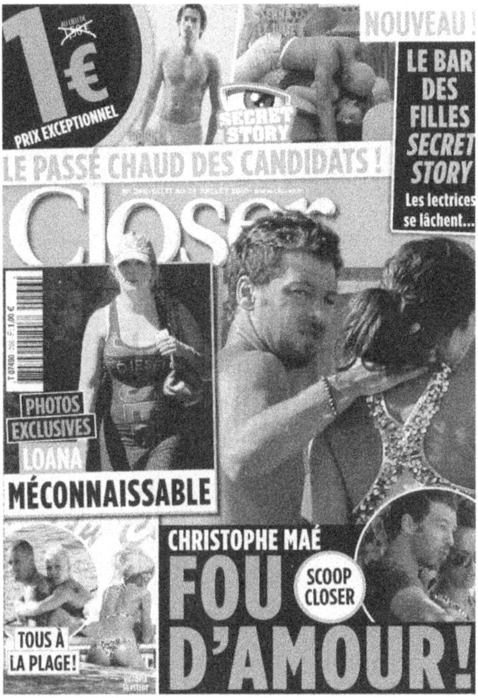

FIG. 25. *Closer*, no. 266, 17–23 July 2010

The sensationalist magazine is, indisputably, a 'people press' and a 'peep-hole press'. As a people press, it is a press that offers the public the chance to satisfy its curiosity about celebrities (people); but as a 'peep-hole press' – literally, a press that 'leers' through the keyhole! – it is a press whose intention is to appear as the only means of satisfying this curiosity. In order to penetrate the lives of celebrities, you have to go through the keyhole of the speciality magazine. The work of the locksmith here usually takes a plural form. As suggested by *Closer*'s graphics, with no fewer than four circles designed to resemble the viewfinder of a camera – one for the price, one for the '*Closer* scoop', two for photographs taken with a telephoto lens – the covers of magazines like this take on the appearance of an opaque rectangular door covered with keyholes, each of which is designed to show us the point of view of the paparazzi lying in wait to snatch these images and which give us glimpses of what might be seen on the other side of the door, inside the magazine, if we are prepared to pay the price (*Closer* offers an 'exceptional' price: with the reduction from €1.50 to €1, they have given us a saving of 50%!).[16] The approach of *professional voyeurism* is explicitly asserted: on the one hand, the terms 'scoop' and 'exclusive photos' suggest the expert monopoly that we have to buy into in order to access the privacy of the stars; on the other, the proliferation of photos, bodies, names, and revelations ('the steamy past of the candidates'; 'Christophe Maé [a French pop star]: madly in love', etc.) demonstrate the magazine's skill with using blatant voyeurism. The latter is also reinforced by a three-way act of mirroring: on the left, we learn that Loana, a former icon of public exhibitionism,[17] is 'unrecognisable'; at the top, we are promised 'news' on the 'steamy past of the candidates' of 'Secret Story' – the reality television programme of the moment, with the all-seeing eye as its logo, that draws on the Big Brother format, also used in so many other countries. Finally, with '(female) readers let themselves go', the magazine's readers themselves are carried away into the endless game of mirrors of 'reality TV' voyeurism, in this game of 'democratising the gaze' and identification that Jean-Claude Kaufmann (2001) and Dominique Mehl (2003) recognised so well. This game is repeated diagonally, in the bottom left of the cover, with the expression 'everyone at the beach', whose delicious ambiguity ('everyone', meaning really everyone, or really 'all the stars') seems to invite the reader on holiday with celebrities – here, with the Swedish model and sex symbol, Victoria Silvstedt.

The people press is a sensationalist press, in the literal double sense of the sensational scoop, and of the sensation of emotion: this form of the press promises to open up a dizzying gap between public and private spheres. The public figures that it displays to us, or rather that it proposes we see through it, are publics, but that which interests this press and its readers is the anecdote, and, above all, the intimate: we follow affairs of the heart and the body, thus inaugurating a new deviation from the Durkheimian concept of the collective conscience: the source of the thrill here is neither the civic goodwill of the ZKM installation, nor the divided social convictions of the *Le Figaro* participatory survey, but the strong and defined states of a public pleasure in private intimacy. The people/peep-hole press has taken the baton from the Sartrian keyhole, but this time without any great risk of it being caught, unless perhaps it falls into the hands of a public that is not its own, and this public reads it in places that are unsuitable, beyond the secret closed doors of its home. This press undertakes the commodification of the keyhole to an extreme degree: by allowing a crowd to simultaneously observe the same scene, it manages to transfer to the keyhole that which provided the display window with its exclusive advantage.

This type of approach appears to be becoming increasingly important, not only in the people press and on reality TV (as has just been examined), but also, and above all, on the internet, on Facebook, blogs, dating websites... in short, these various curiosity devices that bring together the absolute privacy (at least, up until the advent of smartphones) of the domestic world with the absolutely public nature of a public form of media. With these new tools, millions of people can, in the same instant, share the same keyhole; millions of others can view/be offered to be viewed by others in ways that are more or less voluntary or complacent: the voyeurism of some is completed by the forced or consenting exhibitionism of others, and vice versa, thus clouding the definition of and perceptions about 'privacy' (Kessous and Rey 2009). Beyond the curiosity of a *libido-sciendi*, or of the commercial or investigative exploration of the press, today's subjects, thanks to modern media, are able to experience an anecdotal, often playful curiosity, which includes a wealth of identity constructions (Kaufmann 2001), but which may also occasionally produce tragic effects. This was demonstrated to us in the sad story of Tyler Clementi, a homosexual American student who, after discovering that his lovemaking had been filmed without his knowledge and put online by two of his 'friends', ended his life by jumping from a bridge (Foderaro 2010). In a curious reversal of the fairy tale, in this news story it is as if it was not *Bluebeard* and his retrograde morals, but his wife herself, or rather his wife's curiosity, that suddenly became the guilty party responsible for a death (which is also her own, in return).

From *The Saturday Evening Post* to *Closer*, and by passing through *Le Figaro* and *Mediapart*, we have thus examined the ambiguous facets of curiosity. This motive oscillates between rise and fall, between a device for knowledge and a market device for distraction, and between a critical force for civic awareness and a tool for voyeurism which is at best shallow, at worst fatal. On the one hand, curiosity is rich in emancipation: it is curiosity that keeps our mind open to the world, which stimulates us to look around ourselves, to not be taken in, to think outside the box – insofar as showing oneself to be curious, authorising serendipity, being open not only to that which we seek but also to that which we encounter, is perhaps the only way of making discoveries that are worthy of the name. On the other hand, and as Heidegger reminds us, in reviving the Augustinian tradition (which is explicitly cited), curiosity is rich in distraction, namely, in a form of an inclination that, if it is not guided with an adequate sense of purpose, can veer off at any moment, lose itself, or lose us, to the point where we are paradoxically further from this ('closer') proximity to which it was thought to provide access:

> If liberated curiosity concerns itself with seeing, it is not to understand what is being seen, that is, to access a being for its own sake, but only in order to see. It only seeks the new in order to jump to the new from this new towards the new. So if it goes there in order to concern itself with such a viewing, it is not to seize it and to be in the truthful position of knowing, but out of a concern for the possibilities of abandoning oneself to the world. Curiosity is also characterized by a specific *incapacity* to *stay* as close as possible. So too does it no longer seek the leisure of the considered stay, but the uneasiness and excitement which the new always gives it, and the incessant changing of the object that it encounters. Because it does not remain, curiosity concerns itself with the constant possibility of *distraction* (Heidegger 2010: 146).

* * *

What, finally, is curiosity worth? Any promise of curiosity is in danger of arousing an immense disappointment: here is a book which, after having begun with the sacred, has lowered itself inexorably towards the profane, at first with the popular tale of *Bluebeard*, then moving to the inventory of market devices, before finally, after a brief leap into the investigative press, finishing in the inconsequentiality and vulgarity of the people press! Here too is a book which, after giving the impression of managing to break free from the moral sanction that has weighed upon curiosity ever since the Church's founding fathers, closes by coming back, through Heidegger, to this very form of sanction. So many pages just to come back to the starting point! More worrying still is that the disastrous disappointments have been rendered multiple. Between the cover and the present conclusive words extends the much more serious disillusionment of the 'false curiosity' that results from something specific being expected and seeing this expectation going unfulfilled. Unmet expectations are always highly frustrating: 'I am furious that I did not find what I was led to expect; that is, neither the surprises that seemed to be promised to me, nor what I would have liked to see'. For example, this book is quite unembarrassed about saying almost nothing about the social effects of technologies of curiosity. It obscures the subject of the digital divide and the noticeably socially discriminatory character of technologies of curiosity; it does not say enough about the strong powers of distraction associated with these technologies, which diverts actors' attention away from more essential social and political issues. These are legitimate and necessary questions;[18] ignoring them exposes the sociologist to the accusation of failing in his (so-called) duty of criticism or metacriticism (Boltanski 2011).[19]

Even worse, the failure to exhibit a 'curiosity about curiosity' confirms the very failure of the book's project. I wanted to show that curiosity is a widespread social inclination. Now, the only tangible data that I was able to collect in relation to this proposal – my enquiry into the use of the Data Matrix – actually goes against my hypothesis, showing that the propensity towards curiosity and/or the efficacy of curiosity devices is particularly rare and delicate. Today's wives of Bluebeard (including 'bearded ladies': the image here also includes individuals of the male sex!) do not necessarily have the keys to open the doors that they are presented with, and, even when they are provided with them, find the doors too heavy, too complicated, and too slow, while they only have a very absent-minded interest in the keyholes that they are offered and the wonders that gleam at them from the door's other side. However, two things merit attention. First, the logic of seduction (even when non-commercial) operates through its lack of restriction, which involves a quite considerable 'power loss'. From this point of view, at least curiosity is less intrusive and more participatory than classical forms of advertising. Above all, curiosity often functions as serendipity, which also applies to this book. Perhaps from this perspective a curiosity about curiosity is nothing more than a pretext: it is one form of curiosity among others, and it should therefore not distract us from all the other curious things that might cross its path.

Has this last promise been fulfilled, however? Has something been discovered between these pages? From the point of view of readers, at least for some of them, a negative response cannot be excluded. Each of these such responses would thus arise from a different source of disappointment, all equally embarrassing to me, given that I made a contract with the reader to which, although you might have missed it, I have been committed throughout. Of course I imagine that I do not need to be accountable to all those who might complain about being thrown off balance by the piling up of references and objects, by the slightly uneven mixture of a sacred text and profane desires, literature and computer games, sociology and issues of the market, economics and commercial devices; in short, by a visit to a junk shop which strongly resembles a new species of curiosity cabinet. These readers can have no complaints, as they were warned in the very first lines: this book is not for them and if they have read it in spite of everything, the fault is theirs! In contrast, I would be inclined to have more regard for those who might instead think that the journey was perhaps less 'baffling' than was announced, either because I mistakenly lured them with the promise of surprises that did not materialise – 'this book, pah', concludes the reader, 'I knew all this!' – or because the demonstration is unconvincing and scattered with mistakes, blunders, omissions, platitudes, and so on. If I have only stated what is already known; if my text has shortcomings, insufficiencies and contains errors, I could by definition not have anticipated these difficulties. Some people might be infuriated that they did not encounter the Dominique Strauss-Kahn (DSK) affair that was nonetheless promised to them on the back cover, except in two brief allusions, moreover reduced to aspects of form rather than of substance: does misplaced curiosity nowadays still deserve to be punished?! A final disappointment of this type may consist in finding that the content of the book is more limited than might have been suggested by the title. After having first entitled this work 'the sociology of curiosity', conforming to the obvious concerns of my disciplinary and institutional foundations, I changed my mind at the last minute, because, to my mind, it deals not just with sociology but also with the philosophy, anthropology, history, psychology, and economics of curiosity, because I thought that an overly narrow disciplinary restriction would not wholly do my project justice, and because it seemed relevant to play reflexively with the economics of surprise, as presented in chapter 4. I nonetheless remain a sociologist, and, even more narrowly, a sociologist of markets, an affiliation that orients my work and undoubtedly curbs my own curiosity more than I would like, something for which readers from other disciplines, or with no particular disciplinary orientation (or those who are more curious than myself) would have every right to reproach me for. I do not therefore know what to say to all these people, except to repeat that disappointment is part of the game and to suggest to them that in having one's disappointment conjured up lies another lesson in curiosity.

All disappointed curiosity is, as we have seen, extremely ambiguous. In *Bluebeard*, the bodies are for his wife a disappointment, but also a punishment; they are the future image of her own fate, her death. But these same bodies are also an exquisitely perverse surprise for the reader;[20] without them, the tale would lose all its charm. In one way or another, disappointed curiosity cannot therefore be disappointing. In the history of curiosity, disappointment is part of the game, and, because it is present, it only renders more beautiful those rare occasions when it is disappointed or thwarted, and more ardent the more innumerable attempts there are to deny it. Indeed, it is the combination of a thousand disappointments and a few rare moments of satisfied – and fruitful – curiosity, which continually spurs us to begin again, to explore the other side of the door – and to move closer in order to move further away.

APPENDIX

BLUEBEARD

THERE WAS ONCE A MAN WHO HAD FINE HOUSES, BOTH IN TOWN AND country, a deal of silver and gold plate, embroidered furniture, and coaches gilded all over with gold. But this man was so unlucky as to have a blue beard, which made him so frightfully ugly that all the women and girls ran away from him.

One of his neighbors, a lady of quality, had two daughters who were perfect beauties. He desired of her one of them in marriage, leaving to her choice which of the two she would bestow on him. Neither of them would have him, and they sent him backwards and forwards from one to the other, not being able to bear the thoughts of marrying a man who had a blue beard. Adding to their disgust and aversion was the fact that he already had been married to several wives, and nobody knew what had become of them.

Bluebeard, to engage their affection, took them, with their mother and three or four ladies of their acquaintance, with other young people of the neighborhood, to one of his country houses, where they stayed a whole week.

The time was filled with parties, hunting, fishing, dancing, mirth, and feasting. Nobody went to bed, but all passed the night in rallying and joking with each other. In short, everything succeeded so well that the youngest daughter began to think that the man's beard was not so very blue after all, and that he was a mighty civil gentleman.

As soon as they returned home, the marriage was concluded. About a month afterwards, Bluebeard told his wife that he was obliged to take a country journey for six weeks at least, about affairs of very great consequence. He desired her to divert herself in his absence, to send for her friends and acquaintances, to take them into the country, if she pleased, and to make good cheer wherever she was.

'Here,' said he, 'are the keys to the two great wardrobes, wherein I have my best furniture. These are to my silver and gold plate, which is not everyday in use. These open my strongboxes, which hold my money, both gold and silver; these my caskets of jewels. And this is the master key to all my apartments. But as for this little one here, it is the key to the closet at the end of the great hall on the ground floor. Open them all; go into each and every one of them, except that little closet, which I forbid you, and forbid it in such a manner that, if you happen to open it, you may expect my just anger and resentment.'

She promised to observe, very exactly, whatever he had ordered. Then he, after having embraced her, got into his coach and proceeded on his journey.

Her neighbors and good friends did not wait to be sent for by the newly married lady. They were impatient to see all the rich furniture of her house, and had not dared to come while her husband was there, because of his blue beard, which frightened them. They ran through all the rooms, closets, and wardrobes, which were all so fine and rich that they seemed to surpass one another.

After that, they went up into the two great rooms, which contained the best and richest furniture. They could not sufficiently admire the number and beauty of the tapestry, beds, couches, cabinets, stands, tables, and looking glasses, in which you might see yourself from head to foot; some of them were framed with glass, others with silver, plain and gilded, the finest and most magnificent that they had ever seen.

They ceased not to extol and envy the happiness of their friend, who in the meantime in no way diverted herself in looking upon all these rich things, because of the impatience she had to go and open the closet on the ground floor. She was so much pressed by her curiosity that, without considering that it was very uncivil for her to leave her company, she went down a little back staircase, and with such excessive haste that she nearly fell and broke her neck.

Having come to the closet door, she made a stop for some time, thinking about her husband's orders, and considering what unhappiness might attend her if she was disobedient; but the temptation was so strong that she could not overcome it. She then took the little key, and opened it, trembling. At first she saw nothing, because the windows were shut. After some moments she began to perceive that the floor was covered with congealed blood, in which the bodies of several dead women were reflected, ranged against the walls. (These were all the wives whom Bluebeard had married and murdered, one after another.) She thought she should have died for fear, and the key, which she pulled out of the lock, fell out of her hand.

After having somewhat recovered her surprise, she picked up the key, locked the door, and went upstairs into her chamber to recover; but she could not, so much was she frightened. Having observed that the key to the closet was stained with blood, she tried two or three times to wipe it off; but the blood would not come out; in vain did she wash it, and even rub it with soap and sand. The blood still remained, for the key was magical and she could never make it quite clean; when the blood was gone off from one side, it came again on the other.

Bluebeard returned from his journey the same evening, saying that he had received letters upon the road, informing him that the affair he went about had concluded to his advantage. His wife did all she could to convince him that she was extremely happy about his speedy return.

The next morning he asked her for the keys, which she gave him, but with such a trembling hand that he easily guessed what had happened.

'What!' said he, 'is not the key of my closet among the rest?'

'I must,' said she, 'have left it upstairs upon the table.'

'Fail not,' said Bluebeard, 'to bring it to me at once.'

After several goings backwards and forwards, she was forced to bring him the key. Bluebeard, having very attentively considered it, said to his wife, 'Why is there blood on the key?'

'I do not know,' cried the poor woman, paler than death.

'You do not know!' replied Bluebeard. 'I very well know. You went into the closet, did you not? Very well, madam; you shall go back, and take your place among the ladies you saw there.'

Upon this she threw herself at her husband's feet, and begged his pardon with all the signs of a true repentance, vowing that she would never more be disobedient. She would have melted a rock, so beautiful and sorrowful was she; but Bluebeard had a heart harder than any rock!

'You must die, madam,' said he, 'at once.'

'Since I must die,' answered she (looking upon him with her eyes all bathed in tears), 'give me some little time to say my prayers.'

'I give you,' replied Bluebeard, 'half a quarter of an hour, but not one moment more.'

When she was alone she called out to her sister, and said to her, 'Sister Anne' (for that was her name), 'go up, I beg you, to the top of the tower, and look if my brothers are not coming. They promised me that they would come today, and if you see them, give them a sign to make haste.'

Her sister Anne went up to the top of the tower, and the poor afflicted wife cried out from time to time, 'Anne, sister Anne, do you see anyone coming?'

And sister Anne said, 'I see nothing but a cloud of dust in the sun, and the grass greening.'

In the meanwhile Bluebeard, holding a great saber in his hand, cried out as loud as he could bawl to his wife, 'Come down instantly, or I shall come up to you.'

'One moment longer, if you please,' said his wife; and then she cried out very softly, 'Anne, sister Anne, do you see anybody coming?'

And sister Anne answered, 'I see nothing but a cloud of dust in the sun, and the green grass.'

'Come down quickly,' cried Bluebeard, 'or I will come up to you.'

'I am coming,' answered his wife; and then she cried, 'Anne, sister Anne, do you not see anyone coming?'

'I see,' replied sister Anne, 'a great cloud of dust approaching us.'

'Are they my brothers?'

'Alas, no, my dear sister, I see a flock of sheep.'

'Will you not come down?' cried Bluebeard.

'One moment longer,' said his wife, and then she cried out, 'Anne, sister Anne, do you see nobody coming?'

'I see,' said she, 'two horsemen, but they are still a great way off.'

'God be praised,' replied the poor wife joyfully. 'They are my brothers. I will make them a sign, as well as I can for them to make haste.'

Then Bluebeard bawled out so loud that he made the whole house tremble. The distressed wife came down, and threw herself at his feet, all in tears, with her hair about her shoulders.

'This means nothing,' said Bluebeard. 'You must die!' Then, taking hold of her hair with one hand, and lifting up the sword with the other, he prepared to strike off her head. The poor lady, turning about to him, and looking at him with dying eyes, desired him to afford her one little moment to recollect herself.

'No, no,' said he, 'commend yourself to God,' and was just ready to strike.

At this very instant there was such a loud knocking at the gate that Bluebeard made a sudden stop. The gate was opened, and two horsemen entered. Drawing their swords, they ran directly to Bluebeard. He knew them to be his wife's brothers, one a dragoon, the other a musketeer; so that he ran away immediately to save himself; but the two brothers pursued and overtook him before he could get to the steps of the porch. Then they ran their swords through his body and left him dead. The poor wife was almost as dead as her husband, and had not strength enough to rise and welcome her brothers.

Bluebeard had no heirs, and so his wife became mistress of all his estate. She made use of one part of it to marry her sister Anne to a young gentleman who had loved her a long while; another part to buy captains' commissions for her brothers; and the rest to marry herself to a very worthy gentleman, who made her forget the ill time she had passed with Bluebeard.

Moral: curiosity, in spite of its appeal, often leads to deep regret. A thousand examples appear each day. To the displeasure of many a maiden, its enjoyment is short lived. Once satisfied, it ceases to exist, and always costs dearly.

Another moral: apply logic to this grim story, and you will ascertain that it took place many years ago. No husband of our age would be so terrible as to demand the impossible of his wife, nor would he be such a jealous malcontent; he is meek and mild with his wife. For, whatever the color of her husband's beard, the wife of today will let him know who the master is.

C. PERRAULT

NOTES

TEASER

1 This book is part of a longer collective work which I coordinated a few years ago on the 'captation of the public' (Cochoy 2007). 'Captation' is a French word without an exact English equivalent; its meaning corresponds more to 'seducing' than 'capturing', given that it refers to an operation aimed at attracting a public without forcing it (Cochoy 2007).

2 At the risk of a lack of erudition, which is always possible given how difficult it is to prove the inexistence of something, I was unable to identify any general sociological study which deals specifically with this subject (perhaps with the exception of Merton and Barber's remarkable survey (2004) on the related notion of serendipity; see below). Conversely, and as we shall see later, curiosity has been given repeated, and sometimes sustained, attention in history, philosophy, literary criticism, psychology, and psychoanalysis. It is only recently that curiosity appears to have made a notable appearance within sociology with, for example, the works by Beaudoin et al. (2001) on searching for information on the internet, the beautiful study by Nicolas Auray (2006) on exploration practices, or, more recently, research on the attention economy (Goldhaber 1997; Boullier 2009; Kessous et al. 2010). We will see that there is nothing surprising about this 'appearance', given that what all these works have in common is an interest in new technologies. In other words, their interest is in devices whose particular aim is to renew the relationship between people and the world, and which, for this reason, place curiosity at the centre (see fourth and final chapters). Rather than inflicting a long literature review on my readers in the very first pages, and thus risking losing their patience and them abandoning their reading even before being able to discover curiosity in action, I have decided to present and draw on the subjects and references to which I have just alluded throughout the text, where I believe they might best support the thread of my argument.

3 I have given this word the double meaning of logic of movement and logic of action – mobility as movement and mobility as what verges on a motive: a motive for action. I will go into this in further detail in the conclusion, once we have made sufficient progress.

4 This book uses a version of *Bluebeard* edited and made available online by D. L. Ashliman <http://www.pitt.edu/~dash/type0312.html#perrault> [accessed 16 June 2015], with some amendments. I am very grateful for his permission to reproduce this here. This text in turn is based on a version translated by Andrew Lang in *The Blue Fairy Book* (1889). It should also be noted that Ashliman translated and reintroduced the two morals at the end of the tale, which were excluded from Lang's version.
5 For those readers wanting to take the time to read the rest of the tale rather than the summary that follows, I have included the complete version in an appendix.

1. FROM EVE TO BLUEBEARD: THE DIFFICULT SECULARISATION OF CURIOSITY

1 For a complete review of the oral versions that preceded the tale and for an analysis of the changes introduced by Perrault, see Soriano (1977). It must be noted that despite his impressive erudition, Marc Soriano completely forgets the structural link that unites *Bluebeard* and the Bible (as well as other mythological antecedents). It is just as surprising to read that, according to Soriano, 'the concept of "curiosity" weakens the vastly broader topic of the forbidden room' (Ibid: 165), given that we know both the anthropological and religious importance of this motif, and its preeminent role in the tale's structure, in terms of both form and content (see the following analyses).
2 Genesis 3:1–13.
3 Lucas Cranach the Elder, *Adam and Eve* (1526), oil on wood, 117 x 80.5 cm (detail), Courtauld Institute of Art Gallery, London.
4 Gustave Doré and Charles Perrault, *The Fairy Tales of Charles Perrault – Drawings* (1876), Paris, J. Hetzel and Co.
5 Let us not forget that Pandora was the first woman, created on the orders of Zeus, who specifically wanted to get his revenge on man because Prometheus had stolen fire from the gods. Pandora – whose name means 'all gifted' – was sculpted by Vulcan from a mixture of earth and water; Minerva taught her the domestic arts and clothed her; Venus gave her the power of seduction; Mercury inspired her with the art of lying, seductive discourse, and perfidiousness. Zeus tasked Mercury with introducing Pandora to Epimetheus, Prometheus's brother, who was seduced by her and then married her, despite the promise he had made to Prometheus that he would refuse all gifts from Zeus. Pandora brought with her a mysterious box which she had been forbidden to open; as we know, Pandora disobeyed this order, freeing all the evils of mankind – old age, illness, war – with the exception of hope, which lay at the bottom of the box (according to Hesiod, *Works and Days*).
6 Eros, the god of love, who fell in love with the beautiful Psyche, asked her never to try to discover who he was, and concealed his identity in the darkness of the room in

which he came to embrace her every night. However, Psyche's two sisters, mad with jealousy, made her believe that her husband was in fact a horrible monster who would end up devouring her. Poor Psyche, consumed by anxiety, ended up lighting an oil lamp to illuminate the room where her lover was sleeping: she then discovered the most beautiful man she had ever seen. But a drop of burning oil fell on Eros's body, who immediately awoke and fled, furious that Psyche had broken her promise.

7 On Lady Godiva, see chapter 3, note 5.

8 'The Lady of Shalott', a Romantic poem by the English nineteenth-century writer Alfred Tennyson, tells the story of a woman locked up in a castle, isolated on an island in the middle of a river. She is under a curse which forbids her to see the world which stretches out from her window, apart from as an indirect reflection in her mirror. Every day she weaves a magical tapestry, onto which she sews an image of the landscape whose reflection she sees. However, when Lancelot (whom she loves) sings from beneath her window, she cannot resist, and immediately moves forwards to see him, all the while knowing that the curse on her means that she will surely die from allowing herself this simple glance. The mirror suddenly breaks into a thousand pieces. She leaves the castle and takes a boat to join Lancelot's Palace, but dies before reaching it.

9 This particular concept of curiosity served as inspiration for Pascal's famous text on the dangers of 'amusement'.

10 Interestingly, Perrault condemns naive curiosity and says nothing about the morbid form of curiosity, which he activates when condemning its other form!

11 For further clarification on this matter, see the remarkable work by Nicole Jacques-Chaquin on the links between curiosity and demonology (Jacques-Chaquin 1998b).

12 'It is not without just reason that civil laws condemn mathematics so strongly. [...] as God, like the police of Israel judge, issued a very severe ruling against them; that they would be put to death, with their accomplices. But let us imagine it had been allowed amongst men: given that we see that God detests it so, what madness it would be to want to join Christendom, as if we wanted to mix fire and water! And wondrous it is that those from Ephesus, who had given themselves to mad curiosity, after having believed in Jesus-Christ, burnt their books, as Saint Luke recites in the *Acts*. [...] It must even be noted that Saint Luke does not say they were evil or diabolical arts; but he calls them *perierga*, which means frivolous or vain curiosity. What thus is the remedy for obviating such inconveniences? It is that the sobriety recommended by Saint Paul should act like a bridle holding us in pure obedience of God; and to do this, everyone must decide to keep this incalculable treasure of the Gospel in good conscience; as it is certain that the fear of God will act as rampart against all errors. [...] Scholars must give themselves to good and useful study, and not frivolous curiosities, which serve only as silly entertainment. Let great and small, wise men and idiots believe that we are not born to occupy ourselves in useless things, but that the purpose of our exercises must be to edify ourselves and others in the fear of God' (Calvin 1842: 132–134).

13 Incidentally, this point shows that Weber's Protestants are bad Calvinists: if they respected Calvin's word, they would not need to yield to the forms of curiosity involved in searching for signs related to their Election by God!

14 If classification was undertaken, it was secondary, and as Antoine Schnapper (1988: 11) points out very effectively, it was done for artefacts listed in catalogues – it is thanks to this that we know about them: the written description of a collection required a minimal degree of order, although this apparent order was misleading in view of the abundance and proliferation of the items that the cabinets contained. Modern perspectives on the collection came to accentuate this bias by dividing collections, in accordance with contemporary criteria and classifications, both intellectually and physically. This might be, for example, by describing only the works of art and forgetting the rest – all other objects are considered to be less valuable.

15 Museums occupied a pivotal position between the exuberance of cabinets of curiosity and the rigour of taxonomy: 'The paradox of museums lies in their effort to confine knowledge yet simultaneously broaden its parameters. Whereas the ostensibly rigid yoke of authority stabilised the process of collecting nature, the endlessly flexible expression of curiosity adjusted the meaning by constantly finding gaps – unknown details and worlds of speculation – which collectors could fill' (Findlen 1994: 95).

16 The *Encyclopédie* is a famous and ambitious dictionary project edited by Diderot and d'Alembert, and designed to cover the arts and sciences, in keeping with the Enlightenment spirit.

2. BLUEBEARD: TOWARDS THE MARKETISATION OF CURIOSITY

1 Adam claims to have hidden out of fear because he was naked, but perhaps also because he feared God's judgement; he only admits his mistake when pressed with questions, in the tone of 'it wasn't me, it was her!' This is, of course, first the simple effect of being obliged to tell the truth to God, but also, perhaps, the expression of a certain degree of cowardice.

2 The same can be said for the technical paraphernalia that accompanies the character: if the key is the 'fairy', its magic is limited to a very prosaic propensity towards retaining the stain of blood for the sake of intrigue (to bear witness to the mistake but not to change the world); it is a far cry from magic wands, pumpkin carriages, or seven-league boots. Marc Soriano tells us that the very prosaic character of the tale is the result of a very deliberate concern on the part of Perrault, who meticulously tried to rid the popular tale to which *Bluebeard* refers of all of its fairy-tale elements (Soriano 1977: 164).

3 The parallel between the tale and Landru's contemporaries made sense, given that the criminal was given the nickname 'The Bluebeard of Gambais'.

4 Bettelheim is far from being the only psychoanalyst interested in curiosity. This interest is in fact an integral part of the history of psychoanalysis, ever since Freud (1962) linked the desire for knowledge to an earlier experience of childish sexual curiosity. Children are interested in discovering and exploring the genitalia, whether their own or of the opposite sex. In the wake of the master of their manner of thinking, psychiatrists and psychoanalysts have always been interested in curiosity (Winnicott 1953; Dorey 1988; Minard 1995; Collective 1996).

5 Having said that, the anachronistic nature of a contemporary point of view leads us to believe, a little too easily, in the fantastical nature of actual fairy tales and of the creatures which populate them.

6 Let us point out that this analogy did, nonetheless, seduce Marjean Purinton in the context of a study about George Colman's *Bluebeard*, which came after Perrault's (Purinton 2007).

7 See the similarities between both illustrations in Fig. 2: on the left, an authentic cabinet of curiosity mixing, haphazardly, works of art and trivial ornaments, things of value and ordinary objects, medals, shells, paintings, and animals. On the right, the inside of Bluebeard's cabinet (wonderfully interpreted by Gustave Doré) with its spacious receptacles, as richly decorated as they are empty and covered in gold, albeit with a book on the left (perhaps a Bible, as might be suggested by the serpent twisted round a chandelier in the background?). However, the book is only there to bring out the stand on which it rests, and besides, the book's characters have their backs turned.

8 Frans Francken II, *The Cabinet of Rarities*, oil on canvas 74 x 78 cm, Vienna (after 1636), Kunsthistorisches Museum (Inv. N° 1048), <http://www.astronomy2009.it/attach/Content/News/1936/o/2_wunderkammer.jpg>

9 Gustave Doré and Charles Perrault, *Les Contes de Perrault – Dessins* (1876), Paris, J. Hetzel et Cie.

10 The question of the articulations between customary rules of filiation and economic calculation is the subject of a fascinating alternate perspective provided by another famous Perrault tale, *Puss in Boots*. This tale can be read entirely as calling into question the economic effectiveness of birthright, given that in the end the a priori most modest inheritance which is left to the youngest member of the family – the deceased miller's cat – appears to have economic returns that are far greater than the supposedly more considerable assets left to the eldest children to share. Going back to *Bluebeard*, we notice that in the hypothesis which we are examining, birthright would in fact have been inapplicable; given that in the tale, naivety is related to age, imagining two sisters who are equally naive would mean imagining the sisters were twins, and therefore indiscernible in terms of birthright.

11 We can find the same fatal link between forbidden curiosity and the game of mirrors in the 'Lady of Shalott' (see chapter 1, note 8).

12 Of course, self-interest is no more 'natural' than curiosity and can (or must), in order to be effective and to guide action, be itself subject to processes of activation (Hirschman 1977). However, as we have demonstrated, in Bluebeard's time the activation of self-interest started to be based on the actions contained in a series of instances which both frame and extend beyond the sphere of the tale (the growing appeal and availability of consumer goods, and so on). Bluebeard is thus able to consider this disposition as something already existant and operational, and can consequently concentrate on the secondary implementation of curiosity. Note that these dispositions are both 'inside' and 'outside' the actors: just as 'habitus' refers to an external envelope which clothes a person (clothing is the very etymology of the notion (Heran 1987) and to the inner force which 'inhabits him' (if we refer to Bourdieu's theory (1977)), every disposition acts as a resource belonging to the subject, but whose expression relies often on the configuration of the action's context (Lahire 1988).

13 Weariness and curiosity have very strong ties, notably that the first promotes the arousal of the second, as will be presented and explored in greater detail in chapter 4.

14 Here again, as is always the case in stories, it is a question of an important economic motive – that of matching. As I cannot develop the exegesis that this point deserves, I recommend the excellent analysis of the subject by Philippe Steiner (Steiner 2008).

15 At least until halfway through, *Bluebeard* maintains the illusion of a possible choice in her fate, and therefore in the very direction of the tale. This anticipates a literary genre that would later be developed by Raymond Queneau (1967) in the context of the Oulipo. Queneau suggested a story entitled 'A Tale Made Your Way', in which he offered the reader the possibility of putting together their own story through a succession of multiple choices. Nowadays, computing makes this type of literary genre easier to operate: everyone can try this on the website below and will be able to immediately experience the influence that the implementation of a device of pure curiosity is likely to have on every one of us: <http://www.gefilde.de/ashome/denkzettel/0013/queneau.htm> [accessed 9 April 2010].

16 This term is borrowed from the computer game industry, which is very sensitive to the frustration that results from imprisoning players in these linear paths into which literature (by virtue of its very form as a linear, ordered sequence of words which forces the reader to go from the first to the last) has until now condemned them. One of the computer-games universe's greatest achievements is that it invented new ways of scripting works of fiction in which the reader/player now has an infinite number of ways of reaching a specific objective (connoisseurs will recognise the entire evolutionary sequence, ranging from the extremely linear adventures of Lara Croft in

the Tomb Raider saga to missions that can be carried out with almost total freedom, as proposed in the Grand Theft Auto series, to mention just two of the games which have had the greatest impact on the short history of computer games).

17 Although late on we do guess that it was legal business. However, this element only appears for the purposes of the story (to justify Bluebeard's early return at the very moment that his wife has just broken her promise); moreover, the information only stirs up questions instead of answering them: What business? Who is angry with Bluebeard? For what reason? And what if Bluebeard had only invented his trip and the reason for it in order to remain hidden in the vicinity in order to better observe his wife's behaviour?

18 Splitting the view between the outside (the hope of help) and the inside (the threat of Bluebeard) by dividing it between two characters is a real stroke of genius. This method introduces a switching between views, anticipating the use of two cameras during a chase, one to show the fugitive, and the other to show who is chasing him. By segmenting the continuous chase scene into alternate frames, the method means that time can be stretched (we could cheat by separating out the action while increasing its duration and that of the shot). This exploits the fear that is inspired by our restricted access to what is out of shot, thus exacerbating the suspense (to see this being used in a clever way, we can refer to a number of Steven Spielberg's films, in particular *Duel*, the television film to which he owes his rise to fame).

19 If the tale did anticipate the commoditisation that was to come, then it is in the way that today's market sometimes uses a story-based approach with the sense of curious excitement which they share, seemingly connecting them inextricably to one other: 'iPad, my beautiful iPad, don't you see anything coming? This quasi-messianic object, marinated in the greatest secrecy and promoted with the greatest hype, Apple's new tablet seems to concentrate the fantasies of a world which always wants to take mobile subtlety further'. This is how a four-page article began in the newspaper *Libération*, dedicated to the launch of 'the Apple with the golden eggs', as it put it in its mischievous headline (Libération 2010).

3. 'PEEP SHOP'? AN ANTHROPOLOGY OF WINDOW DISPLAYS

1 Even fiction does not escape this constraint, insomuch as the world that we imagine always depends on the very real resources available to us.

2 The word 'surprise' is a wonderful one that means to astonish (to be unexpectedly struck by surprise), to mislead (to do the opposite of a prior expectation), and to captivate (sur-prise: the double seizing of the prospect).

3 More specifically: 'In the 1950s, commercial spaces were clearly identified as urban. It was thus at the heart of this single place that the display had to show what it could do. The writers in the professional press (aimed at small shopkeepers) undertake to define what effect had to be produced by a good window display. A display's effectiveness lay, according to them, in its ability to influence people's movements: therefore it has to attract their attention, bring them to a halt and, in the best case, make them change their itinerary by encouraging them to leave the open space of the street and enter the closed space of the shop. Unlike the publicity poster (of which there are many examples and whose essentially graphic nature make it legible from afar), there is only one window display which can only be deciphered from the pavement in front. A particularly lively and successful window display would at the most attract attention from the other side of the road, encouraging people to cross in order to see from closer up' (Leymonerie 2006: 97).

4 Sartre's scenario can be described as a modern version of the Augustinian position, where the idea of God watching you is actually the root cause of the subject's awareness who, feeling judged, is led to think of, define, and justify himself; further, the *Confessions* are said to be one of the very first occurrences of the subject's introspection.

5 Nor do they exclude other references: this theme of observing things through a keyhole, curiosity as voyeurism and indiscretion, is found in many works and stories which have given it a near-mythical status. *The Golden Ass* by Apuleius has already been mentioned. We should refer to another tale in particular, so clearly does it establish the link between Bluebeard and Sartre's model: the English legend of 'Lady Godiva' and 'Peeping Tom' (the second character appearing in one of the subsequent versions of the original tale). It was said that Lady Godiva was the beautiful wife of Leofric (968–1057), Earl of Mercia and Lord of Coventry, who starved his people by imposing heavy taxes on them. Many times Lady Godiva vainly begged her husband to be less harsh on the population, until eventually he put her to the test, promising to yield to her request if she rode through the town on horseback naked. Godiva took him at his word and crossed the town clad only in her long hair, but not before cleverly telling the inhabitants to lock themselves indoors so that she could avoid being seen. Only one curious person, called Tom, dared to disobey the order and stole a glance at the naked woman... for which he was punished by being struck immediately and suddenly blind (Davidson 1969; Hartland 1890; Mermin 1995; Donoghue 2004).

6 In fact, let us not forget that Bluebeard, whilst appearing threatening, remained extremely vague about the punishment he was going to inflict ('I forbid it in such a manner that, if you happen to open it, you may expect my just anger and resentment'). We might even ask ourselves if there is not in this a secondary motivation for curiosity, pushing us to discover (in a rather masochistic way for the wife and a somewhat sadistic way for the reader), the nature of the punishment incurred!

7 In nineteenth-century France, looking through a keyhole was established in case law as 'unhealthy curiosity'. This form of guilty visual exploration transgressed the 'wall of decency' that Article 330 of the 1810 Penal Code erected between both public spaces (where performing sexual acts constituted indecent assault) and private spaces (where the same practices were lawful and 'stripped the witness of his status of representing the State's watchful eye') (Iacub 2008: 81–82).

8 Incidentally, Perrault uses both variations in equal measure: the first, as we know, in *Bluebeard* and the second in *Donkey Skin*: 'Now, some authors believe that Donkey Skin's people had seen the moment the Prince put his eye to the keyhole; and that, looking from her little window, she had seen this Prince, so young, so handsome, and well-proportioned, that the idea of him stayed with her, and that often the thought of him had made her sigh'. It is unsettling to note that here Perrault depicts the scene later imagined by Sartre (some people saw the Prince looking through the keyhole), even multiplying it (Perrault saw that is was certain authors who had seen that some people had seen that the Prince seeing) and generalising it by reversing it (from the other side of the door, through the 'little window', which is to Donkey Skin what the lock is to the Prince: the subject being watched saw she was being watched).

9 Certainly, and ever since Saint Augustine, the embarrassment of curiosity and one's own secrets appear to be inextricably linked, no doubt because of the extreme significance of the theme of guilt with which it tends to be associated.

10 Starobinski specifically expressed and expanded on his refusal to reduce Rousseau to his psychological and physical afflictions in a scathingly ironic article dedicated to 'Rousseau's illness'. In the article, he draws up 'the rather grotesque list of diagnoses that have claimed to say the last word on Rousseau. Both with respect to his urinary troubles and his psychology: melancholy (1800, Pinel); depressed monomania (1830, Esquirol); degeneracy (1880, in the wake of B. Morel's publications); paranoïa (1889, P. J. Mobius); psychasthenia (1900, by applying Pierre Janet's theories); obsessive spasmodic neurasthenia, arteriosclerosis, and progressive cerebral atrophy on a base of neuroarthritis (1900, Régis); resigned variety of the delirium of interpretation (1909, Sérieux and Capgras); schizophrenia (1918, Demole); latent homosexuality with hysteriform obsessions and reactions (1927, Laforgue); toxic delirium of an interpretative form (1929, Elosu); and more recent experts incline towards "sensitive delirium" as this was defined by Kretschmer' (Starobinski 1961: 69). Starobinski thus justifies his scepticism about Rousseau's clinical exegesis: 'For my part, I have no great liking for the curiosity so often revealed concerning the illnesses of illustrious men. They were men, they had a body, they are dead – in this they resemble everyone else. Perhaps they have striven to become nothing but art and discourse, to dissimulate themselves behind the perfection of their work. [...] The true Rousseau is to be found in the admirable writer, social reformer and pedagogue; the persecuted obsessional character is the man with the urinary infection who is intoxicated by increasing nephritis; his youthful follies are but the psychological consequences of a urethral malformation; admittedly, at certain moments in Rousseau's life, there was delirium, but for this he is not responsible' (Starobinski: 68).

11 In fact, for him, 'Taken separately, neither individual psychology nor sociology offers a satisfactory explanation. If nothing important is to be left out of account, one must resort to a unified method capable of analyzing affective behavior in its social context' (Starobinski 1989: 18).

12 We could say that the 'normal grocer' confronts Starobinski's 'normal man', except that the grocer's profession consists precisely in not reasoning in terms of the average. The grocer adapts himself every time to the person he faces, or rather finds the most systematic and productive way to manage the variation of subjects. The grocer's logic is therefore, in my opinion, somewhat different to the 'normal' attitude described by the literary critic.

13 This, moreover, is where Starobinski begins his inventory, even before outlining the impossible three-part problem: 'Escape the disapproving gaze and surreptitiously take hold of the coveted object: this was a temptation that Jean-Jacques knew and sometimes succumbed to. If occasionally he filched things (usually 'snacks'), it was in order to avoid the shame of revealing his desire. In this way he believed he could achieve immediate ecstasy, without asking anyone's consent and without needing to interpose any coin, an abstract sign that tarnished every pleasure bought with money. Unseen and unidentified: paradoxically, in becoming a thief he abolished crime, simply because he put himself beyond the range of the accusatory gaze. Stealing became an innocent act, but only on condition that consciousness regress in imagination to a stage before it comes to be inhabited by an internalised witness. Jean-Jacques resorted to thievery not in response to a challenge or a penchant for crime but merely to simplify the situation, to get rid of an "inconvenient third party", and he protected himself by taking refuge in a primitive amorality, prior to the knowledge of good and evil'. (Starobinski 1989: 21).

14 For more about a field whose radical characteristics – sexual curiosity on the one hand, moral pressures on the other – make it possible to understand, in a particularly acute way, the imperative of the commercial management of customer discomfort, see Baptiste Coulmont's survey (2007) of the layout of sex shops.

15 As in *Bluebeard*, the layering of instances of observation plays a significant role in the fascination that operates with curiosity and its exegesis: Sartre and Starobinski are interested in the observer who finds himself or believes he is (respectively) being observed. However, they themselves are observers of the scene, who are themselves, or believe they are, being observed by an audience, and who I myself, and then my reader in turn, will investigate or can investigate, thus continuing the game endlessly (if, for example, the reader refers to my analysis and asks himself what the relevance of borrowing this point of view is in the eyes of those that surround him, on whom

his reputation depends). Behind this game of mirrors, what is felt is the excitement of knowledge and of sharing this knowledge: on the one hand, when we desire an object we know nothing (not about what we will truly discover, nor about what others will think), but on the other, acquiring knowledge and possibly sharing it depend on suspending this uncertainty and giving in to the risk of curiosity.

16 Later we will see that after having been insurmountable for a very long time, this constraint has now been removed.

17 It is here that the whole body of urban sociology and anthropology should be referenced. For an overview of the literature, see Sauvageot (2003).

18 Of course, certain window displays involve human figures, but with the occasional exception, as they are usually objectified human figures, taking the form of mannequins.

19 From this point of view, Latour's wordplay suddenly becomes ineffective: of course Starobinki's analysis has 'no object' but only in the material, rather than the figurative sense of the expression: if *The Living Eye* ignores objects, it is in order to clarify a situation that has conferred them no role; in this regard, Starobinski's analysis, far from being inaccurate, is, rather, wholly consistent and relevant.

20 From this point of view, the window display and self-service devices operate in both analogous and distinct ways. They operate analogously because the function of both is to channel the gaze differently – to free from inhibition, and to make the appeal of things take precedence over that which constrains people. Nonetheless, their modi operandi are quite dissimilar. Whereas the window display concentrates gazes like a parabola (making them converge towards a common focus of attention in the hope of using a customer's intersubjectivity to create a shared interobjectivity), self-service aims instead to 'loosen' the gaze and to allow each person to concentrate on the objects that interest them, regardless of the others present. The style of visual layout accompanying the latter has played a considerable role in promoting the acceptance of self-service. Of course there was indeed a reluctance to accept self-service selling because of the loss of service and changes in social status it implied. However, it also emancipated consumers (especially those on the lowest incomes) who became able to make their choices without the intervention, or at times, the uncomfortable judgements, of the shopkeeper and/or other customers (Du Gay 2006). Of course, between service that is paralysing and service that is emancipatory or dangerous (*Bluebeard*) is to be found the problem of shoplifting, the fear of which constituted one of the main obstacles to the development of self-service (Cochoy 2010b).

21 The original text mentions '00' cents. However, this figure must be a typographical error. In fact, if we are given the cheese for free once we have guessed its weight, if we can acquire the same cheese for 00 cents (its exact weight multiplied by 00 cents a pound), and if we fail to guess correctly, then in both cases we obtain the cheese free of charge and the game does not make sense... additionally, there is not the slightest profit for the shopkeeper who gives all his cheese away for nothing (which contradicts a subsequent clarification, according to which according to which 'nearly all the giant cheese [was sold] while it was on display').

22 The key deciding factor between the two figures is liquidity. By matching the company's value to the market's current price and uncoupling it from its fundamentals for a period of time, the highly liquid nature of title deeds puts a premium on the short term and therefore also on market speculation, rejecting the longer-term test of an assessment linked to fundamentals (in case of bankruptcy, for example).

23 Often markets are presented as worlds of rationality in which assessments relating to assets are matched. However, for exactly this reason, markets are also worlds of gambling which introduce forms of curiosity that relate to oneself (will my assessment be right?) and to others (what will be the assessments of the other agents? Where will I position myself in relation to the assessments and the agents?). This is highlighted in the wonderful words of Jacques Crave (2008) in his thesis on the second-hand book market: 'I don't know if you've been to an auction yet? Well, it is very, very unusual – it is nothing like the mechanisms of buying and selling that you might find in an ordinary shop. You don't have time to think. There is enthusiasm, a frenzy amongst those that surround you. You are not making your purchase alone [...] And you are influenced by a range of factors that do not exist when you have the time [...] to read calmly: "Well, I'll think about it, I'll get back to you..." You do not have the time to think: the guy in front of you wants the book and you, you do not want him to have it. So you become willing to invest a lot more money than you had been. Well, it is not that you become willing to invest, it is more that at a given moment you stop thinking [...] And we can far exceed what we were initially willing to pay, especially when we forget the additional fees behind it. Because this goes completely out of the window in the game, in the excitement' (Hélène, book seller and expert in old books, interview, rue Peyras, 30 April 2004). If we 'stop thinking', it is paradoxically because the market is 'thinking heavily' – it draws you into its infinite games of mirrors: markets are indeed places that are just as social as they are economic; they not only gamble with the value of things, they also create an intensely social shared moment through the experience of gambling and the curiosity that is attached to it.

24 Except, of course, in the rather rare and random case when speculation adjusts itself to the deeds' fundamental value.

25 We might object by saying that this vision is rather inexact in the scenario where the aim is to guess the weight of the same initial cheese, given that, because the average of the estimated weights tends to be close to the cheese's real weight, the way the estimates implied by this kind of objective are distributed is perfectly Gaussian (Desrosières 2002). Thus, a player who had access to all of the estimates given by those who preceded him, could very significantly increase his chances of winning by proposing the average of these estimates rather than his own assessment, irrespective of the condition that all of the previous estimates were produced independently (that is based on the cheese and the cheese alone), without considering the estimates made by other players. Therefore, unless the equal treatment of the candidates is distorted by forbidding some people from knowing the estimates of others so as to allow someone else to access them at the end of the game, we return to the situation in which only a direct estimation of the weight of the cheese will prevail.

26 It should be noted that, in neither case – whether we win or lose – does the bet have to be paid for. It is therefore completely free for the winner, given that he did not have to bear the temporary cost of paying for the right to participate.

27 The production of equivalence specific to the market follows an irrefutable logic, if we follow Epictetus: 'For what price do you buy a head of lettuce? An obol. If then someone pays an obol and obtains a head of lettuce but you, not paying an obol, do not obtain one, do not think that you have less than the one who did: for he may have the lettuce, you have the obol, which you did not give' (Epictetus, *Manuel* XXV). But in the scenario where the aim is to guess the weight of the same initial cheese (the terms of exchange having been clearly specified beforehand) we might consider that, for the consumer playing the game, the piece of cheese is 'worth' the money he has to pay in exchange, and that as a result, the actors 'end up quits'. However, Epictetus was only giving the example of the lettuces in order to support the existence of the more discreet and less monetary forms of remuneration associated with exchange, which we must not lose sight of: 'You were not invited to someone's feast? Because you did not give the host the price for which he sells his feast. He sells it for compliments, for a visit, for kindness, dependence' (Ibid). Epictetus' idea is that the balance or imbalance of an exchange must be obvious and relies on a hidden dimension being brought into play (in this case, personal dependencies). Later, we will see that, in our case, monetary equivalence ('money in exchange for cheese') can be called into question according to its specific terms.

28 On the condition of course that we assume that there is a strict substitutability and perfect value equivalence between the money and cheese, which is obviously very unlikely: firstly, the cheese does not have the same liquidity as the money (although it can melt, it is nonetheless highly non-fungible!); secondly, the cheese I am being sold comes with a mark-up, making the value of the cheese that is delivered actually smaller than the value of the bet I agree to in order to receive it; lastly, the preference for cheese decreases the more we obtain. These points are important, and I will come back to them in the next part of the analysis.

29 This calculation should not be excluded: even if the player does not necessarily calculate statistically or probabilistically, it is indeed a calculation that he uses when he tries to 'win his money back'; only one colossal win, which remains a possibility, is needed in order to compensate for all the previous losses (I thank Martin Giraudeau for this remark).

30 Incidentally, this is the only hypothesis capable of taking into account an addiction to gambling: pathological gamblers are well aware that, structurally speaking, they are losers. However, they do not get their satisfaction from their profits but from taking part in the game and from engaging in compulsive curiosity.

31 Let us recall that the spectacular dimension of the game and its consequences as a 'diversion' from personal judgement, and giving in to the sham of idle curiosity was perfectly identified by Saint Augustine.

32 Conversely, the audience is also just as capable of holding the player back if he condemns a passion for the game (here we then find the effect of Sartre's shame being multiplied). Moreover, the development of online games shows to what extent an entirely 'single-player' game, far from allowing the player to concentrate on calculation alone, absorbs him instead in a spiral of his own abandonment.

33 We could even complicate the problem of taking the game's implicit costs into account by extending it to consider the 'opportunity cost' inherent to participation in the game: it in fact only appears to be free; even if playing does not imply spending money, it does take time, and for many participants this time could be put to better use (they could work overtime if they are employed, carry out household chores, find better business opportunities, amuse themselves, or rest, and so on).

34 We find something similar in literature, in the beautiful metaphor provided by Céline, who alludes to the stick plunged into water in order to demonstrate the twisting that needs to be applied to everyday language in order to 'render' it in written form: 'Style, my lady, does indeed stop everyone in their tracks, no one simply comes to it. Because it is a very hard job. It involves taking sentences [...] off their hinges. Or there is another image: if you take a stick and want to make it look straight in water, you have to bend it first because if I put my stick in the water, the refraction will make it appear broken. It has to be broken before it is dipped into water. It is a lot of work. It is the work of the stylist' (Céline 1987: 67–68).

35 It is a very general characteristic of window displays to propose scenarios that make an effort to mimic the effect of a 'projective' mirror, like the presentation of mannequins in clothes shops, for example.

36 From the very start of this analysis, I have chosen to take the article in the *Progressive Grocer* seriously. This is, of course, not a matter of being deceived: the tale oscillates between the 'business case' (which works like a field report) and the 'success story' (which, conversely, works like a rhetorical discourse with a fragile empirical basis). Nonetheless, once we take the article as a generic example of a thousand possible and different situations, examining it allows a certain number of rather general figures to emerge, but which I hope turn out to be useful when studying their more particular and specific manifestations.

37 In the United States, it is the punched-card ballot paper (punched according to one's choice/choices) more than the polling booth that draws the attention, given that it is intrinsically more discreet than the ballot paper. The punched-card ballot, invented in Australia in 1856, was introduced in the US in the second half of the nineteenth century, and the punching machines, which appeared in 1892, became widespread in 1930 (Garner and Spolaore 2005). In France, it was not until 1913 that the polling booth was introduced (Garrigou 2008).

38 On the notion of fun food and its contemporary forms, see De la Ville et al. (2010).

39 We are still far from the interactive window displays of today (Cochoy 2011d).

40 We will meet Alice again and accompany her further in the following chapter.

4. 'TEASING'

1 If this identification is very strong, the nasty surprise will be shared and the tale will seem intolerable; this is where a danger lies – of reading the tale to children who are too young. That is, unless one considers that this is an opportunity for them to grow up, to learn to distinguish between points of view, and to acquire the double skill of being immersed in something while maintaining a critical distance, which is where all the pleasure of literature lies.

2 We could also mention the considerable efforts made by advertising professionals to ban certain misleading advertising practices and even make 'advertising honest': a technique in which the reliability of a particular commitment is less an objective in itself, and more a means of obtaining greater commercial effect – as John E. Powers, one of the founders of modern advertising who played a key role in introducing practices such as free trials or refunds on products in case of an unsatisfied customer, sought to demonstrate (Presbrey 1929: 302, sq.).

3 From this point of view, economists were quicker than sociologists at drawing conclusions from this situation and 'moving on to other things', namely by studying those situations that contradict adverse selection: in particular, they demonstrated that the opposite phenomenon existed – termed 'favourable selection' or 'advantageous selection' – which, for instance, drives those who are least in need of insurance to be the first to acquire it, due to a positive connection between risk aversion and caution in everyday life (Memenway 1990; Chiappori and Salanie 2000; Eisenhauer 2004).

4 As shown by the 'free toy inside' or 'surprises' of our childhood, the over-packaged gifts of McDonald's (Brembeck 2007) and even more so the Kinder eggs of today (Iulio 2011) bring about the very early socialisation of children in commercial curiosity. More generally speaking, on the importance of marketing in the socialisation of childhood, see Cook (2004), Cochoy (2008b), De la Ville (2009), Dupuy (2010), and more.

5 The balance between the pleasure of the wrapping and desire for the object is very subtle and can at any moment tip over towards the frantic destruction of the package that we see in very young children, or, conversely, towards a fetishistic enjoyment of the packaging that has a tendency to replace the object itself. As Roland Barthes noticed with respect to Japanese packages: 'the box operates as a sign: as a cover, screen, mask, it *has value* because of what it conceals, protects and yet points to; it *pulls the wool over our eyes*, if we understand this expression in both the monetary and psychological sense: but even that which it encloses and signifies is postponed for a very long time, as if the package's function was not to protect in space but to delay in time; [...] the content that has been announced flees from wrapping to wrapping and when we finally hold it (there is always *a little something* in the packet) it appears insignificant, derisory, worthless: the pleasure, rightfully belonging to the object, has been taken: the package is not empty but emptied' (Barthes 2007: 65 translation JTL).

6 <http://maxtv80.actifforum.com/avis-de-recherche-f3/monsieur-plus-de-bahlsen-t2591.htm> [accessed 16 May 2015]

7 This comment is somewhat inaccurate, or rather it only applies to the 'generic' definition of advertising that concerns us here. In practice, the advert presents itself in a material form – a poster, brochure, insert (Canu 2007) – often putting it in a position where it is itself 'wrapped' by the newspaper publishing it, the shop sheltering it, the 'package' that goes with it, and so on.

8 The following text refers to and completes two articles published in *Gérer et Comprendre* (Cochoy 2011a) and the *Journal of Marketing Management* (Cochoy 2015).

9 This advert was created by the CLM/BBDO advertising agency and produced by the glamour and fashion photographer Jean-François Jonvelle (Le Monde 1988; Devillers 2001).

10 When referring to *Little Red Riding Hood,* Marc Soriano (1977) reminded us that riddles from the tale's oral versions pepper the main version. From this perspective, it is as if Perrault had carried out a transfer: although he removed the secondary riddles to focus the tale of *Little Red Riding Hood* on the principal plot, he made them instead the principal device in *Bluebeard*.

11 If we look at the referent itself, we notice that in addition to the linguistic element it is a semiological one. Just as Kellogg's increased the number of unpacking motions with its inverted striptease, here the literal striptease refers to the discovery of the message's successive layers of signification and to the revelation of the 'inside story'. We are clearly in the presence of semiological virtuosity, in which the device consists not of playing with one sign as a signifier for another, as in Roland Barthes' (2010) *Mythologies*, but rather in entwining two distinct signifiers – the layered advertisement; the striptease – in such a way that together they lend their form to a signified that is shared, thereby almost stereoscopically reinforcing their own process of signification.

12 In recent years, performativity has drawn considerable attention from specialists in economic sociology because the concept allows them to discuss and ask themselves about the ability of the formulations of the economic sciences to transform the world, rather than simply represent it (Callon 1998). For an introduction to these studies, of which there are too many to mention here, one might consult the different collections of articles dedicated to the topic (MacKenzie et al. 2007; Licoppe 2010; Cochoy et al. 2010).

13 For a history of how decency has been considered in law throughout history, see Marcela Iacub's book, very appropriately called *Through the Keyhole* (Iacub 2008).

14 Marcela Iacub has carefully retraced the legal and social history of the reception of the monokini. Since its first public appearance, this fashion item, invented in 1964, has resulted in a number of legal cases, given its supposedly indecent character. In July 1964 in particular, in order to promote his establishment, the manager of a beach in Cannes had the idea of photographing a young woman, who he had asked to play Ping-Pong in a monokini on the beach in return for payment. Both the employer and employee were found guilty in the County Court, given the intention, in the eyes of the judge, of using this scandalous act for advertising purposes. They were later discharged on appeal 'due to the fact that the spectacle of nudity contained nothing capable of offending a normal or even a delicate sensitivity to decency, unless accompanied by the display of sexual body parts, or lascivious or obscene attitudes or gestures'. This arrest, to which *Myriam* clearly pays a peculiar tribute, was given considerable publicity and played a significant role in the trivialisation of the monokini (Iacub 2008: 170–172).

15 A scandal would emerge, as we shall see later, but locally, without affecting the campaign as a whole or overturning the logic behind it.

16 On the economic contribution of humour to advertising and more generally to the life of organisations, see Alden et al. (1993) and Yarwood (1995), respectively.

17 Note that in *Bluebeard*, this figure had already been introduced: the heroine's friends are the projection of the crowd of other readers. Whether reading the tale or participating in it, everybody wants to know what will be found by using the forbidden key, but no one wants to learn except for by themselves: the premature revelation of a plot's outcome is always perceived as a tragedy, of which we have a recent example; the solution to an Agatha Christie mystery, which for decades had been shown in a London theatre and whose secret the spectators had been invited to keep, was posted on *Wikipedia* (Malkin 2010).

18 For a less schematic presentation of Berlyne's theory, and more generally for a well-informed account about how the discipline of psychology conceives curiosity, see Loewenstein's (1994) impressive review.

19 I am, of course, alluding to a personal anecdote here. When an article in an academic journal was being assessed by reviewers, I received the following anonymous comments (in the spirit of confidentiality appropriate to the procedure, I have deliberately omitted the subject of the article and name of the journal): 'There is a risk that this kind of exercise results in a functionalist account. The researcher – equipped with his or her particular understandings and scientific preferences – provides an interpretation of how things "must have been". [...] Since work within STS has introduced some sensitivities in this respect, it would be unfortunate if the case study was interpreted as a functionalism dressed up in new clothes'. Admittedly, this comment was just one of many, and the journal finally agreed to publish my text. Nonetheless, perhaps this would not have been the case had I not taken care to make amends and accept the censure of my guilty bouts of functionalism!

20 <http://www.dailymotion.com/video/xbcz7_pub-neuf-vous-preferez-les-brunes> [accessed 14 May 2015]

21 Therefore, the homage goes as far as skilfully replaying the idea of the 'private joke' intended for the professionals of advertising that inaugurated *Myriam*, as we shall see later.

22 This campaign is clearly – like *Myriam*, which tried to challenge billboard companies less punctual (than Avenir, see below) – a distorted form of comparative advertising (a form of advertising that is constrained by severe legal restrictions in France). In this respect, like all its fellow adverts, it dances to the tune of the law, proscribing all 'denigration', with the privileged exception granted to 'humour', an opportunity the judge conceded to plaintiffs, given that it is never possible to find a priori in the letter of the law what can or cannot make a judge laugh (Cochoy and Canu 2006).

23 Out of respect for the author quoted and for Saint Augustine, I have taken the liberty to cut out the clarification 'that we would be searching for [...] in vain in the text of Genesis', because this comment, although applicable to certain versions of the Bible, is not to others, such as that by Douay-Rheims, revised by Challoner: 'And the eyes of them both were opened: and when they perceived themselves to be naked, they sewed together fig leaves, and made themselves aprons. Not that they were blind before (for the woman saw that the tree was fair to the eyes, ver. 6), nor yet that their eyes were opened to any more perfect knowledge of good; but only to the unhappy experience of having lost the good of original grace and innocence, and incurred the dreadful evil of sin. From whence followed a shame of their being naked; which they minded not before; because being now stript of original grace, they quickly began to be subject to the shameful rebellions of the flesh'. Now, this version of Catholic tradition – although long after Saint Augustine, given that it dates back to the seventeenth century and to a desire to counter the Reformation – is in fact a translation of the Vulgate; in other words, it is precisely the Latin version of the Bible which the philosopher was familiar with.

24 The circular ambiguity of the dressing/undressing, which neutralises the eroticism and the screening of virtue even as it is being displayed, is inherent to striptease, as was brilliantly noted by Roland Barthes: 'Striptease [...] is based on a contradiction: desexualising the woman at the exact moment when we are undressing her'. And Barthes demonstrated that the removal of the clothes, one by one, has a symmetrical counterpart in the continuous addition of other layers, which conjure up the former: the exoticism, the imposition of a known rite, with the gloves, feathers and fishnet stockings, the layering of the dance (Barthes 2010).

25 Without of course telling us that, from one case to the next, the subject and meaning of the promise have changed: in Genesis, the promise made by Adam and Eve is to abstain from tasting the forbidden fruit; in *Myriam*, despite appearances, the promise is less that made by a female subject, and rather that of the serpent who adopts these traits and does everything in its power to get to taste that commercial offer that he presents.

26 <http://www.jonvelle.com/galerieDinaVierny.php> [accessed 14 May 2015].

27 Genesis has been used in marketing more than we think: let us not forget that 'temptation' is the name that nursery owner Delbard gave to an apple that he created in 1990 by crossing the Grifer and Golden Delicious varieties <http://www.pomme-tentation.com> [Accessed 14 May 2015].

28 It does even more. This leaflet – found in a car dealership while waiting for a repair on my car – recalls the 'within-reach' adverts through which Roland Canu and Alexandre Mallard (Canu and Mallard 2006; Canu 2011b) demonstrated the extreme importance of the following: advertising documents insinuate themselves within commercial interaction; they provide a distraction, they help the customer waiting for an available salesperson to compose themselves, to help them think, to take notes; they also help salespeople to give information to their customers as well as to disengage from interactions that are dragging or that stand little chance of being successful. From this perspective, advertising manipulation takes on an entirely different meaning: it does not involve the mysterious force of symbolic discourse, but rather the physical grasping of advertising, in relation to both supply and demand – in commercial settings, advertising manipulation exists, but it is both material and crossed by the two entities (what I mean by 'crossed' is that supply manipulates demand, and vice versa).

29 Remember that in economics, since Kenneth Arrow (1962), 'moral hazard' refers to opportunistic actions that involve making the most of the incompleteness of a contract, for example by taking more risks once we have insurance cover.

30 I hope I can be forgiven for the slight anachronism in the following parenthetical comment of mentioning brand names, some of which did not yet exist at the time of *Myriam*: it must be understood that here, form is more important than substance!
31 See for example: 'All of Literature might be saying: Larvatus Prodeo, I move forward while pointing at my mask' (Barthes 1972: 32).
32 I chose the expression 'the two-sided public' in order to draw a contrast between targets that are 'cost-free' (the general public) and targets that are commercial (both advertisers and the communicators of advertising that together make up the 'two-sided market' within which advertising is 'negotiated').
33 This method, consisting of layering shifted representations of the same body part so as to give the impression of movement, echoes not only the technique used in cartoons that was perfected at the start of the twentieth century (Laloux 1996) – the use of tracing paper was invented in 1915 – but it also adopts a technique dating back to prehistory, given that it can be found in parietal art (Azéma 2005).
34 Archives from the History of Advertising Trust (HAT), Advertising Association collection (AA), reference number 13/1/3.
35 This little article, barely half a page long and lost amongst the thousands of pages in a magazine that provides a thousand other commercial tricks, had escaped my notice when going through the *Progressive Grocer* page by page, covering the period 1929–59 (admittedly while working on a project that was not about curiosity). I only noticed its existence four years after my investigation, whilst leafing through the magazine's tables of contents that I had photocopied. I was able to obtain the article with the assistance of Berkeley's NRLF librarians, who will never know how satisfying it is to find the needle that pricks one's curiosity amongst a haystack of records!
36 Note that the technique is not limited to the commercial world. In 1933, the English magazine, *The Listener*, reported that the American Federal Ministry of Education had published a brochure on the art of teaching on the radio. Amongst other pieces of advice, it suggested that 'in addition to the regular broadcast announcement [teaching by radio], 'teaser campaigns' may frequently be used advantageously to stimulate interest in broadcasts. Begin with an announcement a week before the broadcast and add an additional announcement each day until seven are given on the day of the broadcast'. And *The Listener* was intrigued to conclude that: '"Teaser" announcements, which aim at catching the listener's attention by a riddling, puzzling or startling allusion, have indeed been tried over here, but they require most cautious and sparing use if they are to avoid arousing hostility' (*The Listener* 1933).
37 <http://www.dailymotion.com/video/x3sco6_fnac-version-1_news> [accessed 16 May 2015] http://www.dailymotion.com/video/x3r6a4_fnac-version-2_news [accessed 16 May 2015]; <http://www.dailymotion.com/video/x3qyqm_fnac-version-3_music> [accessed 16 May 2015]

38 These variations are minimal: the 'butterfly' books in the filmed advert that we have chosen to follow are in others replaced either by flying cameras, or a path paved with flat screens.

39 Let me reveal the anecdote: it was thanks to the use of a high-tech curiosity device, mentioned briefly in the following section, that I was able to identify the song and the singer! (See this chapter, note 45).

40 Kierkegaard, *Either/or*, quoted in Kornberger (2010: 256). I thank the author for having mentioned this text and its relevance to the question of the awakening of curiosity.

41 The connection between boredom and curiosity continues throughout history, as identified and pointed out by Nicole Jacques-Chaquin, who reminds us of the extent to which (in particular in the eighteenth century) boredom intensifies an inclination towards curiosity: '[During the Enlightenment] [i]ntellectual curiosity and its passionate energy [...] appears as the only activity capable of providing a lasting escape from the boredom, which we know is one of the obsessions of the eighteenth century. Unlike other sources of pleasure, it does not become satiated or grow old' (Jacques-Chaquin 1998a: 20). Much later, the link between boredom and curiosity was explored in a different way by behaviourist psychology in attempting to demonstrate, using the experimental method, that boredom is one of the prerequisites of exploratory curiosity (Fowler 1965). In order to reinforce the fascinating relationship between these two opposing dispositions, we might also cite the archetypal literary figures of Faust (encouraged by boredom to make a pact with the Devil so as to undergo new experiences) and Mallarmé's *Sea Breeze* ('The flesh is sad, alas! And I have read all the books. Let's go! Far off. Let's go! I sense that the birds, intoxicated, fly deep into unknown spume and sky!') <http://www.poetryintranslation.com/PITBR/French/Mallarme.htm> [accessed 7 August 2015]. In light of the lessons of history, psychology, and literature, all in all we can only hope that sociology in turn will get to grips with this question seriously, in its own way, so as to explain to us the delicate link between habituation and exploration processes.

42 As was noted by Siegfried Kracauer (2005), in a beautiful text on boredom, 'even if a subject would like to do nothing, things are done to him'. Fnac's scenography consists precisely in operating both levers simultaneously: it is a matter of 'creating the boredom' of the subject (representing the waiting) in order to better be able to undo it (stirring curiosity).

43 For an in-depth exploration of the different facets and uses of serendipity, see Andel and Bourcier (2009) and Andel and Bourcier (2011).

44 Merton discovered the term himself through serendipity when attempting to found the sociology of the sciences, while thinking about the unforeseen consequences of social action (Shulman 2004).

45 See the applications 'Shazam' and 'Soundhound'.
46 See the applications 'Around me', 'Fonefood', 'LocalPicks', 'Locly', and so on.
47 See respectively 'Panomarascope' and 'Peak.ar', 'Pocket Universe Astronomy', 'Sun Seeker', 'Nearest Tube', and 'Velib'.
48 The questionnaire was designed in collaboration with the École Nationale Supérieure des Sciences Agronomiques of Bordeaux and its students, who carried out the survey in November 2009 under the supervision of Fédéric Couret and Alexander Lee. The statistical analysis was carried out with the help of Jan Smolinski. The focus groups were led with the assistance of Aurélie Lachèze. This survey would not have been possible without the support of the *Œnotrace* (a pseudonym) project of wine geo-traceability and all its partners and participants, of which there are too many to list here. I warmly thank all these people and institutions.
49 For more detailed results from the study, see the following three references, from which I have taken certain elements: Cochoy (2011c); Cochoy (2012); and Cochoy (2014).
50 'The term agencement denotes a form of arrangement that acts and at the same time imposes a certain format on the action. Saying that an agencement is a market-agencement (as opposed to agencements that can be for example qualified as altruistic, political or scientific) means specifying that it is structured to direct the collective action towards the establishment of bilateral commercial transactions. This structuring of collective action is achieved through a series of specific framings, which contribute to giving collective action the specific format that it should have' (Callon 2015).
51 The adapted French idiom meaning 'the straw that broke the camel's back'.
52 In 2009, a study carried out in Japan showed that 78.3% of Japanese people knew that their mobile phones were equipped with a QR-code reader and that 84.7% of these people had used it <http://whatjapanthinks.com/2009/07/05/qr-code-reading-phones-held-by-almost-four-in-five-japanese/> [Accessed 14 May 2015].

5. 'CLOSER'

1 For a recent exception, see Manguel 2015.
2 I would also like to confess my own curiosity from my own modest position, given how often subjects of research have a deeply biographical dimension. Here, curiosity will have served not only as a theme and a lure, but also as method: the elements that this book has touched upon are not so much objects that the sociologist has gone looking for, in line with his interests and research programme, as a series of events, images and texts found along the way, purely serendipitously, during his professional and personal journey.

3 What makes the door-closer ideal is that it offers universal access, even if Bruno Latour correctly demonstrated that its technical imperfections often lead to the movements of the weakest being jeopardised (Latour 1988).

4 On 4 July 2011, the British daily newspaper *The Guardian* revealed that its rival newspaper, the *News of the World,* had hacked the voicemail of Milly Dowler, a thirteen-year-old teenager murdered in 2002. The affair shocked the public and led to the revelation of widespread illegal phone hacking carried out by the tabloid, in collusion with police officers and political complacency, to the extent that the media group owned by the magnate Rupert Murdoch was shaken to its foundations, as was the British political class (for a summary of the affair, see LeMonde.fr (2011)).

5 These two forces are closely linked: a radical innovation of form, such as the invention of a new product (the people carrier in the car market, 3D for the cinema industry, body movement recognition replacing 'joysticks' in the computer game sector), at the same time involves an economy of surprise.

6 By the qualification of people, I mean operations that are far from limited to the professional training brought to mind by this expression, encompassing rather all procedures which, within a wide range of different relationships, involve providing others with skills, values, motives, reasons, impulses (and so on) that they would otherwise not possess.

7 One should perhaps add sensations to this list (Sauvageot 2003) – that is to say, the complete list of auditory, gustatory, olfactory, tactile, and visual perceptions that occur upstream of emotions, as something more corporeal and infra-cognitive. For some years now, sensations have played a major role in the social organisation of markets, and thus in awakening curiosity, via the development of atmospheric marketing (Grandclément 2004) and sensory marketing (Hultén et al. 2009), not forgetting the emerging approach of neuromarketing (Fugate 2007; Lee et al. 2007).

8 To pursue this attempt at semantic precision would of course require additional research that could well entail using sources of inspiration other than the current body of social sciences. In fact, forging ahead could paradoxically involve returning to old references: it would not only be a case of reconnecting with Weber (as we have just seen) but also of reactivating, in a new way, the programme of the seventeenth-century moralists. We know the extent to which authors such as La Bruyère, La Fontaine, or La Rochefoucault excelled in the art of painting people's moral portraits, which we could define as practising a kind of inner ethnography of human motives. It would be a matter of recovering this source of inspiration whilst revisiting it: this would involve concerning ourselves (as was the case long ago) with the 'moral traits' driving social practices, but understanding the word 'trait' less as an 'inner characteristic' and more as an 'externally circulating arrow' – in other words, a moral element that is recovered or constructed and brought into play through relational artefacts in order to redefine economic and social relationships.

9 Unless we returned to the Freudian hypothesis of infantile sexual curiosity (Freud 1962), or, even more unlikely, unless we endow the reader of the advert with a paedophilic inclination.

10 Note that this sales pitch, which aims to render curiosity innocent (even holy) by evoking its social benefits, reminds us of Francis Bacon's argument – him being the first to find a means of 'saving' curiosity from religious condemnation, by highlighting its contribution to the expression of Christian charity.

11 'No, and despite appearances, "Le Canard" [the duck] has not come to paddle in the net', it reads. This single-page website, with only a few links to click on (with nevertheless one link too near to that week's front page which gives access to other front pages), and as a consequence, eminently 'iconoclastic' – in the sense of informational radicalism – to put things in the wordplay so beloved of this medium, arouses curiosity in perhaps a far more subtle and effective way than many other media forms <http://www.lecanardenchaine.fr/> [Accessed 14 May 2015].

12 The Karachi affair concerned an attack on the town in 1995 which left 14 French people dead, and which some people attributed to the payment of commissions being suspended, apparently to have been paid in the context of arms deals; these commissions would have led to return commissions for French political figures (*Mediapart* 18 November 2010). The Mediator affair concerned a healthcare scandal, involving the drug of the same name, the use of which may have led to several hundred deaths (*Mediapart* 16 November 2010).

13 I am referring to the classical objection made by Pierre Bourdieu (1979), according to whom 'public opinion does not exist', except as an aggregate effect of people's responses to surveys that make them give their opinions, often in spite of themselves.

14 Of course, there is sometimes a distance between the fictitious and real 'I'. As we can see, the person who clicked (a sociologist of curiosity) is an atypical reader, who was evasive, perhaps even embarrassed about having to give his opinion about this question, but who wants to know the answer for his investigation: thus, between the two screenshots, he let some time pass, to the point that nearly 200 people expressed their opinion in the interval!

15 Of course, the old-fashioned letter to the editor anticipated this sort of device, but had such a time delay that it was not able to contribute to arousing the public in an instant.

16 It is not by chance that *Closer*, along with its rivals *Public* and *Voici*, was one of the first organs of the press to experiment with using Data Matrix-type codes in France, especially to spread videos that complemented the printed magazine (AFMM 2007).

17 Loana was the winner of the first reality television programme in France, *Loft Story*, which continuously filmed the 'private–public life' of a group of young people and broadcast it to the general public.

18 In my defence, I have nonetheless tackled these questions, thanks especially to *Closer*, which saved me, *in extremis*, from the accusation of having forgotten the issue of entertainment (an issue which has admittedly already been tackled with Saint Augustine, but so long ago that my reader may have forgotten!). I also touched on the social dimension in my detour via the quantitative survey, even if the latter showed the entirely secondary and inconclusive contribution of most of the classical social variables with respect to the propensity towards curiosity.

19 I subscribe without reservation to sociologists' duty of vigilance, and even to their duty of engagement, as long as they are sure of their 'science,' and sure that they are acting wisely (two points which, on a purely personal level, and in spite of the desire shared by myself and all my colleagues to do the best sociological work possible, often leads me to act with a certain amount of restraint). This said, having come to the social sciences from the world of contemporary literature, I have always been astonished to observe that in sociology the word 'criticism' has hardly any meaning beyond that of the very narrow and negative 'denunciation' or 'objection,' whilst in literature it has a much more positive and constructive meaning. A literary critic (in the academic rather than the journalistic sense of the word) would find little point in criticising a work without having a high opinion of its qualities. Thus, in literature, 'criticism' does not aim to pass judgement on its subject, still less to undertake political or moral policing, but rather to explore 'what is at work within the work,' namely, how texts are organised, how they function, what complex relationships the writing may have with its sources, and via what means, for the production of which effects, and so on and so forth. Even though I have left literature, I have retained this concept of criticism. I see my work as a sociologist as similar to that of a literary critic who must first write the book that he intends to critique (to gather data by means of an investigation and order them into a narrative) and then conduct this critique with the aim of elucidating rather than denouncing his subject. It is this type of method that I have endeavoured to follow here, by thinking that it ought to be possible to practise sociology in the manner of Jean Starobinski, to adopt a model encountered in this book.

20 Incidentally, there is a beautiful sense of anticipation here, certainly operating in a different register to the surrealist wordgame, the 'exquisite corpse' – a game in which the goal of the participants is to write a sentence collectively, with each subsequent player starting from the last word written by the previous player, without any knowledge of what has come before.

BIBLIOGRAPHY

AFMM, 'Opération "Flashcode". Retours d'expérience', *Communiqué de presse*, Association Française du Multimédia Mobile <http://blu-project.typepad.com/blu_mobile/files/afmm_appm_flashcode.pdf> [accessed 3 January 2011]

AFOM, *Livre blanc sur le sans contact mobile* <http://nfcclub/upload/nfcclub/common/cms/AFOM_NFC.pdf> [accessed 3 January 2011]

Akerlof, G. A., 'The Market for "Lemons": Quality Uncertainty and the Market Mechanism', *Quarterly Journal of Economics*, 84.3 (1970), 488–500

Alden, D. L., W. D. Hoyer, and C. Lee, 'Identifying Global and Culture-Specific Dimensions of Humor in Advertising: a Multinational Analysis', *Journal of Marketing*, 57.2 (1993), 64–75

Allison, A, 'Portable Monsters and Commodity Cuteness: Pokémon as Japan's New Global Power', *Postcolonial Studies*, 6.3 (2003), 381–95

Amine, A., and L. Sitz, 'Émergence et structuration des communautés de marque en ligne', *Décisions Marketing*, 46 (2007), 63–75

Andel, van P., 'Anatomy of the Unsought Finding. Serendipity: Origin, History, Domains, Traditions, Appearances, Patterns and Programmability', *The British Journal for the Philosophy of Science*, 45.2 (1994), 631–48

Andel, van P., and D. Bourcier, eds., *De la sérendipité dans la science, la technique, l'art et le droit, leçons de l'inattendu* (Chambéry: L'Act Mem, 2009)

——— eds., *La sérendipité: le hasard heureux* (Paris: Hermann, 2011)

Andrieu, F., O. Badot, and S. Macé, 'Hypermodernité et distribution: Le cas du est Edmonton Mall', *Revue Management et Avenir*, 2.2 (2004), 27–50

Arnoldi, J., and Ch. Borch, 'Market Crowds Between Imitation and Control', *Theory, Culture & Society*, 24.7.8 (2007), 164–80

Arrow, K. J., 'Uncertainty and the Welfare Economics of Medical Care', *American Economic Review*, 53.5 (1963), 941–73

Auray, N., 'Une autre façon de penser le lien entre technique et politique: les technologies de l'internet et le réagencement de l'activité autour de l'exploration', Working paper, *Economics and Social Sciences*, 18, Telecom Paris (2006)

Auray, N., 'Pirates en réseau: prédation, détournement et exigence de justice', *Esprit*, (2009), 168–80

——— 'Les Technologies de l'information et le régime exploratoire', in A. van P., and D. Bourcier, eds., *La sérendipité: le hasard heureux* (Paris: Hermann, 2011), pp. 329–43

Austin, J. L., *Philosophical Papers* (London: Oxford University Press, 1961)

Azéma, M., 'Et si… les hommes préhistoriques avaient inventé le dessin animé et la bande dessinée?', *Préhistoire, art et sociétés*, vol. LIX (2005), 55–69

Ball, Ph., *Curiosity: How Science Became Interested in Everything* (Chicago: Chicago University Press, 2013)

Barthes, R., *Le Degré zéro de l'écriture* (Paris: Seuil, 1972)

——— *Roland Barthes by Roland Barthes* (Berkeley: University of California Press, 1977)

——— *Camera Lucida* (New York: Hill and Wang, 1981)

——— *L'empire des signes* (Paris: Seuil, 2007 [1970])

——— *Mythologies*, Jacqueline Guittard, trans. (Paris: Seuil, 2010 [1957])

Barry, A., and L. Kimbell, 'Pindices', in B. Latour, and P. Weibel, *Making Things Public, Atmospheres of Democracy* (Cambridge, MA: MIT Press, 2005), pp. 872–73

Baudrillard, J., *Consumer Society: Myths & Structures* (London: Sage, 1998 [1970])

——— *For a Critique of the Political Economy of the Sign* (Missouri: Telos Press Ltd., 1981 [1972])

Beaudoin, V., D. Cardon, and A. Mallard, 'De clic en clic. Créativité et rationalisation dans les usages des intranets d'entreprise', *Sociologie du travail*, 43.3 (2001), 309–26

Beauvois, J.-L., and R.-V. Joule, *Petit raité de manipulation à l'usage des honnêtes gens* (Grenoble: Presses Universitaires de Grenoble, 1987)

Belk, R. W., M. Wallendorf, and J. F. Sherry Jr., 'The Sacred and Profane in Consumer Behavior: Theodicy on the Odyssey', *Journal of Consumer Research*, 16.1 (1989), 1–38

Benedict, B. M., *Curiosity: A Cultural History of Early Modern Inquiry* (Chicago: University of Chicago Press, 2001)

Berlyne, D. E., 'Novelty and Curiosity as Determinants of Exploratory Behaviour', *British Journal of Psychology*, 41 (1950), 68–80

——— 'A Theory of Human Curiosity', *British Journal of Psychology*, 45 (1954), 256–65

——— *Conflict Arousal and Curiosity* (New York: McGraw-Hill, 1960)

Besançon, J., O. Borraz, and C. Grandclément-Chaffy, *La sécurité alimentaire en crises, les crises, Coca-Cola et listeria de 1999–2000* (Paris: L'Harmattan, 2004)

Bettelheim, B., *The Uses of Enchantment: The Meaning and Importance of Fairy Tales* (New York: Random House, 1976)

Boltanski, L., *On Critique: A Sociology of Emancipation*, G. Elliot, trans. (Cambridge, MA: Polity Press, 2011 [2009])

Bonnin, G., 'Des instrumentalistes aux chineuses: quatre figures de la mobilité en magasin', *Sciences de la société*, 56 (2002), 43–60

Boullier, D., 'Les industries de l'attention: fidélisation, alerte ou immersion', *Réseaux* 154.2 (2009), 231–46

Bourdieu, P., *Outline of a Theory of Practice* (Cambridge, MA: Cambridge University Press, 1977 [1972])

——— 'Public Opinion Does Not Exist', in A. Mattelart, and S. Siegelaub, eds., *Communication and Class Struggle* (New York: International General, 1979), pp. 124–30

——— *Distinction: A Social Critique of the Judgment of Taste* (London: Routledge, 1984 [1979])

——— ed., *Photography: A Middle-Brow Art* (Stanford, CA: Stanford University Press, 1996 [1965])

Boutet, M., 'S'orienter dans les espaces sociaux en ligne: l'exemple d'un jeu', *Sociologie du travail*, 50.4, October–December (2008), 447–70

Brembeck, H., 'To Consume and be Consumed: Birthday Parties at McDonald's', in H. Brembeck, K. Ekström, and M. Mörck, eds., *Little Monsters (De)coupling Assemblages of Consumption* (Berlin: Lit Verlag, 2007), pp. 67–84

Brives, Ch., *Des levures et des hommes, anthropologie des relations entre humains et non humains au sein d'un laboratoire de biologie*, PhD thesis, Université de Bordeaux II, 2010

Bromberger, Ch., *Le Match de football: ethnologie d'une passion partisane à Marseille, Naples et Turin* (Paris: Éditions de la MSH, 1995)

Butler, J., 'Performative Acts and Gender Constitution: An Essay in Phenomenology and Feminist Theory', *Theatre Journal*, 40.4 (1988), 519–31

Callon, M., 'Introduction: The Embeddedness of Economic Markets in Economics', in M. Callon, ed., *The Laws of the Markets* (Oxford: Blackwell, 1998), pp. 2–57

——— 'What Does it Mean to Say that Economics is Performative?' in D. MacKenzie, F. Muniesa, and L. Siu, eds., *Do Economists Make Markets? On the Performativity of Economics* (Princeton, NJ: Princeton University Press, 2007), pp. 311–57

——— 'Revisiting Marketization: From Interface-markets to Market-agencements', *Consumption, Markets and Culture* (2015), forthcoming

Callon, M., and B. Latour, '"Thou Shall not Calculate!" or How To Symmetricalize Gift and Capital', *Revue du MAUSS semestrielle*, 9 (1997), 45–70. English version available at: <http://www.bruno-latour.fr/sites/default/files/downloads/P-71%20CAPITALISME-MAUSS-GB.pdf> [accessed 15 May 2015]

Callon, M., C. Méadel, and V. Rabeharisoa, 'The Economy of Qualities', *Economy and Society*, 31.2 (2002), 194–217

Calvignac, C., *Qu'offre la demande? Socio-économie de l'innovation par l'usager,* PhD thesis, Université Toulouse II, 2010

Calvin, J., 'Traité ou avertissement contre l'astrologie qu'on appelle judiciaire et autres curiosités qui règnent aujourd'hui au monde', in *Œuvres françoises de Jean Calvin recueillies pour la première fois, précédées de sa vie par Théodore de Bèze et d'une notice bibliographique par P. L. Jacob, bibliophile* (Paris: Librairie Charles Gosselin, 1842)

Canu, R., *Publicités et travail marchand: la manipulation des documents publicitaires sur le marché des télécommunications (2003–2007)*, PhD thesis, Université Toulouse II, 2007

Canu, R., and F. Cochoy, 'La loi de 1905 sur la répression des fraudes: un levier décisif pour l'engagement politique des questions de consommation?' *Sciences de la société*, 62 (2005), 69–91

Canu, R., and C. Datchary, 'Journalistes et lecteurs-contributeurs sur mediapart', *Réseaux*, 160.2 (2010), 195–223

Canu, R., and A. Mallard, 'Que fait-on dans la boutique d'un opérateur de télécommunications? Enquête ethnographique sur la mise en référence des biens marchands', *Réseaux*, 24.135.136 (2006), 161–92

Carroll, L., *Alice's Adventures in Wonderland* (New York: Sam'l Gabriel Sons & Co., 1916)

Cazelles, B., and B. Wells, 'Arthur as Barbe-Bleue: The Martyrdom of Saint Tryphine (Breton Mystery)', *Yale French Studies*, 95 (1999), 134–51

Céline, L.-F., *Le style contre les idées: Rabelais, Zola, Sartre et les autres* (Paris: Complexe, 1987)

Chabault, V., *La Fnac entre commerce et culture: parcours d'entreprise, parcours d'employés* (Paris: Presses Universitaires de France, 2010)

Chamberlin, E. H., *The Theory of Monopolistic Competition: A Reorientation of the Theory of Value* (Cambridge, MA: Harvard University Press, 1962 [1933])

Chandler, A. D. Jr., *The Visible Hand: The Managerial Revolution in American Business* (Cambridge, MA: The Belknap Press of Harvard University Press, 1977)

Chiapello, È., *Artistes versus managers: le management culturel face à la critique artiste* (Paris: Métailié, 1998)

Chiappori, P., and B. Salanie, 'Testing for Asymmetric Information in Insurance Markets', *The Journal of Political Economy*, 108 (2000), 56–78

Cochoy, F., 'De l'embarras du choix au conditionnement du marché. Vers une socio-économie de la décision', *Cahiers internationaux de sociologie*, 106 (1999), 145–73

——— *Une sociologie du packaging, ou l'âne de Buridan face au marché* (Paris: Presses Universitaires de France, 2002)

——— 'Is the Modern Consumer a Buridan's Donkey? Product Packaging and Consumer Choice', in K. Ekström, and H. Brembeck, eds., *Elusive Consumption* (Oxford and New York: Berg Publisher, 2004), pp. 205–27

——— 'A Brief Theory of the "Captation" of the Public: Understanding the Market with Little Red Riding Hood', *Theory, Culture & Society*, 24.7.8 (2007a), 213–33

——— 'A Sociology of Market-Things: On Tending the Garden of Choices in Mass Retailing', in M. Callon, F. Muniesa, and Y. Millo, eds., *Market Devices* (Sociological Review Monographs) (London: Blackwell, 2007b), 109–29

——— 'Calculation, Qualculation, Calqulation: Shopping Cart's Arithmetic, Equipped Cognition and Clustered Consumers', *Marketing Theory*, 8.1 (2008a), 15–44

——— 'Hansel and Gretel at the Grocery Store: *Progressive Grocer* and the Little American Consumers' (1929–1959), *Journal of Cultural Economy*, 1.2 (2008b), 145–63

——— 'Driving a Shopping Cart from STS to Business, and the Other Way Round: On the Introduction of Shopping Carts in American Grocery Stores (1936–1959)', *Organization*, 16.1 (2009), 31–55

——— '"How to Build Displays that Sell"': The Politics of Performativity in American Grocery Stores (*Progressive Grocer*, 1929–1946)', *Journal of Cultural Economy*, 3.2 (2010a), 299–315

——— 'Reconnecting Marketing to "Market-Things": How Grocery Equipments Drove Modern Consumption', in Araujo L., and Kjellberg, H., eds., *Reconnecting Marketing to Markets: Practice-based Approaches* (Oxford: Oxford University Press, 2010b), pp. 29–49

——— 'Les trente ans de Myriam, ou les fabuleux dessous du teasing publicitaire', *Gérer et comprendre*, 104 (2011a), 4–13

——— 'Modernizing the Grocery Trade with Cartoons in Wartimes: Humor as a Marketing Weapon, *Progressive Grocer* (1939–1945)', in C. McLean, F.-R. Puyou, P. Quattrone, and N. Thrift, eds., *Imagining Organizations* (London: Routledge, 2011b), pp. 173–88

——— *Sociologie d'un 'curiositif': Smartphone, code-barres 2D, et self-marketing* (Lormont, Le Bord de l'eau, 2011c)

——— '*In Datamatrix Veritas*? Managing Wine Flow and Information Overflow with a Two-Dimensional Barcode', in B. Czarniawska, and O. Löfgren, eds., *Managing Overflow* (New York: Routledge, 2012), pp. 52–67

——— 'Consumers at Work, or Curiosity at Play? Revisiting the Prosumption/Value Co-Creation Debate with Smartphones and 2D Barcodes', *Marketing Theory*, 7 July 2014 (online version): <http://mtq.sagepub.com/content/early/2014/07/07/1470593114540676.full.pdf+html> [accessed 10 August 2015], 1–21

——— 'Myriam's "Adverteasing": on the Performative Power of Marketing Promises', *Journal of Marketing Management*, 31.1.2 (2015), 123–40

Cochoy, F., and R. Canu, 'La publicité comparative ou comment se faire justice à soi-même en passant par le droit', *Revue française de sociologie*, 47.1 (2006), 81–115

Cochoy, F., M. Giraudeau, and L. McFall, eds., *The Limits of Performativity: Politics of the Modern Economy* (Abingdon: Routledge, 2014)

Cochoy, F., and C. Grandclément, 'Publicizing Goldilocks' Choice at the Supermarket: The Political Work of Shopping Packs, Carts and Talk', in B. Latour, and P. Weibel, eds., *Making Things Public: Atmospheres of Democracy* (Cambridge, MA: MIT Press, 2005), pp. 646–59

Cochoy, F., and M. Lalanne, 'Enquêtes sur les vitrines du marché: afficher, emballer, étiqueter', *Sciences de la société*, 80 (2011), 3–9

Cochran, Th. C., *Business in American Life: A History* (New York: Mc Graw Hill, 1972)

Collectif, 'La curiosité ou l'interdit du regard', *Cliniques méditerranéennes*, Strasbourg, 51.52 (1996), 51–62

Conein, B., and M. Latapy, 'Les usages épistémiques des réseaux de communication électronique: le cas de l'open-source', *Sociologie du travail*, 50.3 (2008), 331–52

Cook, D. T., *The Commodification of Childhood: The Children's Clothing Industry and the Rise of the Child Consumer* (Durham, NC: Duke University Press, 2004)

Cooren, F., 'Froideur des passions et chaleur des calculs. L'économie d'une révolution permanente', Paper presented at *Exercices de métaphysique empirique (autour des travaux de Bruno Latour)*, Centre Culturel International de Cerisy-la-Salle, Cerisy-la-Salle, 29 June 2007

——— *Action and Agency in Dialogue: Passion, Incarnation and Ventriloquism* (Amsterdam and Philadelphia: John Benjamins Publishing Co., 2010)

Coris, M., 'La culture du don dans la modernité. Les communautés du logiciel libre', *Réseaux*, 24.140 (2006), 161–190

Coulmont, B., *Sex-Shops: une histoire française* (Paris: Dilecta, 2007)

Crave, J., *Le "Livre-échange": relations marchandes autour du livre de seconde main*, PhD thesis, Université Toulouse II, 2008

Czarniawska, B., *Cyberfactories: How News Agencies Produce News* (Cheltenham, Edward Elgar, 2011)

Daston, L., and K. Park, *Wonders and the Order of Nature, 1150–1750* (Cambridge, MA: MIT Press, 1998)

Davidson, H. R. E., 'The Legend of Lady Godiva', *Folklore*, 80.2 (1969), 107–21

De Blic, D., and C. Lemieux, 'Le scandale comme épreuve. Éléments de sociologie pragmatique', *Politix*, 71.3 (2005), 9–38

De la Ville, V.-I., 'L'enfant dans l'espace commercial: éléments pour une mise en perspective…', *Management & Avenir*, 21.1 (2009), 157–71

De la Ville, V.-I., G. Brougère, and N. Boireau, 'How can Food become Fun? Exploring and Testing Possibilities', *Young Consumers*, 11.2 (2010), 117–30

Debord, G., *Society of the Spectacle* (Detroit, MI: Black and Red Press, 1983 [1967])
Desrosières, A., *The Politics of Large Numbers: A History of Statistical Reasoning*, C. Naish, trans (Cambridge, MA: Harvard University Press, 2002 [1993])
Devillers, S., 'Avec Myriam, la pub a tenu ses promesses', *Le Figaro*, August (2001)
Didier, E., 'Do Statistics "Perform" the Economy?' in D. MacKenzie, F. Muniesa, and L. Siu, eds., *Do Economists Make Markets? On the Performativity of Economics* (Princeton, NJ: Princeton University Press, 2007), pp. 276–310
Dion Le-Mée, D., *La foule dans un contexte commercial: concept, mesure, effets sur les comportements*, PhD thesis, Université de Rennes I, 1999
Donoghue, D., 'Lady Godiva: A Literary History of the Legend', *Albion: A Quarterly Journal Concerned with British Studies*, 36.1 (2004), 90–1
Dorey, R., *Le désir de savoir: nature et destins de la curiosité en psychanalyse* (Paris: Denoël, 1988)
Du Gay, P., 'Le Libre-service. La distribution, les courses et les personnes', *Réseaux*, 24.135.136 (2006), 33–58
Dupuy, A., *La Place du plaisir dans la socialisation alimentaire des enfants et des adolescents*, PhD thesis, Université Toulouse II, 2010
Eisenhower, J., 'Risk Aversion and the Willingness to Pay for Insurance: A Cautionary Discussion of Adverse Selection', *Risk Management and Insurance Review*, 7 (2004), 165–75
Eroglu, S. A., and G. D. Harrell, 'Retail Crowding: Theoretical and Strategic Implications', *Journal of Retailing*, 62.4 (1986), 346–63
Eroglu S. A., and K. A. Machleit, 'An Empirical Study of Retail Crowding: Antecedents and Consequences', *Journal of Retailing*, 66.2 (1990), 201–21
Eroglu S. A., K. A. Machleit and T. F. Barr, 'Perceived Retail Crowding and Shopping Satisfaction: the Role of Shopping Values', *Journal of Business Research*, 58 (2005), 1146–53
Farrell, J., *Paranoia and Modernity: Cervantes to Rousseau* (Ithaca, NY: Cornell University Press, 2005)
Ferrand, L., 'Comprendre les effervescences musicales. L'exemple des concerts de rock', *Sociétés*, 104.2 (2009), 27–37
Field, E., *Advertising: The Forgotten Years* (London: E. Benn, 1959)
Findlen, P., *Possessing Nature: Museums, Collecting, and Scientific Culture in Early Modern Italy* (Berkeley: University of California Press, 1994)
Floch, J. -M., 'Êtes-vous arpenteur ou somnambule? L'élaboration d'une typologie comportementale des voyageurs du métro', in J.-M. Floch, ed., *Sémiotique, marketing et communication* (Paris: Presses Universitaires de France, 1990), pp. 19–48
Foderaro, L., 'Private Moment Made Public, Then a Fatal Jump', *The New York Times*, 29

September 2010, <http://www.nytimes.com/2010/09/30/nyregion/30suicide.html?_r=0> [accessed 13 August 2015]

Foucault, M., 'The Use of Pleasure', *The History of Sexuality Series*, vol. 2, R. Hurley, trans (New York: Pantheon Books, 1985)

——— *The Order of Things*, A. Sheridan, trans (New York: Vintage, 1973 [1966])

Fournier, A., 'Ce que révèlent les "journaux de guerre afghans"', *LeMonde.fr*, July (2010)

Fowler, H., *Curiosity and Exploratory Behavior* (New York: Macmillan, 1965)

Freidson, E., *Profession of Medicine: A Study of the Sociology of Applied Knowledge* (Chicago: University of Chicago Press, 1988)

Freud, S., *Three Essays on the Theory of Sexuality*, J. Strachey, trans (New York: Basic Books 1962 [1905])

Frohlich, X., 'Food's Little Black Box: A History of the FDA's "Nutrition Facts" Label', working paper, MIT, Cambridge, MA (2007)

Fugate, D. L., 'Neuromarketing: a Layman's Look at Neuroscience and its Potential Application to Marketing Practice', *Journal of Consumer Marketing*, 24.7 (2007), 385–94

Gaglio, G., 'La dynamique des normes de consommation: le cas de l'avènement de la téléphonie mobile en France', *Revue française de socio-économie*, 2 (2008), 181–98

Garner, Ph., and E. Spolaore, 'Why Chads? Determinants of Voting Equipment Use in the United States', *Public Choice*, 123.3.4 (2005), 363–92

Garrigou, A., *Les Secrets de l'isoloir* (Paris: Thierry Magnier, 2008)

Geertz, C., 'The Bazaar Economy: Information and Search in Peasant Marketing', *American Economic Review*, 68.2 (1978), 28–32

Girard, R., *Deceit, Desire and the Novel: Self and Other in Literary Structure*, Y. Freccero, trans (Baltimore, MD: The Johns Hopkins University Press, 1965 [1961])

Giraudeau, M., J. -P. Gond, and D. Martin, 'Disciplining Students and Markets: How to Embed Newcomers into Economics Thanks to "Market Games"', working paper, CERTOP, Université Toulouse II, 2007

Glad, P. W., 'Progressives and the Business Culture of the 1920s', *The Journal of American History*, 53.1 (1966), 75–89

Glass, J. M., 'Notes on the Paranoid Factor in Political Philosophy: Fear, Anxiety, and Domination', *Political Psychology*, 9.2 (1988), 209–28

Godart, F., *Sociologie de la mode* (Paris: La Découverte, 2010)

Goldhaber, M. H., 'The Attention Economy and the Net', *First Monday*, 2.4, (1997) <http://firstmonday.org/htbin/cgiwrap/bin/ojs/index.php/fm/article/viewArticle/519/440> [accessed 16 May 2015]

Gomart, É., and A. Hennion, 'A sociology of Attachment: Music Amateurs, Drug Users', *The Sociological Review*, 47.S1 (1999), 220–47

Grandclément, C., 'Climatiser le marché. Les contributions des marketings de l'ambiance et de l'atmosphère', *Ethnographiques.org*, November (2004) <http://www.ethnographiques.org/2004/Grandclement> [accessed 16 May 2015].

——— 'Wheeling Food Products Around the Store... and Away: The Invention of the Shopping Cart (1936–1953)', Paper presented at the *Food Chains Conference: Provisioning, Technology, and Science*, Hagley Museum and Library, Wilmington, DE, 2–4 November 2006

——— *Vendre sans vendeurs: sociologie des dispositifs d'achalandage en supermarché*, PhD thesis, École Nationale Supérieure des Mines de Paris, 2008

Grousset-Charrière, S., *La Socialisation élitaire des étudiants aux États-Unis. Le cas des 'Final Clubs', sociétés secrètes de Harvard*, PhD thesis, Université Toulouse II, 2010

Harrison, P., 'Curiosity, Forbidden Knowledge, and the Reformation of Nature Philosophy in Early Modern England', *Isis*, 92.2 (2001), 265–90

Hartland, E. S., 'Peeping Tom and Lady Godiva', *Folklore*, 1.2 (1890), 207–26

Heidegger, M., *Être et temps*, E. Martineau, trans, 2010, <http://metataphysica.free.fr/Heidegger/Etre%20et%20Temps.pdf> [accessed 16 May 2015]

Heilbrunn, B., 'Porno chic ou addiction choc?', *Libération*, 25 October 2002

Hemenway, D., 'Propitious Selection', *The Quarterly Journal of Economics*, 105 (1990), 1063–69

Hennion, A., *La Passion musicale. Une sociologie de la médiation* (Paris: Métailié, 1993)

Hennion A., and C. Méadel, 'In the Laboratories of Desire. Advertising as an Intermediary Between Products and Consumers', *Réseaux*, 1.2 (1993), 169–92

Heran, F., 'La seconde nature de l'habitus: tradition philosophique et sens commun dans le langage sociologique', *Revue française de sociologie*, 28.3 (1987), 385–416

Hertz, E., *The Trading Crowd: An Ethnography of the Shanghai Stock Market* (Cambridge: Cambridge University Press, 1998)

Hirschman, A. O., *The Passions and the Interests: Political Arguments for Capitalism Before its Triumph* (Princeton, NJ: Princeton University Press, 1977)

Houdard, S., 'La Bible, le curieux et la vérité. Connaissance et scepticisme au XVIe siècle', in N. Jacques-Chaquin, and S. Houdard, eds., *Curiosité et* Libido sciendi *de la Renaissance aux Lumières*, vol. 1 (Fontenay-aux-Roses: ENS Éditions, 1998), pp. 35–71

Hughes, Th. P., *Networks of Power: Electrification in Western Society, 1890–1930* (Baltimore, Johns Hopkins University Press, 1983)

Hung, K., 'Framing Meaning Perceptions with Music: The Case of Teaser Ads', *Journal of Advertising*, 30.3 (2001), 39–49

Hultén, B., N. Broweus, and M. Van Dijk, *Sensory Marketing* (Basingstoke, Hampshire: Palgrave Macmillan, 2009)

Iacub, M., *Par le trou de la serrure. Une histoire de la pudeur publique (XIXe–XXIe siècle)* (Paris: Fayard, 2008)

Impey, O., and A. Macgregor, eds., *The Origins of Museums: The Cabinet of Curiosities in Sixteenth- and Seventeenth-Century Europe* (Oxford: Clarendon Press, 1985)

Iulio, S., and N. Diasio, 'Fun Food From Ritual to Performance: An Anthropological and Communicational Analysis of Kinder Sorpresa Commercials', in K. M. Ekström, and B. Tufte, eds., *Children, Media and Consumption* (Göteborg: The International Clearing House on Children, Youth and Media/UNESCO, 2007), pp. 161–77

Iulio, S., 'La Publicité pour les aliments destinés aux enfants entre risques, plaisirs et divertissement: le cas de Kinder', *Cahiers de l'OCHA*, (2011), 57–63

Iulio, S., and C. Vinti, 'La Publicité italienne et le modèle américain: le débat entre "techniciens publicitaires" et "artistes" (1948–1960)', *Vingtième siècle, revue d'histoire*, 101 (2009), 61–80

Iulio, S., 'Publicité et culture enfantine: sur l'usage des contes de fées dans les contes adressés aux enfants', Actes du colloque international, *L'édition pour la jeunesse entre héritage et culture de masse*, 25–27 November (2004)

Jacques-Chaquin, N., 'La curiosité, ou les espaces du savoir', in N. Jacques-Chaquin, and S. Houdard, eds., *Curiosité et* Libido sciendi *de la Renaissance aux Lumières*, vol. 1 (Fontenay-aux-Roses: ENS Éditions, 1998a), pp. 13–32

——— 'La Passion des sciences interdites: curiosité et démonologie (XVe-XVIIIe siècles)', in N. Jacques-Chaquin, and S. Houdard, eds., *Curiosité et* Libido sciendi *de la Renaissance aux Lumières*, vol. 1 (Fontenay-aux-Roses: ENS Éditions, 1998b), pp. 73–107

Jenkins, R. V., 'Technology and the Market: George Eastman and the Origins of Mass Amateur Photography', *Technology and Culture*, 16.1 (1975), 1–19

Katona, G., *The Powerful Consumer* (New York: McGraw-Hill Book Co., 1960)

Kaufmann, J.-C., *Corps de femmes, regards d'hommes* (Paris: Nathan, 1998)

——— 'Voyeurisme ou mutation anthropologique?', *Le Monde*, 11 May 2001

Kenny, N., *The Uses of Curiosity in Early Modern France and Germany* (Oxford: Oxford University Press, 2004)

Kessous, E., and B. Rey, 'Économie numérique et vie privée', *Hermes*, 53 (2009), 49–54

Kessous, E., K. Mellet, and M. Zouinar, 'L'économie de l'attention: entre protection des ressources cognitives et extraction de la valeur', *Sociologie du travail*, 52.3 (2010), 359–73

Keynes, J. M., *The General Theory of Employment, Interest and Money* (New York: Harcourt Brace and Co., 1936)

Kjellberg, H., 'Marketing on Trial: The SAS EuroBonus Case', in L. Araujo, J. Finch, and H. Kjellberg, eds., *Reconnecting Marketing to Markets: Practice-based Approaches* (Oxford: Oxford University Press, 2010), pp. 181–203S

Kornberger, M., *Brand Society: How Brands Transform Management and Lifestyle* (Cambridge: Cambridge University Press, 2010)

Kracauer, S., *The Mass Ornament: Weimar Essays* (Cambridge, MA: Harvard University Press, 2005)

Lahire, B., *The Plural Actor* (Malden, MA: Polity Press 2011 [1998])

Laloux, R., *Ces dessins qui bougent 1892–1992: cent ans de cinéma d'animation* (Paris: Dreamland, 1996)

Lancaster, K., 'Socially Optimal Product Differentiation', *American Economic Review*, 65.4 (1975), 567–85

Lang, A., *The Blue Fairy Book*, 5th edn (London and New York: Longmans, Green, and Company, 1889), pp. 290–95

Latour, B., *We Have Never Been Modern* (Cambridge, MA: Harvard University Press, 1993)

——— 'Mixing Humans and Nonhumans Together: The Sociology of a Doorcloser', *Social Problems*, 35.3 (1988), 298–310

——— 'The Berlin Key or How to do Words with Things', in P. M. Graves-Brown, ed., *Matter, Materiality and Modern Culture* (London: Routledge, 1991), pp. 10–21

——— 'The "Pedofil" of Boa Vista: A Photo-Philosophical Montage', *Common Knowledge*, 4.1 (1995), 145–87

——— 'On Interobjectivity', *Mind, Culture, and Activity: An International Journal*, 3.4 (1996), 228–69

——— 'Factures/Fractures From the Concept of Network to that of Attachment', *Res*, 36 (1999), 20–31

——— *Pandora's Hope: Essays on the Reality of Science Studies* (Cambridge, MA: Harvard University Press, 1999)

——— *Reassembling the Social: An Introduction to Actor-Network Theory* (Oxford: Oxford University Press, 2005)

Latour, B., and P. Weibel, eds., *Making Things Public: Atmospheres of Democracy* (Cambridge, MA: MIT Press, 2005)

Laurent, S., 'Affaire Woerth: si vous avez raté un épisode', *LeMonde.fr*, 1 September (2010) <http://www.lemonde.fr/politique/article_interactif/2010/09/01/affaire-woerth-si-vous-avez-rate-un-episode_1405471_823448.html> [accessed 16 May 2015]

Le Bon, G., *The Crowd: A Study of the Popular Mind*, with a New Introduction by Robert K. Merton (New York: Viking Press, 1960)

Le Monde, 'Étoiles des murs', *Le Monde*, 28 September (1988)

——— 'La stratégie bien rodée de Wikileaks', *LeMonde.fr*, 26 July (2010) <http://www.lemonde.fr/technologies/article/2010/07/26/la-strategie-bien-rodee-de-wikileaks_1392088_651865.html> [accessed 16 May 2015]

——— 'L'affaire des écoutes, le scandale qui menace l'empire Murdoch', *LeMonde.fr*, 18 juillet (2011) <http://www.lemonde.fr/europe/article/2011/07/18/le-scandale-qui-menace-l-empire-murdoch_1549009_3214.html> [accessed 16 May 2015]

Lee, N., A. J. Broderick, and L. Chamberlain, 'What is "Neuromarketing"? A Discussion and Agenda for Future Research', *International Journal of Psychophysiology*, 63.2 (2007), 199–204

Lendrevie, J., and A. de Baynast, *Publicitor* (Paris: Dunod, 7th edn, 2008)

Leymonerie, C., 'La Vitrine d'appareils ménagers. Reflet des structures commerciales dans la France des années 1950', *Réseaux*, 24.135.136 (2006), 93–124

Libération, 'iPad, l'ardoise sur laquelle on peut tabler', *Libération*, 5 April (2010), 4

Licoppe, Ch., *La Formation de la pratique scientifique: le discours de l'expérience en France et en Angleterre (1630–1820)* (Paris: La Découverte, 1996)

——— 'La Construction conversationnelle de l'activité commerciale. "Rebondir" au téléphone pour placer des services', *Réseaux*, 24.135.136 (2006), 125–60

——— Numéro spécial un tournant performatif? Retour sur ce que "font" les mots et les choses, *Réseaux*, 163.5 (2010)

Lilti, A., 'The Writing of Paranoia: Jean-Jacques Rousseau and the Paradoxes of Celebrity', *Representations*, 103 (2008), 53–83.

Loewenstein, G., 'The Psychology of Curiosity: A Review and Reinterpretation', *Psychological Bulletin* 116(1) (1994), 75–98

MacKenzie, D., and Y. Millo, 'Constructing a Market, Performing Theory: The Historical Sociology of a Financial Derivatives Exchange', *American Journal of Sociology*, 109.1 (2003), 107–45

MacKenzie, D., F. Muniesa, and L. Siu, eds., *Do Economists Make Markets? On the Performativity of Economics* (Princeton, NJ: Princeton University Press, 2007)

Maillet, Th., *Le Marketing et son histoire, ou le mythe de sisyphe réinventé* (Paris: Pocket, 2010)

Malkin, R., 'Wikipédia révèle le secret de "La Souricière" d'Agatha Christie', *Rue 89*, 1 September (2010)

Mallard, A., *Le Cadrage cognitif et relationnel de l'échange marchand: analyse sociologique des formes de l'organisation commerciale*, Post-doctoral research paper (Université Toulouse II, 7 May 2009)

Manguel, A., *Curiosity* (New Haven, CT: Yale University Press, 2015)

Mantoux, A., 'Myriam: wuand la publicité tient ses promesses', *Lesechos.fr*, 3 August (2010) <http://www.lesechos.fr/entreprises-secteurs/tech-medias/actu/020662466960-myriam-quand-la-publicite-tient-ses-promesses.htm> [accessed 16 May 2015]

Marchand, R., *Advertising the American Dream: Making Way for Modernity, 1920–1940* (Berkeley: University of California Press, 1986)

Marcuse, H., *One-Dimensional Man* (Boston: MA, Beacon Press, 1964)
Marion, G., *Idéologie marketing* (Paris: Eyrolles, 2004)
Martin, D., *Les options fondamentales de la finance moderne. Domestication sociologique d'un produit financier*, PhD thesis, Université Toulouse II, 2005
McFall, L., 'The Language of the Walls: Putting Promotional Saturation in Historical Context', *Consumption, Markets and Culture*, 7.2 (2004), 107–28
McKendrick, N., J. Brewer, and J. H. Plumb, *The Birth of a Consumer Society: The Commercialization of Eighteenth-Century England* (Bloomington: Indiana University Press, 1982)
Mehl, D., 'Le public de Loft Story: distance et connivence', *Médiamorphoses*, Hors série (2003), 71–168
Mellet, K., 'Aux sources du marketing viral', *Réseaux*, 157.158 (2009), 268–92
Menon, S., and D. Soman, 'Managing the Power of Curiosity for Effective Web Advertising Strategies', *Journal of Advertising*, 31.3 (2002), 1–14
Mermin, D., 'Godiva's Ride: Women of letters in England, 1830–1880', *The American Historical Review*, 100.2 (1995), 521–22
Merton, R. K., and E. Barber, *The Travels and Adventures of Serendipity* (Princeton, NJ, and Oxford: Princeton University Press, 2004)
Miller, D., *A Theory* of *Shopping* (Ithaca, NY: Cornell University Press, 1998)
Minard, M., ed., *De la curiosité en psychiatrie* (Ramonville-Saint-Agne: Erès, 1995)
Mukerji, Ch., *From Graven Images: Patterns of Modern Materialism* (New York: Columbia University Press, 1983)
Ourdan, R., 'Wikileaks: dans les coulisses de la diplomatie américaine', *LeMonde.fr*, 28 November (2010) <http://www.lemonde.fr/international/article/2010/11/28/wikileaks-dans-les-coulisses-de-la-diplomatie-americaine_1446078_3210.html> [accessed 16 May 2015]
Parasie, S., *Et maintenant une page de pub! Une histoire morale de la publicité à la télévision française (1968–2008)* (Paris: INA, 2010)
Péninou, G., 'Evolution de l'intellectualité publicitaire', *Revue française du marketing*, 191.1 (2003), 13–19
Pérec, G., *Things: A Story of the Sixties; A Man Asleep*, D. Bellos, and A. Leak, trans (Boston, MA: David R. Godine, 1990 [1965])
Perrot, M., *Faire ses courses* (Paris: Stock, 2009)
Piette, A., *Anthropologie existentiale* (Paris: Pétra, 2009)
Polanyi, K., *The Great Transformation* (Boston, MA: Beacon Press, 1957 [1944])
Pomian, K., *Collectors and Curiosities: Paris and Venice, 1500–1800* (Cambridge, MA: Polity Press, 1990)
Pomian, K., 'Histoire naturelle: de la curiosité à la discipline', in P. Martin and D. Moncond', eds., *Curiosité et cabinets de curiosités* (Neuilly: Atlande, 2004), pp. 15–42

Pradelle, de la, M., *Les Vendredis de Carpentras: faire son marché, en Provence ou ailleurs* (Paris: Fayard, 1996)

Presbrey, F., *History and Development of Advertising* (Garden City, NY: Doubleday, 1929)

Purinton, M. D., 'George Colman's "The Iron Chest" and "Blue-Beard" and the Pseudoscience of Curiosity Cabinets', *Victorian Studies*, 49.2 (2007), 250–57

Queneau, R., 'Un conte à votre façon', in *Contes et propos* (Paris: Gallimard, 1981), pp. 221–26

Rochet J.-Ch., and J. Tirole, 'Platform Competition in Two-Sided Markets', *Journal of the European Economic Association*, 1.4 (2003), 990–1029

Roth, C., D. Taraborelli, and N. Gilbert, 'Démographie des communautés en ligne: Le cas des wikis', *Réseaux*, 26.152 (2008), 205–40

Saint Augustine, *The Confessions of Saint Augustine*, E. B. Pusey, trans (Stilwell, KS, Digireads, 2005)

Sartre, J.-P., *Being and Nothingness*, H. E. Barnes, trans (New York: Washington Square Press, 1984 [1943])

Sauvageot, A., *Figures de la publicité, figures du monde* (Paris: Presses Universitaires de France, 1987)

——— *L'Épreuve des sens: de l'action sociale à la réalité virtuelle* (Paris: Presses Universitaires de France, 2003)

Schmidt, C., *La Sémantique économique en question: recherche sur les fondements de l'économie théorique* (Paris: Calmann-Lévy, 1986)

Schnapper, A., *Le Géant, la licorne, la tulipe. Collections françaises au XVIIe siècle* (Paris: Flammarion, 1988)

Schwarzkopf, S., 'Containment via Edutainment: The British Advertising Industry's Reaction to the Rise of Consumer Movements in the US and the UK (1930–1960)', Paper presented at the *Annual Conference of the Economic History Society*, Royal Holloway University of London, 2–4 April 2004

Senior, C., and N. Lee, 'A Manifesto for Neuromarketing Science', *Journal of Consumer Behaviour*, 7.4.5 (2008), 263–71

Shapin, S., and S. Schaffer, *Leviathan and the Air-Pump: Hobbes, Boyle, and the Experimental Life* (Princeton, NJ: Princeton University Press, 1985)

Shapiro, C., and J. E. Stiglitz, 'Equilibrium Unemployment as a Worker Discipline Device', *American Economic Review*, 74.3 (1984), 433–44

Shulman, J. L., in R. K. Merton, and E. Barber, *The Travels and Adventures of Serendipity* (Princeton, NJ, and Oxford: Princeton University Press, 2004), pp. XIII–XXV

Simmel, G., 'The Sociology of Secrecy and of Secret Societies', *The American Journal of Sociology*, 11.4 (1906), 441–98

Sinclair, U., *The Jungle* (New York: Oxford University Press, 2010 [1906])

Sitz, L., 'Les Mondes de marque: L'exemple Apple', *Décisions Marketing*, 52, October–December (2008), 19–30

Smith, W. R., 'Product Differentiation and Market Segmentation as Alternative Market Strategies', *Journal of Marketing*, 21.1 (1956), 3–8

Sombart, W., *Le Bourgeois. Contribution à l'histoire morale et intellectuelle de l'homme économique moderne* (Paris: Petite Bibliothèque Payot, 1966)

Soriano, M., *Les contes de Perrault: culture savante et traditions populaires* (Paris: Gallimard 1977 [1968])

Stanziani, A., *Histoire de la qualité alimentaire (XIXe–XXe siècles)* (Paris: Seuil, 2005)

Starobinski, J., *The Living Eye* (Cambridge, MA: Harvard University Press, 1989)

——— 'The Illness of Rousseau', *Yale French Studies*, 28 (1961b), 64–74

Steiner, P., 'Le Marché comme arène et les technologies sociales d'appariement', *Sciences de la société*, 73 (2008) 41–60

Strasser, S., *Satisfaction Guaranteed: The Making of the American Mass Market* (New York: Pantheon Books, 1989)

Tarde, G., 'Les Crimes des foules', *Archives d'anthropologie criminelle et des sciences pénales*, 7.40 (1892), 353–86

Tarde, G., *L'Opinion et la foule* (Paris: Le Sandre, 2006 [1901])

Tasitano, M., *La Curiosité, Apulée et Augustin* (Lagrasse, Verdier, 1989)

The Listener, 'Week by Week', *The Listener*, 6 September, 243 (1933), 340

Thérenty, M. E., and A. Vaillant, *1836: l'an I de l'ère médiatique. Analyse littéraire et historique de la presse* (Paris: Nouveau Monde éditions, 2001)

Thévenot, L., 'Pragmatic Regimes Governing the Engagement with the World', in K. Knorr-Cetina, T. Schatzki, and E. v. Savigny, eds., *The Practice Turn in Contemporary Theory* (London: Routledge, 2001), pp. 56–73

Thomas, G., 'Plaintes troubles contre le patron de WikiLeaks', *Le Monde*, 23 August (2010)

Underhill, P., *Why We Buy: The Science of Shopping* (New York: Simon & Schuster, 1999)

Vatin, F., *La Fluidité industrielle: essai sur la théorie de la production et le devenir du travail* (Paris: Méridiens-Klincksieck, 1987)

Veblen, T., *The Theory of the Leisure Class* (Oxford: Oxford University Press, 2013 [1899])

Vergnon, G., 'Le "poing levé", du rite soldatique au rite de masse. Jalons pour l'histoire d'un rite politique', *Le Mouvement social*, 212, July–September (2005), 77–91

Wacquant, L., 'An Inventive and Iconoclastic Scientist', *Berkeley Journal of Sociology*, 46 (2002), 177–79

White, H. C., 'Where do Markets Come From?', *American Journal of Sociology*, 87 (1981), 507–47

Wilkins, B. T., 'The Nature of Rousseau', *The Journal of Politics*, 21.4 (1959), 663–84

Winnepennickx-Kieser, J., *La Perception d'un cadeau offert par une entreprise au consommateur: regards croisés de l'anthropologie et du marketing*, PhD thesis, IAE de Toulouse, 2008

Winnicott, D., 'Transitional Objects and Transitional Phenomena', *International Journal of Psychoanalysis*, 34 (1953), 89–97

Wilson, T. P., *The Cart that Changed the World: The Career of Sylvan N. Goldman* (Norman: University of Oklahoma Press, 1978)

Yarwood, D. L., 'Humor and Administration: A Serious Inquiry into Unofficial Organizational Communication', *Public Administration Review*, 55.1 (1995), 81–90

MATTERING PRESS TITLES

On Curiosity
The Art of Market Seduction

FRANCK COCHOY

Practising Comparison
Logics, Relations, Collaborations

EDITED BY
JOE DEVILLE, MICHAEL GUGGENHEIM, AND ZUZANA HRDLIČKOVÁ

Modes of Knowing
Resources from the Baroque

EDITED BY
JOHN LAW AND EVELYN RUPPERT

Imagining Classrooms
Stories of Children, Teaching, and Ethnography

VICKI MACKNIGHT

www.ingramcontent.com/pod-product-compliance
Lightning Source LLC
Chambersburg PA
CBHW032347280326
41935CB00008B/483